About Island Press

Since 1984, the nonprofit Island Press has been stimulating, shaping, and communicating the ideas that are essential for solving environmental problems worldwide. With more than 800 titles in print and some 40 new releases each year, we are the nation's leading publisher on environmental issues. We identify innovative thinkers and emerging trends in the environmental field. We work with world-renowned experts and authors to develop cross-disciplinary solutions to environmental challenges.

Island Press designs and implements coordinated book publication campaigns in order to communicate our critical messages in print, in person, and online using the latest technologies, programs, and the media. Our goal: to reach targeted audiences—scientists, policymakers, environmental advocates, the media, and concerned citizens—who can and will take action to protect the plants and animals that enrich our world, the ecosystems we need to survive, the water we drink, and the air we breathe.

Island Press gratefully acknowledges the support of its work by the Agua Fund, Inc., The Margaret A. Cargill Foundation, Betsy and Jesse Fink Foundation, The William and Flora Hewlett Foundation, The Kresge Foundation, The Forrest and Frances Lattner Foundation, The Andrew W. Mellon Foundation, The Curtis and Edith Munson Foundation, The Overbrook Foundation, The David and Lucile Packard Foundation, The Summit Foundation, Trust for Architectural Easements, The Winslow Foundation, and other generous donors.

The opinions expressed in this book are those of the author(s) and do not necessarily reflect the views of our donors.

SPRAWL
REPAIR
MANUAL

SPRAWL
REPAIR
MANUAL

GALINA TACHIEVA

Contributors
Judith I. Bell, Maria Elisa Mercer,
Rachel D. Merson Zitofsky
with
Eusebio Azcue and Chris Ritter

Washington | Covelo | London

Published by Island Press

Island Press, 1718 Connecticut Ave., NW, Suite 300, Washington, DC 20009.

Library of Congress Cataloging-in-Publication Data

Tachieva, Galina.
Sprawl repair manual / Galina Tachieva.
 p. cm.
Includes bibliographical references and index.
ISBN-13: 978-1-59726-731-1 (cloth : alk. paper)
ISBN-10: 1-59726-731-7 (cloth : alk. paper)
ISBN-13: 978-1-59726-732-8 (pbk. : alk. paper)
ISBN-10: 1-59726-732-5 (pbk. : alk. paper) 1. Cities and towns--United States--Growth. 2. Sustainable development--United States. 3. Social justice--United States. 4. Citizenship--United States. I. Title.
HT384.U5T33 2010
307.1'214--dc22
                    2010015762

Printed on recycled, acid-free paper

Design by Duany Plater-Zyberk & Company

Manufactured in the United States of America

10 9 8 7 6 5

C E N T E R
——FOR——
A P P L I E D
T R A N S E C T
S T U D I E S

The production of this book was made possible with support from the Center for Applied Transect Studies. CATS promotes research, publication, tools, and training for the design, coding, building, and documentation of transect-based communities. The publishing program at CATS was funded with proceeds from the Richard H. Driehaus Prize. www.transect.org

TABLE OF CONTENTS

ACKNOWLEDGEMENTS

This manual was created with a sense of urgency. A desire to reform sprawl is in the air across the country, from Long Island to Texas, from the southern tip of Florida all the way to Portland. A growing number of initiatives are focused on solving the pressing economic, social, and environmental problems of sprawl. To aid those initiatives and take advantage of the unique opportunities that now exist, this book provides a collection of sprawl repair tools and the lessons learned from built retrofit projects.

The inspiration for the book emerged in April 2008 at the Congress for the New Urbanism (CNU) in Austin, where the Sprawl Retrofit Initiative began with several dozen participants. We gathered to discuss the urgency of repairing sprawl, our experiences with retrofit projects, and how to move forward. In June 2009, at the Congress in Denver, we presented a first draft of the *Sprawl Repair Manual*. Since then we have been hard at work on the book, with input from the CNU Sprawl Retrofit Initiative. A sprawl repair listserv has hosted widely ranging discussions on the topic (see below for details). Many of the ideas debated in this correspondence have found places in the manual, and its success as a practical guide will be due in large part to the contributions of many experts and practitioners.

Many of the techniques demonstrated in the book are derived from the work and built projects of Duany Plater-Zyberk & Company (DPZ) over the last twenty years. This effort would not have been possible if the book had not been produced in our office. I was able to dedicate consistent focus and attention because my partners, especially Elizabeth Plater-Zyberk and Andres Duany, were so generous, patient, and supportive. Judith I. Bell, Maria Elisa Mercer, and Rachel D. Merson Zitofsky – a dedicated, talented, and savvy team – worked closely with me, and we received invaluable contributions from illustrators Eusebio Azcue and Chris Ritter. The team was supported and encouraged by the entire office.

Brian Falk at the Center for Applied Transect Studies was a thoughtful and challenging advisor on all issues related to writing, content, and publishing, and Heather Boyer was an enthusiastic supporter and sponsoring editor at Island Press.

While more deserve to be thanked for their contributions, I would like to specifically mention these individuals, as each of them has contributed in a special way: John Anderson, Ellen Dunham-Jones, Robert Gibbs, Sara Hines, Mike Lydon, Joshua Martin, Michael Mehaffy, Leslie Pariseau, Daniel Slone, Sandy Sorlien, Emily Talen, Dhiru Thadani, June Williamson, and, from the DPZ office, Torika Alonso-Burford, Alice Enz, Eduardo A. Pardo Fernandez, Xavier Iglesias, Matt Lambert, Chien Nguyen, Atul Sharma, Shannon Tracy, Max Zabala and our interns Marcos Bode, Scott Douglass, Scarleth Lazo, Megan Recher, and Laura Valla.

I am also very grateful to my family for their understanding and support.

This manual is intended to be a dynamic document, updated with new techniques and strategies as they emerge. I hope that at some point it will become available electronically, so that supplemental information can be easily added and accessed.

With that in mind, I look forward to readers' comments. Please send your feedback directly to me, at galina@dpz.com. If you would like to join the Sprawl Retrofit Initiative listserv, please send an e-mail request to Retrofit-Repair-subscribe@dpz.com.

I hope this manual will be helpful to all who are concerned about the consequences of sprawl and are driven to repair our sprawling state of affairs.

Galina Tachieva
Miami, 2010

FROM SPRAWL TO COMPLETE COMMUNITIES

This manual provides guidance for transforming fragmented and inefficient development into complete communities that are livable and robust. Polemical as well as practical, the manual will equip design professionals, developers, regulators, and citizens with strategies drawn from successful built projects.

Sprawl is a pattern of growth characterized by an abundance of congested highways, strip shopping centers, big boxes, office parks, and gated cul-de-sac subdivisions – all separated from each other in isolated, single-use pods (figure 1-1). This land-use pattern is typically found in suburban areas, but also affects our cities, and is central to our wasteful use of water, energy, land, and time spent in traffic. Sprawl has been linked to increased air and water pollution, greenhouse gas emissions, loss of open space and natural habitat, and the exponential increase in new infrastructure costs. Social problems related to the lack of diversity have been attributed to sprawl, and health problems such as obesity to its auto-dependence.

In contrast, complete communities have a mix of uses and are walkable, with many of a person's daily needs – shops, offices, transit, civic and recreational places – within a short distance of home. They are compact, so they consume less open space and enable multiple modes of transportation, including bicycles, cars, and mass transit. A wide variety of building types provides options to residents and businesses, encouraging diversity in population. This mix of uses, public spaces, transportation, and population makes complete communities economically, socially, and environmentally sustainable (figure 1-2).

The promise of suburbia has been eroding for decades, but reached a critical point with the mortgage meltdown of 2008. A record number of homes went into foreclosure and entire subdivisions and commercial developments began to fail. Yet the expanse of sprawl represents a vast investment, and cannot be simply abandoned or demolished. Pragmatism demands the reclamation of sprawl through

1-1. Sprawl: fragmented, car-dependent single uses

1-2. Complete community: balanced, connected, compact

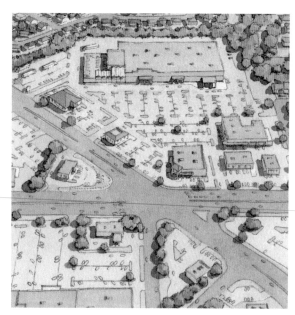

1-3. Commercial sprawl

1-4. Complete community

redevelopment that introduces mixed uses and transportation options. It must be acknowledged, however, that portions of sprawl may remain in their current state, while others may devolve, reverting to agriculture or nature. The design and regulatory strategies and incentives shown here are intended for the places that are best suited to be urbanized because of location or existing investment.

The history and consequences of suburban development, specifically sprawl, are well documented. Numerous books articulate the trajectory of sprawl within its historical context – from the Federal Housing Administration's mortgages for new construction, the subsidies of the interstate highway system, and the tax laws allowing accelerated depreciation of commercial development, to the evolution of Euclidean zoning's separation of uses and the cultural mandate for separation by race. Recent publications put forward the need to redevelop sprawl and what specifically should be repaired; among these are *Greyfields into Goldfields* and *Malls into Main Streets*, reports by the Congress for the New Urbanism. *Retrofitting Suburbia: Urban Design Solutions for Redesigning Suburbs*, by Ellen Dunham-Jones and June Williamson, explains why we need to retrofit sprawl and documents successful examples of retrofits through illuminating and comprehensive analysis.

The *Sprawl Repair Manual* seeks to expand the literature as a guide that illustrates how to repair the full range of suburban conditions, demonstrating a step-by-step design process for the creation of more sustainable communities. This is a framework for designing the interventions, incorporating them into the regulatory system, and implementing them with permitting strategies and financial incentives.

The proposed approach addresses a range of scales from the region down to the community, street, block, and building. The method identifies deficiencies in typical elements of sprawl, and determines the best remedial techniques for those deficiencies. Also included are recommendations for regulatory and economic incentives.

Lessons learned from history guide this methodology. Rather than the instant and total overhaul of communities, as promoted so destructively in American cities half a century ago, this is a guide for incremental and opportunistic improvement.

Most of the diagrams have been conceptualized and generalized to make them applicable to a wider range of situations. In some cases the real conditions were simplified to make the components and their deficiencies easily identifiable, and the techniques explicit. All techniques are shown with two- and three-dimensional drawings and diagrams, in a declension from the most general to the most specific (figures 1-3 and 1-4).

CHOICES

There are two primary options for growth: conventional sprawl development and complete communities.

Sprawl abandoned the neighborhood structure in favor of car-dependent patterns. When driving is mandatory for almost all daily activities, carbon emissions are higher. With the price of gasoline rising, long commutes to or from exurban locations become economic disadvantages. Because sprawl developments are not compact, they consume excessive amounts of farmland and valuable natural areas.

Studies have shown that sprawl is damaging to both physical and social health, isolating people in car-dominated environments where they are deprived not only of the physiological benefits of walking, but also of the natural human interactions typical of complete communities.[1] This is especially relevant to aging residents, who lose their independence when they can no longer drive, and need to leave their suburban houses for retirement communities. Children and younger adults are also vulnerable to the car-dependence of sprawl. In 1969, 90 percent of all children walked to school, as schools were part of complete neighborhoods, but in 2002 only 31 percent walked to school.[2]

Sprawl developments, particularly in exurban areas, suffered some of the highest foreclosure rates, and many have also seen dramatic increases in crime rates, some greater than 30 percent.[3] Many homes, and even entire subdivisions, have been abandoned, creating the effect of sporadic and dispersed occupancy typical of the consequences of natural disasters. Christopher Leinberger, visiting fellow at the Brookings Institution, predicts that the suburbs on the fringes, poorly served by public transport, will suffer a very visible decline as low-income populations move in and these areas become "magnets for poverty, crime, and social dysfunction."[4]

Nonetheless, the development industry continues to produce sprawl, with the support of the financial industry, planning practices, and government policies. Sprawl remains cheaper to plan, easier to finance, faster to permit, and less complicated to build, primarily due to the regulations governing development. It is simpler to attach the freestanding, isolated, single-use components of sprawl to the already subsidized and prolific highway system than to assemble these elements into real neighborhoods and towns. Sprawl is extremely inflexible and will not mature into vibrant urbanism on its own. Without precise design and policy interventions, sprawl might change – a strip shopping center might be scrapped and replaced with a lifestyle center when the next owner comes along – but it is unlikely to produce walkable, sustainable urbanism.

In contrast to sprawl, complete communities are economically robust because they include a variety

1-5. Mashpee Commons, Massachusetts, 1960s shopping center

1-6. Transformation into a town center in the 2000s

of businesses that support daily needs, and nearby residents work at and patronize those businesses. They are socially healthy because many generations with diverse incomes and backgrounds live and interact within them. Complete communities are livable because of their comfortable human scale. They are environmentally superior because they are compact, saving land and natural resources. Vehicle miles traveled (VMT) are reduced by as much as 30 percent, resulting in less pollution and less energy used.[5]

Complete communities also support walking and physical activity, which have been proven important to public health and general well-being. A multidisciplinary team of researchers from the University of Miami has determined that communities with a mix of uses and good connectivity, block structure, public spaces, and transit proximity have residents who are more likely to walk, less likely to be overweight, and have greater social and community interactions.[6] The researchers worked with the Florida Department of Health to create evidence-based criteria for the Surgeon General's Seal of Walkability so the general public would know what to look for in a community.

The demand for complete communities is greater than the current supply. According to Todd Litman, founder of the Victoria Transport Policy Institute, in 2009 North-American households were evenly divided in their preferences for sprawl or smart growth in the form of walkable, diverse neighborhoods. He predicts that by 2030, more than two-thirds will prefer smart growth.[7] This manual shows one way to meet the growing needs for walkable environments by repairing sprawl into complete communities.

SPRAWL REPAIR DEFINED

Sprawl repair transforms failing or potentially failing, single-use, and car-dominated developments into complete communities that have better economic, social, and environmental performance.

The objective of the sprawl repair strategy is to build communities based on the neighborhood unit, similar to the traditional fabric that was established in towns and cities prior to World War II. The primary tactic of sprawl repair is to insert needed elements – buildings, density, public space, additional connections – to complete and diversify the mono-cultural agglomerations of sprawl: residential subdivisions, strip shopping centers, office parks, suburban campuses, malls, and edge cities. By systematically modifying the reparable areas (turning subdivisions into walkable neighborhoods, shopping centers and malls into town centers) and leaving to devolution those that are irreparable (abandonment or conversion to park, agricultural, or natural land), sprawl can be reorganized into complete communities.

To identify the proper targets for repair, it is essential to understand the form and structure of sprawl in the American built environment. Sprawl can take place in intensely urban areas, but most is found in suburban areas. There are three generations of suburbia that vary in form as related to urbanity and walkability: pre-war suburbs, post-war suburbs, and the late 20th-century exurbs. While the pre-war suburbs are often complete communities, the latter two types abandoned the pedestrian-centered neighborhood structure in favor of auto-centric dispersion.

The pre-war suburbs include patterns of growth that can be defined as suburban, but are not sprawl per se (figure 1-7). In the U.S., the first suburbs sprang up in the nineteenth century along the newly built railroad lines, as compact, middle-class communities assembled around stations (examples include Lake Forest and Riverside in Illinois and Forest Hills in Queens, New York) (figure 1-8). These were modeled after the suburbs built in England in the eighteenth century

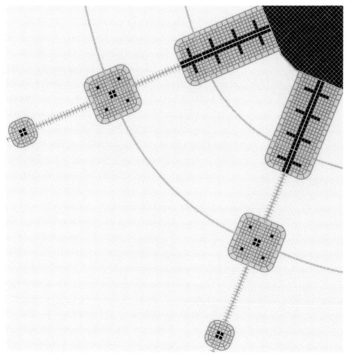

1-7. First-generation suburbs: traditional growth patterns formed streetcar and railroad communities outside the city limits

1-8. Forest Hills, New York

■ Traditional urban core

■ First-generation suburbs

■ Railroad or streetcar lines

□ Undeveloped land

to serve the London bourgeoisie, and inspired development outside of cities in other parts of the world.[8] With the invention of the electric streetcar, another group emerged closer to the city and accessible to a more diverse economic and social population than the railroad suburbs (examples include Cleveland Park in Washington, DC, the Country Club District in Kansas City, Missouri, and Brookline, outside of Boston, Massachusetts).[9] These developments depended on their proximity to rail stops, and maintained an urban structure for pedestrian walkability and a mixture of daily uses. In the beginning of the 20th century, yet another type of development joined the suburban echelons; communities such as Bloomfield Hills, Michigan, and Coral Gables, Florida, were designed to accommodate the automobile, but still consisted primarily of mixed-use, compact, and diverse neighborhoods.

In stark contrast to the pre-war suburbs, the second generation of suburbs was single-use, low-density development spurred by new incentives from the federal mortgage system and the increase in automotive infrastructure and use (figure 1-9). The second-generation

suburbs began to develop in the 1920s, but flourished after the end of World War II, when, under the auspices of national defense, the federal government created the interstate highway system, the largest infrastructure project the country had ever seen. Ironically, the main achievements of this monumental effort were to facilitate personal mobility and undermine the fundamental walkability of American urbanism.

Levittown, built on Long Island, New York, in 1948, was the preeminent example of a community dependent on the nation's new commitment to the car (figure 1-10). Conceived as an innovative and affordable master-planned community based on the mass production of housing, Levittown was the prototype of the post-war American suburb, and ultimately became the symbol of the ascent and failure of sprawl. Levittown's thousands of identical houses on identical lots transmogrified the American dream of the earlier suburbs by making everything within them subordinate to the automobile, including the residents.

Though Levittown had schools, shopping centers, and park areas, its master plan ignored the traditional

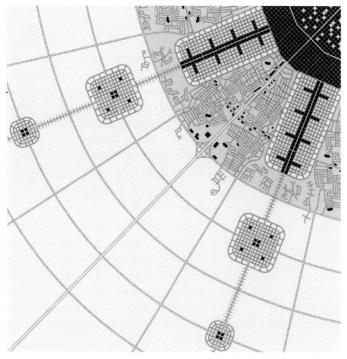

1-9. Second-generation suburbs: conventional suburban development created car-dependent sprawl along new highways

1-10. Levittown, New York

© 2009 Google, Map Data © 2009 Tele Atlas

▨ Decline in urban core

▨ Second-generation suburbs

▨ Highways and interchanges

▢ Undeveloped land

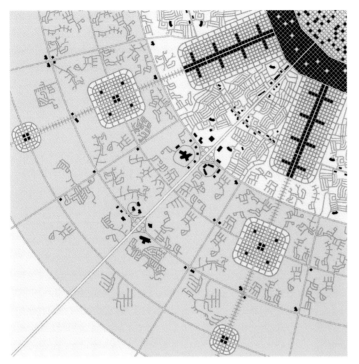

1-11. Third-generation suburbs: the exurbs

1-12. Tyson's Corner, Virginia

 Decline in urban core

 Third-generation suburbs

 Highways and interchanges

Undeveloped land

neighborhood structure, and the community was created only for families who owned cars. The use of the automobile eliminated the need for convenient proximity of the elements of everyday life, and the walkable compactness of the pre-war suburb gave way to sprawl. In the wake of its 60th birthday in 2008, Levittown adopted an environmental program, aimed "to persuade residents to upgrade their homes, improving energy efficiency and cutting fuel bills."[10] As logical and noble as such efforts are, especially in this time of climate change and amidst the (first) great recession of the 21st century, Levittown and suburbs of its kind will need more than the "greening" of individual buildings. They will need a major repair of the overall urban structure, because even if buildings are made more efficient, driving is not reduced, and the environmental, societal, and economic burden of sprawl will remain.

The second generation of suburbs has been blighted by traffic, obsolete housing stock, and inadequate amenities, and has been leapfrogged by newer sprawl out in the exurbs. These places are the urgent contenders for repair, as their deficiencies prohibit them from respond-

ing to the changing demographics of a fast-aging and more diverse population. Mashpee Commons in Cape Cod, Massachusetts, one of the first redevelopments of a greyfield (obsolete, underutilized land) in the country, represents the potential to revitalize this generation of suburbs. It is a retrofit in which a dead shopping center built in the 1960s was transformed into a town center in the 1980s (figures 1-13 and 1-14).

The last generation, or third-ring suburbs (figures 1-11 and 1-12), flourished from the 1980s through the early 2000s on the exurban edge. Until recently, these suburbs have been highly competitive and in good physical shape, due in part to potent owners' associations that enforced special standards and bylaws to maintain quality within the developments. The developments are often gated, single-use housing pods or commercial agglomerations such as strip shopping centers, malls, corporate campuses, or entire edge cities, and all are reachable only by automobile.

Repairing these suburbs will require a proactive, visionary approach that anticipates the potential economic decline and devaluation of developments. Urban planners, business owners, developers, and municipal governments must anticipate their failure and intercede. An example of a farsighted repair of a still-successful mall and its surroundings is Downtown Kendall in Miami-Dade, Florida, where the county, chamber of commerce, and landowners worked together to outline a long-term plan for the transformation of this edge city into a transit-oriented, regional center (figures 1-15 and 1-16).

Repair of some places will be physically and economically more feasible (e.g., the perfectly located mall waiting to be connected to the surrounding suburban fabric), while others will be more likely to wither than evolve. These are the isolated, disconnected, exurban fringes where the application of the neighborhood structure will be least feasible. And if residents and businesses migrate en masse from these fringes, because of unemployment, foreclosures, or social instability, these places may well be transformed back to agriculture or nature. Nationally and internationally, the "shrinking cities" initiative (started by cities like Youngstown, Ohio) focuses on programs for managing the devolution (reduction of the physical infrastructure) of urban and suburban areas experiencing economic and population decline.[11] In comparison to other countries (mainly in Europe), where a negative population change is the predominant reason for "shrinking cities," the population in the U.S. is expected to continue growing, creating the potential for repair and intensification of some areas.[12]

This manual concentrates mainly on strategies for densification of sprawl, but acknowledges that some re-greening and de-densification initiatives are

1-13. Mashpee Commons, 1960: strip shopping center

1-14. Mashpee Commons, 2000s: transformed into a town center

valid alternatives to blight and depopulation in the suburbs. Examples are given for contracting cities and suburbs at the regional scale (chapter three, "Repair at the Regional Scale"), as well as instructions for re-platting deserted properties to larger lots to be used for gardens or larger family compounds (chapter six, "Repair at the Block Scale").

Areas where the crisis is most acute – where traffic congestion, falling real estate values, outdated infrastructure, and lack of public amenities become unbearable – as well as the places with regional importance and manageable ownership patterns, should be given priority for sprawl repair. As discussed at greater length in chapter three, "Repair at the Regional Scale," priorities for sprawl repair or devolution must be set at the regional level. However, the subject of devolution is sensitive and relatively new, and is best addressed at the community scale, where residents, associations, property owners, and developers can make decisions locally.

© 2009 Google, Map Data © 2009 Tele Atlas

1-15. Downtown Kendall, Florida: edge city in the process of sprawl repair

1-16. New street in Downtown Kendall

CHALLENGES

Experience with retrofit projects shows there are numerous challenges to overcome in the process of sprawl repair. The first challenge is financial, as sprawl repair requires considerable initial investment. It becomes more financially feasible, however, when analyzed from a long-term perspective and when compared to conventional suburban development. The increased density and mixed uses, for example, reduce the cost of infrastructure per capita.

Land-use segregation and imbalance in the form of single-use concentrations (shopping centers, residential enclaves, and office parks) fragment the built environment. In addition, economic and market differences cause further separation and the existing ownership patterns are often disjointed. These factors create the need for coordinated and expensive land acquisitions, placing pressures on affordability of housing and further complicating the prospects for repairing the existing fabric.

Transportation constraints include the lack of connectivity and permeability in existing suburban thoroughfare patterns. There is rarely a continuous network to allow for multiple choices of movement, only a sparse arrangement of highways, collectors, and cul-de-sacs confining the traffic stream to limited channels of high speed and congestion. Interweaving the thoroughfare network will be challenging, and in some cases impossible. Many properties will need to be acquired, and many rights-of-way will need to be modified before achieving any meaningful connectivity.

Open space management in sprawling areas usually does not amount to continuous and significant environmental preserves. Haphazard sprawl development has disconnected natural areas, with the result that neither the human nor natural habitat has retained its integrity. There is no hierarchy in the treatment of open space; swales, berms, and wild vegetation are permitted in urbanized areas, while massive impervious surfaces encroach on sensitive natural networks.

Excessive requirements for on-site parking reduce the potential for increasing density and varying building types. Most conventional zoning codes require on-site parking and do not allow shared parking ratios, thus limiting development to low structures with parking lots or high-rises with parking decks. There is no incentive for mid-size buildings with lower parking ratios that will more evenly distribute construction through the suburban fabric.

Existing land-development regulations promote the separation of uses. The regulatory emphasis is still on the quantitative criteria, rather than physical design. The result is sprawl that is neither urban nor rural in character, but rather an ambiguous mixture in which roadways and parking lots have priority over the buildings that form the public space. New codes are needed to allow the retrofit of these elements into more sustainable communities.

In addition to municipal ordinances, many gated communities, as found in the second- and third-ring suburbs, are protected by homeowners' association covenants, which leave few legal means for retrofit. Together with the overhaul of the regulatory framework that supports sprawl, identifying the legal methods for sprawl repair will be essential to its successful implementation.

However, the most important reason for the inefficiency of suburban sprawl is the absence of neighborhood structure. The diverse and compact neighborhood unit, which is the building block of smart growth, has been abandoned and even outlawed, leading to the fractured and inefficient landscape of suburbia. Establishing neighborhood structure and connecting it to the larger region is the greatest design challenge encountered in sprawl repair.

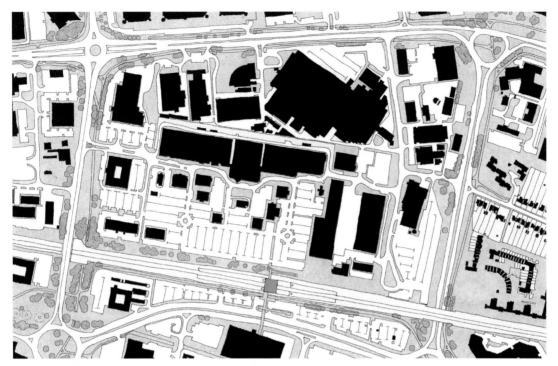

1-17. Greyfield site next to a train station

◼ Existing buildings   ▥ Train station

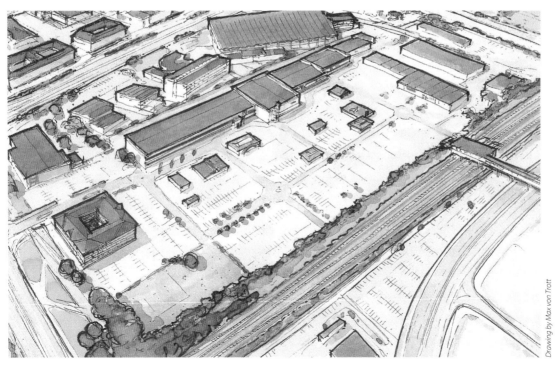

1-18. Overscaled parking and dispersed buildings underutilize the site

Drawing by Max von Trott

OPPORTUNITIES

Energy costs are rising, meaning long commutes are becoming unaffordable. A changing climate compels us to pollute less. We need to increase physical activity to overcome the epidemic of obesity and chronic diseases. Entire residential and commercial developments are failing. The economics of sprawl are not working. These are the obvious justifications for sprawl repair. But there are other reasons that, while less obvious, are equally compelling.

The emergence of a new class of buyers – economically farsighted, environmentally conscious, and socially active – is creating a major shift in the housing market. Baby Boomers (those born between 1946 and 1964) and their Millennial progeny (born between 1976 and 2000) represent more than 135 million people, many of them with an orientation toward diverse, compact urbanism – Boomers because they're retiring and want the convenience, sociability, and stimuli of a complete community, and Millennials because they are young and want the excitement and job opportunities of urban environments.[13] Trends such as these, along with economic and environmental forces that make exurban development unsustainable, will lead builders, developers, and the private sector at large to pursue sprawl repair aggressively. Combined with public policy, such a shift would be very powerful. This manual addresses these opportunities by showing techniques for the transformation of sprawl into communities that are attractive to these buyers.

As Ellen Dunham-Jones and June Williamson assert in *Retrofitting Suburbia*, the population of 21st-century suburbia is very different from the stereotype of fifty years ago that depicted the suburbs as predominantly white, middle-class families with children. Together with the quantitative and generational shifts, the growing presence of ethnic minorities accustomed to less driving and living and working in less space will contribute to new opportunities for engaging different cultures. The sprawl repair techniques provide a variety of ways to expand the range of public spaces and more affordable building types to accommodate the housing and business needs of a diverse, multiethnic population.

The need to accommodate population growth is another obvious reason for sprawl repair. By 2025, the population of the U.S. is expected to increase by 70 million – equal to the combined current populations of California, New York, and Florida.[14] According to Arthur C. Nelson of the Metropolitan Research Center at the University of Utah, the U.S. will reach 400 million people in 2037. Of the next 100 million people, only 12 percent will have children, as most of the population will fit into the categories of empty nesters or single-person households. He predicts a dramatic shift in the market toward more urban environments, as the demand for single-family housing will plummet.[15] According to Nelson, inner cities and first-generation suburbs will not have sufficient housing supplies to satisfy the need of the market, and "two-thirds or more of the next 100 million people and associated jobs are likely to locate in existing second-tier (1950–2000) suburbs." The manual demonstrates how growing housing needs can be satisfied by intensification of sprawling developments in the second and third tiers of suburbs, especially near places with potential for transit.

The required infrastructure for conventional development is excessive – in most cases overscaled – and can be utilized in the redevelopment process. As an example, sprawl's wide thoroughfares can easily accommodate transit infrastructure and bicycle lanes as well as cars. Vast parcels of deteriorating commercial buildings and parking lots are ready to be urbanized and become centers for the adjacent suburban communities. Furthermore, aging residents will prefer to retire in their suburban homes, which are the largest personal investments for most of these residents. If amenities and services are provided through repair strategies, it may become possible for millions of seniors to retire in place and invest in their current communities instead of moving.

Hundreds of new communities that are compact, pedestrian-friendly, and mixed-use have been built in the last three decades and are ready to be used as models for sprawl repair. They differ from

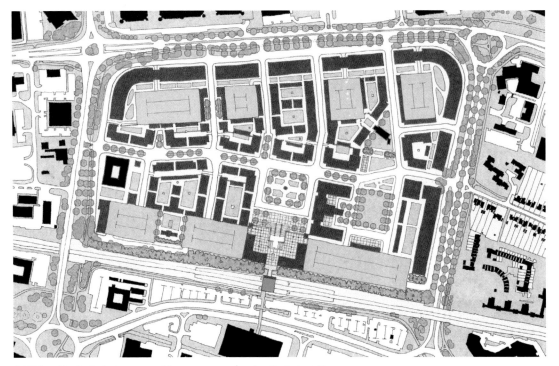

1-19. Transit-oriented urban core with a new square framing the train station

■ Existing buildings   ■ Proposed buildings   ■ Train station   ■ Parking garages

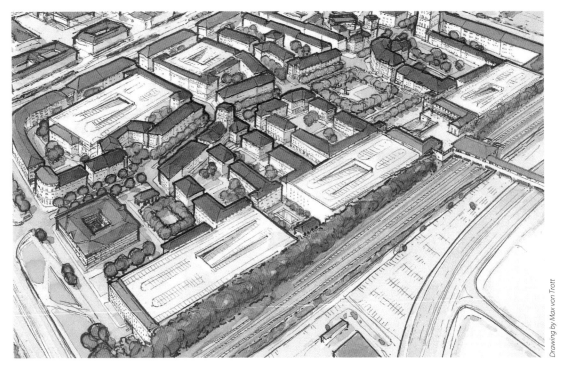

1-20. Final stage of greyfield repair with parking lot developed and buildings replaced

sprawl in fundamental ways, among the most significant of which is their capacity for intensification and incorporation of public transit. The experience of building these communities has provided practical tools that are applicable to sprawl repair and are explained in this manual.

Sprawl repair is an economic necessity, but also provides the opportunity for economic growth. As observed in a study by the Brookings Institution's Metropolitan Policy Program, the employment decentralization that started in the 1960s became a substantial phenomenon for most metropolitan regions through the 1990s and 2000s, with the result that most businesses were located outside of city limits.[16] This manual emphasizes the use of existing employment and commercial hubs as anchors to be redeveloped into complete communities with balanced uses and

transportation options. Many existing buildings can also be rehabilitated for new businesses. Existing jobs can be saved, and new green jobs can be created in the process of transforming sprawl.

Beginning in 2008, the retail industry experienced unprecedented upheaval, creating an opportunity to reform the conventions of large-scale commercial overdevelopment. General Growth Properties, the second-largest mall owner in the U.S., filed for bankruptcy in April 2009, but had recently started a program to retrofit many of its megaretail hubs into mixed-use centers. This practice, together with the redevelopment of existing employment hubs, should be supported and incentivized.

Proximity to agricultural land is one of the few advantages exurban developments have over urban centers. Some, therefore, have the potential to be retrofitted for

1-21. Infill as repair of a corporate office park: Legacy Town Center, Plano, Texas

local food production. They have abundant open space, and they are close to the edges where they can easily interface with agriculture. It may be also easier to adapt these areas for irrigation, whether natural or manmade, or introduce grey-water recycling. The next American rural village might not be designed from scratch; it may be a model of repaired suburban sprawl.

The regulatory environment that supports sprawl has already begun to change. Form-based codes have been approved in many municipalities around the U.S. More than 80 cities, such as Petaluma, California, Montgomery, Alabama, and Miami, Florida, have adopted or are currently adopting the SmartCode, a model, form-based comprehensive ordinance that replaces use- and density-based ordinances and enables the development of mixed-use, traditional neighborhoods. This shift in the regulatory framework makes smart growth development legal again and assists sprawl repair initiatives.

Regional planning allows for the choice of sustainable growth instead of sprawl, as it provides coordination between municipalities and jurisdictions. Counties across the nation are adopting regional smart growth policies. In Sacramento, California, an association of local governments completed a "Blueprint of the Future" for the six-county metropolitan region. The plan covers growth until 2050, and encourages compact developments near mass transit, thus saving $8 billion in construction costs for freeways, utilities, and other infrastructure.[17] In Florida, the Treasure Coast Regional Planning Council is a unique four-county collaboration on strategic regional planning that has been effective in providing comprehensive planning assistance, urban design, town planning, and redevelopment initiatives, as well as model regulatory documents.[18]

Statewide planning practices can provide discipline and coordination on a large scale. If an entire state embraces policies that do not foster sprawl, the repair of suburbia will be more feasible, as state resources will be channeled to incentivize sustainable growth. Projects such as Envision Utah and Louisiana Speaks endeavor to create coordinated solutions for their states' growth and outline opportunities for infill and repair.

At the federal level, agencies have come together to address growth in a holistic, multi-disciplinary manner that should help with sprawl repair. In 2009, the U.S. Department of Housing and Urban Development (HUD), the U.S. Department of Transportation (DOT), and the Environmental Protection Agency (EPA) announced an interagency partnership for sustainable communities. Their goal is to coordinate federal housing, transportation, and other infrastructure investments to protect the environment, promote equitable development, and help address the challenges of climate change. The growing awareness of climate change presents an opportunity to create complete and sustainable communities through redevelopment, as new smart growth policies become the norm.

This is an opportunity for sprawl repair initiatives to be combined with federal funding, and possibly legislation. However, without the clear goals of physical change through sprawl repair, funding and legislation will not be sufficient to achieve the repair of our unsustainable suburbs. Concrete, practical tools are needed, and this manual provides a full range – from the region, where federal and state incentives will be needed, to the single structure, where private investments and individual commitments will be required.

CHAPTER TWO

THE SPRAWL REPAIR METHOD

Sprawl repair begins with analysis at the regional scale (figure 2-1). Complete communities – cities, towns, villages – are identified for preservation and emulation, and unsustainable but salvageable sprawl elements are identified for repair. For sprawl elements that are beyond repair, the decision must be made whether to leave them as they are, convert them to farmland, or let them devolve into open space.

The sprawl repair method is comprised of urban design, regulatory, and implementation techniques. The final products of sprawl repair are communities in which people live better, drive less, and, as a result, save energy and resources, ultimately contributing to a healthier environment. Prioritizing the use of resources, value engineering, demolition, and process modeling are focused on making sprawl repair more economical. The process leading from the state of sprawl to the state of repaired, sustainable urbanism is dependent on the specifics of the target and its site – the physical boundaries, regional context and connectivity, ownership pattern, demographics, politics, and economic potential, as well as different construction methods and available technology, materials, and workforce. As a result, sprawl repair strategies take a variety of paths – some more direct and expeditious, while others may consist of

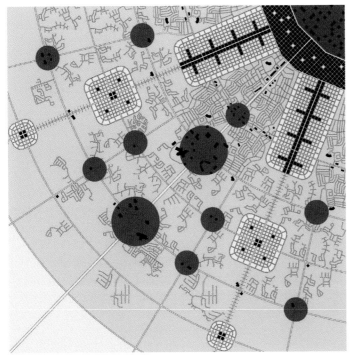

Repair in urban core

Communities for preservation and emulation

Sprawl development

Sprawl repair targets

Sprawl as is or devolution

Undeveloped land

2-1. Sprawl repair targets: commercial, employment, and transportation nodes with the best potential for redevelopment

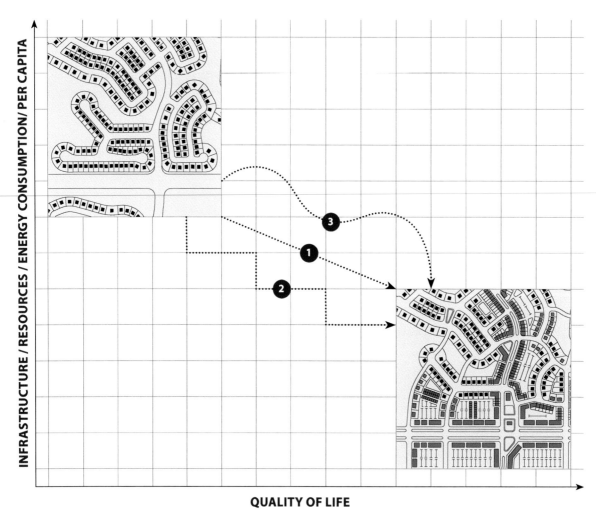

2-2. Conceptual representation of possible paths of sprawl repair and their effects on resource use and quality of life

1. Direct process of sprawl repair
2. Phased process of sprawl repair
3. Indirect process of sprawl repair

gradual and slower steps. Regardless of its path, the final state of the repaired sprawl element is a part of a complete community that needs fewer resources and provides a better quality of life.

Figure 2-2 shows the transformation of a sprawl repair target into a part of a complete community. The change of quality of life is represented along the horizontal axis, while the vertical axis shows the quantitative change in the reduction of energy, resources, and infrastructure use per capita after the transformation. The process of transformation is shown in multiple paths direct (the straight line), phased (the stepped line), and indirect (the circuitous line). The direct path represents a case in which economics and timing support one big-effort, single-phase, radical repair. The phased path includes several steps, with portions of the project developed at different times. The indirect path represents a sequence of changes that bring the project closer to the final repaired state, but in a longer, incremental progression of trial and adjustment. No matter which path is chosen, the final result is a positive qualitative change from sprawl to walkable urbanism.

Figures 2-3, 2-4, and 2-5 compare selected urban indicators before and after sprawl repair. They illustrate the redevelopment potential of sprawl as expressed by changes of urban indicators. In all cases the density increases substantially, sufficient to support transit. It should be emphasized that transit works at a larger, regional scale, coordinated between retrofitted nodes. For example, a minimum density of 15 units to the acre can support a frequent local bus service.[1] The cases shown analyze occupant densities, rather than resident or employee densities, because the sprawl elements had single uses. In all cases, the occupant density, meaning people residing and working in an area per acre, increases dramatically (more than doubles), showing the redevelopment potential of these repair sites.

Two critical metrics shown in the figures are the length and surface of thoroughfares per capita before and after sprawl repair. In all cases, these measurements decrease. Similar reductions can be expected for other infrastructure, meaning less infrastructure is required per capita when a sprawl element is repaired with the demonstrated techniques. In the long run, such repair is less expensive and more efficient than employing methods that create sprawl.

It is important to note that in addition to increased transit-supportive density and developable real estate, these transformations add civic space, a variety of uses, and space for urban agriculture, ultimately improving the quality of life for residents and workers.

SINGLE-FAMILY SUBDIVISION				
TRANSFORMATION	CATEGORIES	BEFORE	AFTER	IMPROVEMENT OF URBAN INDICATORS
	Site acreage, acres	131	131	1.0
	Total built area,[1] sq. ft.	2,305,000	3,219,000	1.4
	Total building footprint,[2] sq. ft.	433,000	807,000	1.9
	Total building area,[3] sq. ft.	549,000	1,249,000	2.3
	Total occupant load, occupants	2,000	7,000	3.4
	Occupant density, occupants per acre	16	55	3.4
	Parking area per capita, sq. ft. per occupant	64	66	1.0
	Thoroughfare area per capita, sq. ft. per occupant	773	216	0.3
	Thoroughfare length per capita, ft. per occupant	6	2.2	0.4

1 Total built area comprises all construction, including buildings, parking, and thoroughfares.
2 Total building footprint comprises all building footprints, regardless of use.
3 Total building area comprises all building square footage. Garages of single-family residences are included.

2-3. Quantitative comparison of urban indicators in a single-family subdivision

TRANSFORMATION	CATEGORIES	BEFORE	AFTER	IMPROVEMENT OF URBAN INDICATORS
	Site acreage, acres	126	126	1.0
	Total built area,[1] sq. ft.	3,490,000	6,780,000	1.9
	Total building footprint,[2] sq. ft.	530,000	1,610,000	3.0
	Total building area,[3] sq. ft.	1,450,000	5,440,000	3.8
	Total occupant load, occupants	15,000	29,000	2.0
	Occupant density, occupants per acre	115	235	2.0
	Parking area per capita, sq. ft. per occupant	88	57	0.6
	Thoroughfare area per capita, sq. ft. per occupant	52	33	0.6
	Thoroughfare length per capita, ft. per occupant	0.7	0.5	0.7

1 Total built area comprises all construction, including buildings, parking, and thoroughfares.
2 Total building footprint comprises all building footprints, regardless of use.
3 Total building area comprises all building square footage. Parking decks are included.

2-4. Quantitative comparison of urban indicators in a business park

TRANSFORMATION	CATEGORIES	BEFORE	AFTER	IMPROVEMENT OF URBAN INDICATORS
	Site acreage, acres	230	230	1.00
	Total built area,[1] sq. ft.	5,150,000	14,500,000	2.8
	Total building footprint,[2] sq. ft.	1,290,000	3,770,000	2.9
	Total building area,[3] sq. ft.	1,770,000	11,500,000	6.5
	Total occupant load, occupants	19,000	50,000	2.6
	Occupant density, occupants per acre	84	216	2.6
	Parking area per capita, sq. ft. per occupant	77	66	0.9
	Thoroughfare area per capita, sq. ft. per occupant	100	55	0.6
	Thoroughfare length per capita, ft. per occupant	1.00	0.4	0.4

1 Total built area comprises all construction, including buildings, parking, and thoroughfares.
2 Total building footprint comprises all building footprints, regardless of use.
3 Total building area comprises all building square footage. Parking decks are included.

2-5. Quantitative comparison of urban indicators in a shopping mall

TWO MODELS

Complete communities consist of corridors, districts, and neighborhoods. These elements have defined edges and connect to form balanced urban and rural systems (figure 2-6).

Corridors are natural or manmade pathways such as greenways, creeks, wetlands, boulevards, or rail lines. Corridors can serve as transportation infrastructure for a region, linking neighborhoods, towns, and districts, or as a framework of continuous open space providing protection for wildlife and environmental networks. With the ascent of sprawl, manmade corridors such as highways and arterial roads have been overcome by strip commer-

cial development. At the same time, natural corridors in the form of greenways and creeks have been obliterated by leapfrogged development and pavement.

Districts are places where one predominant use is concentrated, such as college campuses or medical facilities. Districts are necessary elements of healthy regions and, while predominantly single-use, they can be organized in an urban structure similar to a neighborhood to fit within the surrounding context. The type of planning that produced sprawl has affected districts as well, suburbanizing them into isolated and car-dependent enclaves located far away from urban cores and residential areas. New universities have become commuter hubs in the

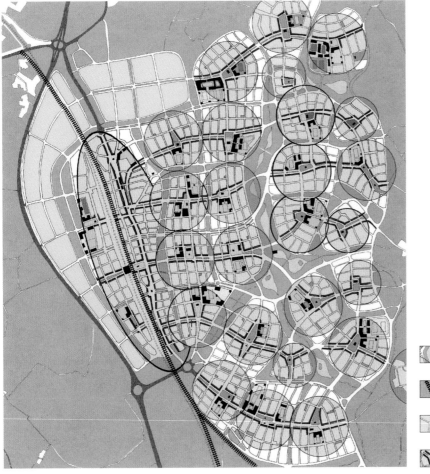

Natural corridor

Manmade corridor

District

Neighborhood

2-6. Complete communities consist of distinct corridors, districts, and neighborhoods far-flung exurbs where everyone needs a car and the campuses have been overwhelmed by parking lots and garage structures.

The pre-war planning methodology used the neighborhood as the primary unit of growth. All uses within a neighborhood were close to each other, as people needed to reach them by foot. Streetcars connected neighborhoods, while railroads connected towns and cities. Post-war development policies and practices drastically departed from this discipline, as the car provided long-distance mobility. This liberated planning from the restrictions of walkable distances between destinations, and sprawl was born (figure 2-7).

The repair of sprawl is most effective when it is applied at all scales of development – from the region, because transit should be handled at a larger scale, to the block and the building, because interventions may start small for lack of resources. Nevertheless, the neighborhood is the essential increment, because walkability and, most importantly, sustainable growth can be achieved only at this level. The traditional neighborhood model has many advantages over the conventional sprawl model of planning. The core principles and goals of the sprawl repair process are inspired by and based on the attributes of the neighborhood model.

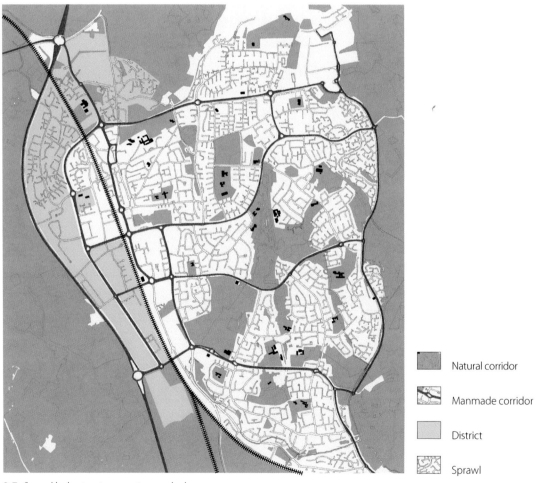

Natural corridor

Manmade corridor

District

Sprawl

2-7. Sprawl lacks structure, centers, and edges

NEIGHBORHOOD UNIT MODEL

The neighborhood unit is a comprehensive planning increment (figure 2-8). When combined with others of its kind, it becomes a town or a city. When freestanding in the landscape, it is a village or a hamlet. The neighborhood unit model has the following attributes:

- The physical size of the neighborhood is defined by a five-minute walk from its geographic center to its edge, covering approximately a quarter of a square mile.
- The basic needs of daily life are available in close proximity. The neighborhood offers transit, employment, and shopping, plus civic and leisure activities.
- Streets form a connected network, providing alternate routes that help to disperse traffic, and are equitable for vehicles, pedestrians, and bicyclists.
- Diversity in the type, size, and disposition of buildings, streets, and open spaces creates many options in environments, experiences, functions, uses, prices, and populations.
- These attributes contribute to the conservation of energy, natural resources, farmland, open spaces, time, and money.

SPRAWL MODEL

Sprawl development is not organized in a neighborhood structure (figure 2-9). Though conventional suburban subdivisions are often called "neighborhoods," they do not have the characteristics traditionally found in neighborhoods. In contrast to the neighborhood model, sprawl has the following attributes:

- Commercial, residential, and civic uses are separated from each other with no regard for distance.
- Daily needs are accessible only by car.
- Roads are arranged in a discontinuous pattern that reduces the choice of route and mode of transport, and creates congestion.
- The elements of sprawl are separate pods containing singular building types, sizes, and dispositions, leading to a limited range of environments, experiences, functions, uses, prices, and populations.
- These attributes contribute to the less-efficient use of energy, natural resources, farmland, open spaces, time, and money.

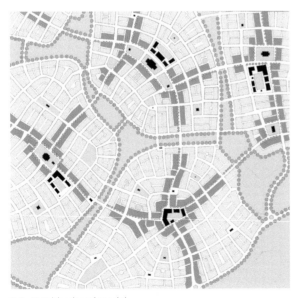

2-8. Neighborhood model

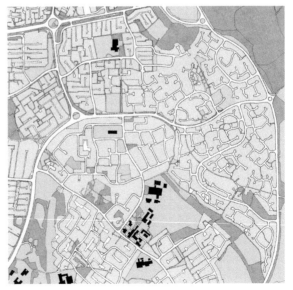

2-9. Sprawl model

Figures 2-10, 2-11, and 2-12 illustrate the differences between two models of planning. The neighborhood unit model is on the left side of the diagrams, while the sprawl model is on the right. Both communities contain the same elements – houses, offices, a school, shopping, and open space – but the elements are organized differently.

Neighborhood   Sprawl

2-10. Comparison of uses

Figure 2-10 demonstrates the mix of uses in a traditional neighborhood – a main street and square lined with shops, apartments, and offices, with blocks of houses behind the main street and a school on the edge. The sprawl model includes the same uses, but they are segregated – the houses, offices, and stores form separate pods, each surrounded by parking. The school is on the edge, as in the other model, but cannot be directly accessed from the residential area.

1. School
2. Houses
3. Shops
4. Civic building
5. Offices

Neighborhood   Sprawl

2-11. Comparison of connectivity

Figure 2-11 illustrates the urban fabric of both models – the street network in the traditional neighborhood is well connected, with all uses mixed together and accessible to each other by car, bicycle, or on foot, while the sprawl model imposes isolation at every point with a sequence of dead-end pods that are not accessible to one another except through the collector road.

 Streets
Cul-de-sacs

Neighborhood   Sprawl

Figure 2-12 shows the shorter travel distances in traditional urbanism versus the redundant and longer trips required in sprawl. The first diagram demonstrates a trip from a house to the shops, the route kept within the neighborhood. In the sprawl example, the same trip goes through the collector road, increasing traffic. This system not only requires driving, but also imposes dependence and isolation on people who are too young, too old, too sick, or too poor to drive.

■- ➤   Travel distance between home and work

2-12.   Comparison of trip lengths

Without the clarity of the neighborhood structure, conventional suburban development blurs the boundaries and characteristics of neighborhoods, corridors, and districts, and sprawls across the land. For example, strip commercial development often makes incursions into residential areas, and because the commercial and residential building types (but not their uses) are incompatible, the desire for separation grows ever stronger. The suburban edge is diluted in its interface with the natural boundaries; sprawl leapfrogs other sprawl and encroaches in areas that need to be protected, such as productive farmland and natural habitat. Sprawl repair identifies and enhances centers and edges; it takes the elements of sprawl and transforms them into complete communities – neighborhood centers, town centers, regional urban cores, and transit corridors, connected into a healthy regional structure.

As sprawl has eroded the built environment, it has also corrupted common conceptions. Terms such as "neighborhood" and "center" once had clear and commonly understood meaning. But developers of sprawl have created so many single-use housing pods, and called them "neighborhoods," and so many strip malls, and called them "town centers," that the terms have lost much of their value. Another benefit of sprawl repair

is to reclaim the meaning of terms such as these, and make them useful again. A center is a focal point (and often a gathering place), not necessarily a geographic mid-point, where a variety of housing and commercial and civic amenities are provided for surrounding suburban developments. The sprawl repair method identifies rural centers (hamlets that serve rural communities), neighborhood centers (repaired commercial and residential nodes with potential for transit, serving several suburban communities), town centers (repaired, larger-scale commercial nodes with potential for transit, serving several suburban communities), and regional urban cores (repaired employment and commercial hubs, serving a region). Sprawl repair techniques are dedicated to transforming:

- Single-use residential and commercial developments (nodes at important thoroughfares, which are concentrations with potential for higher density, mixed use, and transit) into rural centers, neighborhood centers, town centers, and regional urban cores;
- Strip commercial corridors into transit corridors and networks; and
- Commuter-oriented districts into more walkable and complete urbanism.

TECHNIQUES

The sprawl repair method is based on urban design, regulation, and implementation techniques.

These are the same instruments that have made sprawl the prevalent form of development. But when focused on retrofit and redevelopment, these tools transform the existing physical environment from sprawl to complete communities.

URBAN DESIGN TECHNIQUES

Sprawl repair should be designed at all urban scales, including repair of a regional domain, transforming sprawl elements at the community scale, and re-configuration of conventional suburban blocks and the reuse, expansion, and adaptation of single structures.

The urban design method at the regional scale

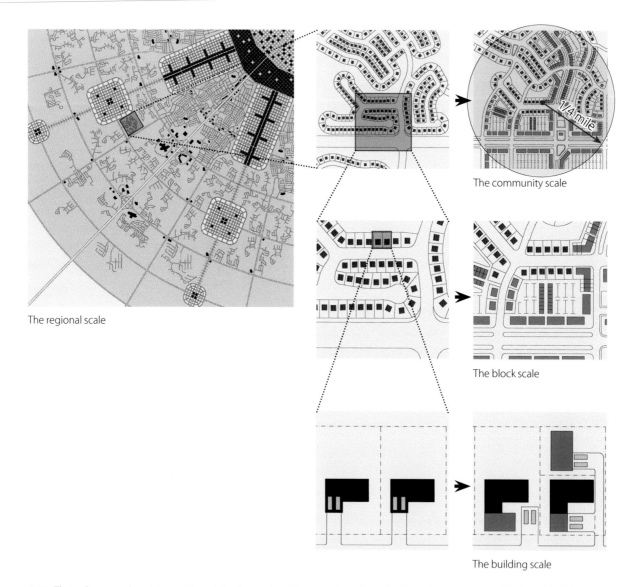

The regional scale

The community scale

The block scale

The building scale

2-13. These diagrams show interventions at the four scales of the sprawl repair method – region, community, block, and building

includes several steps that produce a document mapping the structure of sprawl repair (figure 2-13). The steps determine the physical boundaries of the regional domain, delineate the areas to be preserved and reserved, prioritize the salvageable commercial and employment nodes, determine the potential transit and infrastructure networks, identify the sprawl repair targets, and, after the transfer of development rights, assemble the final sector map. Two additional tools, the Sprawl Repair Assessment Tool and the Sprawl Repair Void Analysis, assist the urban design process at the regional scale. Chapter three, "Repair at the Regional Scale," illustrates these steps and tools.

Urban design at the community scale concentrates on restructuring sprawl into neighborhoods, transit corridors, and well-balanced districts that have short walking distances to daily needs and provide healthier environments to a multigenerational population. It has long been established that most people will choose not to walk if a destination is more than five minutes away (roughly a quarter of a mile). The distance covered in this five-minute walk is commonly called a pedestrian shed, and is usually represented (in planning documents) by a circle with a quarter-mile radius (figure 2-14). Larger circles of a half-mile radius are used when the pedestrian sheds are

centered on a transit stop, as people are willing to walk longer to such destinations. Delineating the pedestrian sheds for the potential neighborhoods and town centers happens at the regional scale (see chapter three, "Repair at the Regional Scale, Step Five: Identify the Sprawl Repair Targets"), but their detailing and urban design happen at the community scale. The pedestrian shed is a simple but essential tool in the pursuit of order and walkability in auto-oriented suburban environments.

After the pedestrian sheds are determined, the neighborhoods and town centers are shaped using a range of urban design techniques. They include introducing new building types to allow a greater mix of uses, connecting and improving thoroughfares to be more pedestrian friendly, and rationalizing parking to accommodate future urbanization and eliminate underutilized parking.

Defining open and civic space is an essential urban design technique that involves the creation of a hierarchy of well-defined spaces for common use. The integration of local food production is becoming a predominant trend and is recommended for all repair sites, as they can easily accommodate gardens and allotments, even while their urbanism is being redesigned.

The repair at the community scale is closely interrelated with the redesign of the full range of suburban

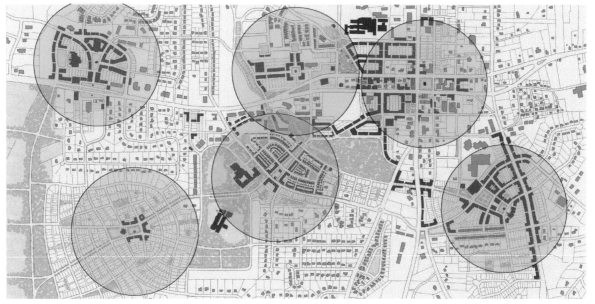

2-14. The sprawl repair method uses pedestrian sheds to delineate neighborhoods and town centers, which should be connected by transit

thoroughfares. Designed exclusively for cars, with only velocity and capacity in mind, suburban thoroughfares must be repaired into complete streets, meaning they safely and comfortably accommodate pedestrians, bicyclists, public transit, and vehicles. The urban design interventions are aimed to achieve specific character – fast and dangerous suburban thoroughfares are redesigned into pedestrian- and bike-friendly streets where vehicular traffic is accommodated without sacrificing the built environment around it. In most cases, the existing rights-of-way are kept the same, as well as the pavement width of the thoroughfares, because the proposed design changes are handled within the existing parameters. The conversion of suburban intersections into more urban and pedestrian-friendly types is also demonstrated.

Urban design at the block scale deals with techniques for transforming blocks into smaller urban increments and preparing them to become part of a future pedestrian-friendly urban fabric. Large suburban megablocks are broken down into a finer grain of smaller blocks by introducing new streets and passages, thereby establishing a coherent pattern for further redevelopment.

Repair at the building scale complements the community and block scales, as it deals with the main building stereotypes that define sprawl. These emblematic structures, via modest urban design interventions, have the potential to contribute to a more diverse, harmonious, and walkable urban fabric. Rather than being demolished, existing suburban buildings are repurposed and/or lined with new structures, often taking advantage of suburbia's typically excessive setbacks (the distances between buildings and property lines) and parking lots.

REGULATORY TECHNIQUES

Even though sprawl has proven low performance, it is still difficult to approve and finance mixed-use, walkable, and diverse projects. Furthermore, it is impossible to repair sprawl using most existing zoning practices and policies, as they are still suburban in nature. A total overhaul of current zoning practices is required for an effective intervention in suburbia. As this is impossible to do in a single, sweeping motion, new codes must be adopted one municipality, or even one project, at a time, as overlay districts, in parallel, or in place of existing codes. In all cases, these codes must powerfully incentivize smart growth rather than sprawl.

To overcome the difficulties related to building and maintaining sprawl, a gradual process of adopting form-based codes has been started by some municipalities and cities. Form-based codes regulate the form of the built environment, allowing and encouraging good place making. A model form-based code is the SmartCode, a comprehensive ordinance that enables smart growth community patterns and the transformation of sprawl into walkable urbanism.[2] The code includes a special sector (Sprawl Repair Sector G-5) that is assigned to areas that are currently single use and have disconnected conventional development patterns, but have the potential to be completed or redeveloped into neighborhoods and urban centers.

The Sprawl Repair Module has been created as a special "plug-in" to the SmartCode to activate the technology for repair as a part of the code. The module presents a sequence of techniques for retrofitting the sprawl elements into complete communities. It operates at the scale of the region, community, block, building, and thoroughfare.

Some of the sprawl areas will be up-zoned to accommodate higher but well-designed density, and allow the introduction of mixed uses and transit. This creates the regulatory basis for successional growth and the transformation of sprawl elements into viable neighborhoods with more transportation and housing choices. Conventional suburban blocks may be reconfigured to receive higher densities and additional uses.

At the scale of the building, the most important issues will be to allow flexible uses within existing structures (houses becoming live-work units, big-box retail becoming office space or a civic building), and increased density within existing parcels and lots (a mansion turned into multifamily housing or an assisted living facility, or the addition of accessory units).

Another important task is to create standards to calm and repair dangerous thoroughfares and make them safe for walking and bicycling while creating connections between residential areas, shops, workplaces, schools, civic buildings, and recreation.

The SmartCode and the Sprawl Repair Module operate according to the rural-to-urban transect (the Transect), an organizational framework and planning

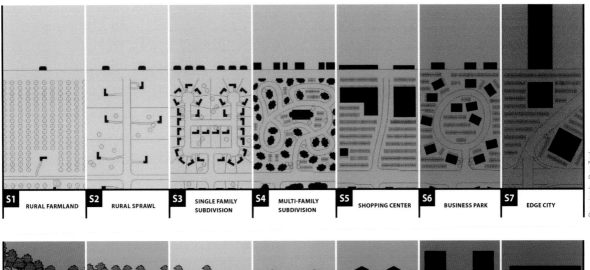

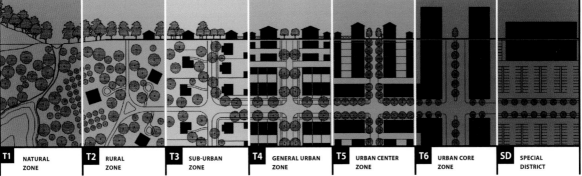

2-15. Comparison of the Transect in sprawl and in traditional urbanism, showing the lack of direct correlation between the two

T1 NATURAL ZONE consists of lands approximating or reverting to a wilderness condition, including lands unsuitable for settlement due to topography, hydrology, or vegetation.

T2 RURAL ZONE consists of sparsely settled lands in open or cultivated states. These include woodland, agricultural land, grassland, and irrigable desert. Typical buildings are farmhouses, agricultural buildings, cabins, and villas.

T3 SUB-URBAN ZONE consists of low-density residential areas, adjacent to higher zones that have some mixed use. Home offices and outbuildings are allowed. Planting is naturalistic and setbacks are relatively deep. Blocks may be large and the roads irregular to accommodate natural conditions.

T4 GENERAL URBAN ZONE consists of a mixed use but primarily residential urban fabric. It may have a wide range of building types: detached and sideyard houses, and townhouses. Setbacks and landscaping are variable.

T5 URBAN CENTER ZONE consists of higher-density, mixed-use buildings that accommodate retail, offices, townhouses, and apartments. It has a tight network of streets, with wide sidewalks, steady street tree planting, and buildings set close to the sidewalks.

T6 URBAN CORE ZONE consists of the highest density and height, with the greatest variety of uses, and civic buildings of regional importance. It may have larger blocks; streets have steady street tree planting and buildings are set close to wide sidewalks. Typically only large towns and cities have an Urban Core zone.

SPECIAL DISTRICTS consist of areas with buildings that do not conform to one or more of the six normative Transect zones.

Note: Definitions adapted from SmartCode v9.2

methodology that enables the comprehensive and effective redevelopment of our sprawling communities into more sustainable patterns. The Transect is not a mandatory tool to be imposed on planners and local governments. A transect is a concept originally used by ecologists to describe distinct natural habitats, but has been extended to cover the human habitat. The Transect,

as it relates to the built environment, organizes structural elements according to an increasing density and complexity, from the countryside to the urban core.

The lack of rural-to-urban logic in sprawl is one of the fundamental differences from traditional urbanism (figure 2-15). The Transect is broken into zones, each representing a complex habitat of different building types,

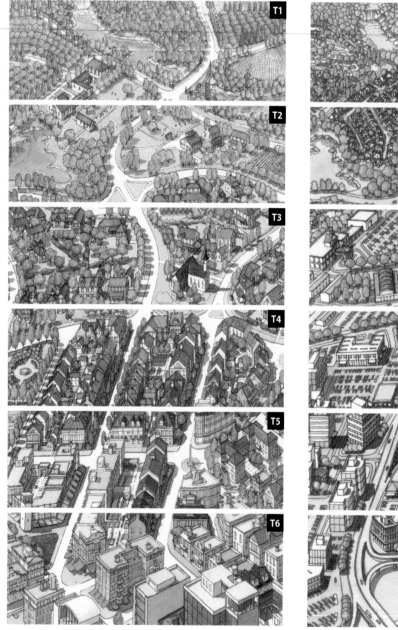

2-16. Transect of traditional urbanism

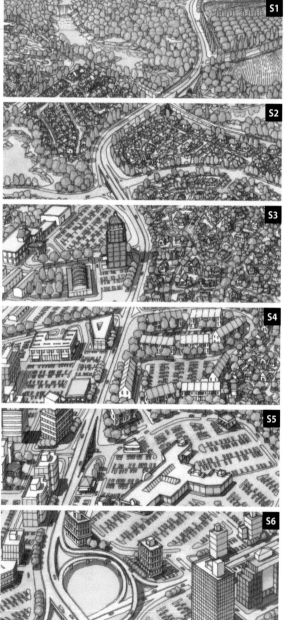

2-17. Transect of sprawl

streetscapes, and public spaces (figure 2-16). This is in contrast to sprawl, in which each element is a single-use agglomeration, usually a monoculture of a single building type (figure 2-17). The Transect zones represent zoning conditions that are similar to the ones administered by conventional zoning codes, except they include not only the building use, density, height, and setback requirements, but also how buildings relate to each other and how together they shape the public realm.

Sprawl elements cannot be repaired in isolation; they must always be considered in the context of the community scale. Single-use and typologically monotonous areas need to be balanced with other required elements and uses to form the full range of Transect zones appropriate to complete communities. For example, a residential-only suburban enclave, which accommodates only low-density housing (defined as T3, Sub-Urban zone) needs to be rebalanced with other uses and building types found in T4, General Urban, and T5, Urban Center zones. Commercial enclaves, such as malls and office parks, which exemplify the intensity of T6, Urban Core zone, need to be rebalanced with the lower-intensity Transect zones, like T3, T4, and T5. The distribution and ratios of Transect zones within the plan will be defined by a process of local adjustment and calibration of existing conditions and by the densities necessary for transit.

The Sprawl Repair Module indicates the proportions of Transect zones that need to be added or rebalanced in order to transform the sprawl repair target into a mixed-use, diverse, and transit-ready community.[3] The zoning modifications, together with the urban design adjustments, such as connecting streets and creating public space, are reflected in specific regulating plans. Chapter four, "Repair at the Community Scale," demonstrates several examples of regulating plans of repaired sprawl elements.

IMPLEMENTATION TECHNIQUES

Sprawl has been encouraged for decades through policies and legislation, and its repair must also be encouraged, even directly incentivized. The two main techniques to encourage and incentivize the private sector are easier permitting and infrastructure funding.

Permitting and incentivizing the repair of strategically located commercial nodes – malls, regional shopping centers, employment hubs, edge cities (agglomerations of high-intensity uses in suburban or exurban areas) – should be the first on the list of sprawl repair interventions. Repair of these elements not only promises maximum return on investment but has the potential to galvanize the transformation of vast swaths of nearby sprawl development. These nodes represent the largest monetary and real estate investments in suburbia, and in most cases they are still under single ownership. If they are redeveloped as complete town centers, with residential and office components to supplement the retail, transit between these intensified nodes will become viable.

Smaller commercial entities are the next targets, and failing residential subdivisions are last. The choices for the latter will include: evolution into mixed-use neighborhood centers if they have potential for intensification and transit, or devolution – abandonment or conversion to park or agricultural land.

A practical outline of incentives for implementation is presented in chapter four, "Repair at the Community Scale." The strongest incentive for repair of commercial nodes is public money for infrastructure, but it should be available for only the most environmentally responsible and well-designed projects, because those will have the greatest positive and far-reaching effect on their larger contexts. In addition, public-private partnerships can be effective, and government-funding programs are available for some projects (Tax Increment Financing, Business Improvement Districts, Energy Efficiency and Conservation Block Grants, etc.). Some of these have already been used in retrofitting projects and can be helpful in the transitional time when such projects are still the exception.

To change the entrenched sprawl system, it may be necessary to introduce legislation. The "Florida Sprawl Repair Act," developed for the Florida Department of Community Affairs, provides a list of incentives that can be implemented at different levels of government.[4] It has not yet been adopted into law, but it can be pursued as such and used as a template by other states. The document contains protocol for repairing malls and suggestions for funding, management, partnerships, phasing, and implementation.

CHAPTER THREE

REPAIR AT THE REGIONAL SCALE

To be most effective, sprawl repair must begin at the regional scale and consider the larger context – existing infrastructure, thoroughfare connectivity, potential for transit, and goals for preservation and regeneration of natural systems. The objective is to analyze transportation, other infrastructure, and natural areas as a complete system and to identify the nodes best suited for repair.

Parts of suburban sprawl have the potential to be transformed into desirable urban nodes because they contain employment concentrations and have potential for economic growth. Ideal examples are located along thoroughfare networks that support transit or can be repaired to accommodate it.

Demographic and economic projections are critical factors when making decisions at the regional scale.

The analysis must cover two contradictory tendencies that make the case for sprawl repair. First, according to the U.S. Census, between 1999 and 2009 most growth has happened in suburban areas, and the projections are that suburban expansion will continue. Second is the convergence in the coming decades of the two largest generations in U.S. history, the aging Baby Boomers and the Millennials, both of whom have very specific preferences for urban places. Many people are interested in the more diverse, sustainable lifestyles urban areas offer. But existing cities and downtowns may not have the capacity to absorb the millions of people who will be looking for diversified living arrangements.

Sprawl repair as a regional strategy is the answer to the demographic challenges. The existence of jobs within a suburbanized region is the driver behind any

Drawing by James Wassell

3-1. Regional plan using natural boundaries to prevent continued sprawl development

such strategy, because retail and residential development are typically driven by the job market. The redevelopment of sprawl reverses the process that started sprawl in the post war years – housing was the first element to move out of the city, followed by shopping centers and malls, and finally joined by offices and workplaces. The repair starts with the areas that hold the strongest potential for employment and for supporting viable urban centers that will sustain economic growth and minimize the need for long commuter trips.

Existing employment-only districts, such as California's Silicon Valley and edge cities, are promising yet challenging targets for urbanization. Edge cities with high concentrations of Class A office space and/ or regional shopping destinations, such as Tyson's Corner in Virginia, can be converted into urban cores with higher-density living arrangements and new green jobs and technologies. In times of tightened economic circumstances, such ambitious projects may not seem feasible, but the goals of sprawl repair should be set high enough to satisfy the needs of future generations. In the context of a promising regional economy, social stability and political will for such projects may attract incremental investment over a longer span of time. The Millennials will be attracted to such hubs, as will the Baby Boomers, who will be seeking opportunities for active retirement, lifelong learning, and social interaction.

Sprawl repair at the regional scale starts with the delineation of the urbanized areas in conjunction with environmental evaluation of the region and projections of demographics, transportation needs, and economic growth. The urban boundary model, conceptualized by Ebenezer Howard, uses statistical projection to delineate the urbanized area. The rural or natural boundary model, developed by Benton MacKaye, uses cultural and ecological criteria to prioritize open space to be protected from urbanization.[1] The two models are typically used in combination, but for the sprawl repair process the rural boundary approach is more practical, as the borders between developed and undeveloped areas in sprawl are already diluted, and the imposition of an urban boundary may be either redundant or politically impossible. The rural boundary method allows for the identification and reclamation of environmentally sensitive open-space networks that were damaged and obscured by sprawl. Such systems can be delineated and mapped as areas to be repaired and preserved in perpetuity. One example is the reduction of impervious parking lots of malls and strip shopping centers, which results in relief of stress on the watershed.

The repair at the regional scale identifies for redevelopment existing commercial nodes based on efficient spacing for transit. After their transformation, these nodes will become mixed-use neighborhood centers, town centers, and regional urban cores, ideally in proximity to transit stops.

SECTOR MAPPING

To identify the logical places for retrofit and repair, the mapping of the region should integrate analysis of projected economic and demographic growth, existing transportation, infrastructure, commercial nodes, natural resources, housing, and job concentrations.

The resulting sector map, with identified targets for sprawl repair, can accompany the comprehensive plan for a particular county or region and can be a powerful tool for metropolitan planning organizations (MPOs) when setting goals for their long-range transportation plans (figure 3-2). The targets will be the logical places for private development and public investment in services, utilities, and green (open space and natural elements) and grey infrastructure (manmade infrastructure), as well as financial and permitting incentives from specific federal, state, or local sources. Adopting form-based codes at the community scale will help municipalities with the implementation of sprawl repair at the regional scale.

Following is a step-by-step description of the sprawl repair process at the regional scale, using a hypothetical portion of a region as an example. Depending on the conditions of a given region, some steps may be used out of sequence or omitted entirely, but when tailored to the needs of the region, they offer a useful repair protocol. The first six steps provide the basis for the sector map, which is finalized in the last, seventh step.

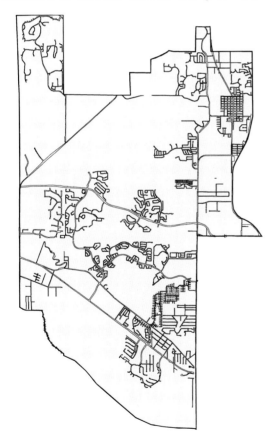
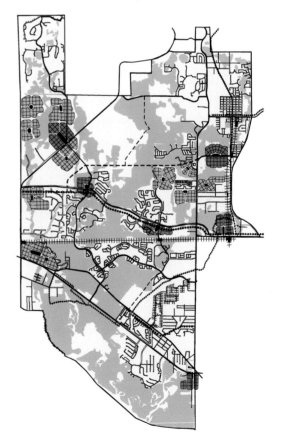

 Existing sprawl   Neighborhood centers   Town centers Preservation areas Multimodal connections

3-2. Example of sector mapping of a suburbanized county

STEP ONE: DETERMINE SPRAWL REPAIR DOMAINS

The process begins with the delineation of the various sprawl repair domains within a region. These may or may not coincide with existing municipal boundaries, which are political constructs that do not always correspond to the geography or patterns of development. Mapping entire suburban regions for sprawl repair is possible but focusing on domains, or areas smaller than entire regions, is more practical. The domains for sprawl repair are chosen for their potential to become mixed-use and transit-connected nodes for the larger region. These domains can be larger than or coincide with the sprawl repair sectors, which are the specific areas where sprawl repair will take place and where regulatory reforms will be focused.

Within a given domain, the areas identified as sprawl repair sectors are individual agglomerations of single-use, disconnected commercial and residential enclaves, strip commercial corridors, and commuter-oriented districts that have the potential to be transformed into neighborhood and town centers, regional urban cores, transit corridors, and well-balanced districts.

At this first step, it is important to identify the existing thoroughfare system, which is limited to a few types carrying high volumes of traffic – freeways, arterials, collectors, locals, and cul-de-sacs (see chapter five, "Repair of Thoroughfares and Parking," for descriptions and discussions of types of thoroughfares). Ideally, this incomplete network will be repaired to support a multimodal transportation network and walkable fabric.

3-3. Step One: Determination of sprawl repair domains

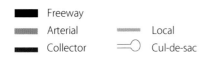

▮▮▮ Freeway
▮▮▮ Arterial   ▬▬▬ Local
▮▮▮ Collector   ⊃◯ Cul-de-sac

☐ Identify the regional domain with its geographical boundaries and its potential growth areas.
☐ Identify the sprawl repair sector as a target for regional redevelopment.

STEP TWO: DELINEATE PRESERVATION AND RESERVATION AREAS

Next in the process is the identification of open space to be preserved, reserved, or repaired. Some of these environmentally and culturally significant lands, such as jurisdictional wetlands and those under conservation easements, are already protected by law. These should be mapped as preservation areas. Others, such as floodplains and view corridors, should be, but are not yet, protected from development, and are candi-

dates for transfer of development rights (discussed in step six). These are in the reservation areas.

The portions of open space networks that should have been preserved, but are damaged and in need of repair and restoration, will be allocated to the reservation areas. Once the rehabilitation process begins, the land will become a part of the preservation areas.

3-4. Step Two: Delineation of preservation and reservation areas

■ Preservation Area
▨ Reservation Area

☐ Identify areas where development should not occur.
☐ Analyze open space for potential watershed restoration, daylighting of bodies of water, and other retrofitting strategies.

STEP THREE: PRIORITIZE THE COMMERCIAL AND EMPLOYMENT NODES

Commercial nodes and employment clusters are identified and prioritized according to their regional importance, as they will become the town centers, the neighborhood centers, and regional urban cores. Parts of the U.S. retail market are overdeveloped, with a great surplus of commercial establishments ranging in size and service area from convenience stores to regional malls (figure 3-5). Many of these service areas overlap, creating the conditions for retail oversaturation and mutual extinction (for description of the retail types see chapter four, "Repair at the Community Scale: Shopping Center"). In this context, the choice of commercial targets for repair and redevelopment is of strategic importance to the region, and needs to be carried out methodically.

The regional commercial nodes that have the best locations for transit and job generation (malls, employment hubs, regional power centers) and potential for financial incentives are assigned the highest priority for retrofit and will become regional urban cores and town centers. The second tier of commercial nodes that serve smaller areas but have the capacity to receive new uses, building types, and added density – while connecting to the adjacent residential enclaves – are assigned moderate priority. These can be strip shopping centers or suburban office parks. Low priority will be given to the small commercial establishments that typically occur at intersections at the entrances of residential subdivisions. These intersections can be transformed into neighborhood centers that simultaneously serve several enclaves (see chapter four, "Repair at the Community Scale: Single-Family Subdivision").

RETAIL TYPE			SIZE (square feet)		SERVICE AREA (radius)		REPAIR PRIORITY		
SYMBOL	SPRAWL TYPE	REPAIRED TYPE	MINIMUM	MAXIMUM	MINIMUM	MAXIMUM	LOW	MODERATE	HIGH
	Convenience Store	Corner Store	1,500	2,500	1/4 mile	1 mile	X		
	Convenience Center	Main Street /Neighborhood Center	10,000	30,000	1 mile	2 miles		X	
	"Neighborhood Center"	Town Center	60,000	120,000	2 miles	5 miles			X
	Community Center	Town Center	150,000	500,000	4 miles	7 miles			X
	Regional Center	Town Center	600,000	1.5 M	5 miles	15 miles			X
	Power Center	Regional Urban Core	500,000	1.5 M	5 miles	15 miles +			X
	Employment Center	Regional Urban Core	N/A	N/A	5 miles	15 miles			X

3-5. Commercial types classified and prioritized for sprawl repair

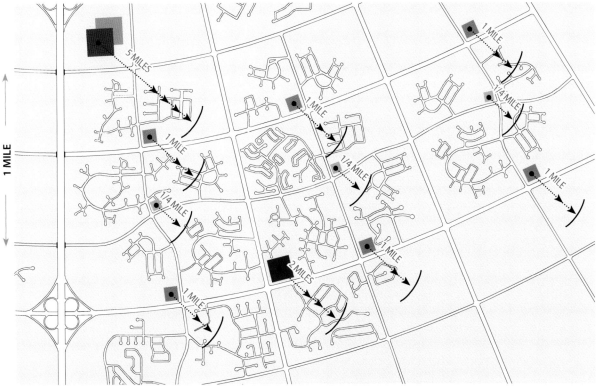

3-6. Step Three: Classification of retail types and ranking of priority for sprawl repair

 Service Area Radius (not to scale)

Convenience Store
Convenience Center
"Neighborhood Center"
Community Center
Regional Center
Power Center
Employment Center

☐ Analyze the existing system of commercial and employment nodes, including service areas.

☐ Identify the high-priority targets for redevelopment and repair: employment hubs and regional shopping centers that can be transformed into regional urban cores and town centers.

☐ Identify the moderate-priority nodes for redevelopment and repair: strip shopping centers and office parks that can be transformed into main streets and neighborhood centers.

☐ Identify targets to be given low priority for redevelopment and repair: convenience stores, gas stations, subdivision entrances that can be transformed into corner stores.

STEP FOUR: PRIORITIZE THE POTENTIAL TRANSIT AND INFRASTRUCTURE NETWORKS

Adapting auto-oriented thoroughfare networks to rational, multi-modal transportation systems is fundamental to sprawl repair at the regional scale. The potential transit routes are identified as an overlay of scarce and disconnected, sprawling thoroughfare systems. New transit connections, as well as new streets and roads, are added to form truly functional networks and create conditions to disperse traffic and reduce congestion. Improving street connectivity also improves the pedestrian experience.

The most logical locations for transit within the metropolitan region are the corridors that connect existing urban cores (traditional cities and towns) with the potential regional urban cores, town centers, and neighborhood centers (those repaired from sprawl elements that will accommodate high enough residential densities to make transit viable). Transit-supportive densities vary according to the type of transit. For example, light rail requires a minimum of nine dwelling units per acre, while frequent local bus systems require 15.

Public transportation strategies can include heavy rail alongside or within existing freeways. Light rail should be considered along arterials, where the commercial nodes with potential for retrofit are located.

But before rail is chosen, bus transit should be analyzed as a cheaper alternative, especially in the transitional period of urban intensification while the mixed-use nodes are being built. Rail may be considered a better environmental choice, depending on the source of power, but both rail and bus systems should be employed to create an extensive network of mass transit. Bus Rapid Transit (BRT) can happen along arterials or collectors, later to be supplemented or replaced by light rail. BRT can be complemented by circulator bus networks to gather passengers from the future neighborhood centers that will be organized around the medium-priority commercial nodes. When light rail arrives, it can share stops with the BRT and circulator buses, forming multi-modal hubs and sub-regional destinations.

This step also includes the analysis and prioritization of other significant infrastructure necessary for the conveyance of water, communications, and energy, as well as additional transportation networks such as regional trails, canals, airports, and bridges. These networks are essential components in the sprawl repair process at the regional scale, and should be coordinated and planned concurrently.

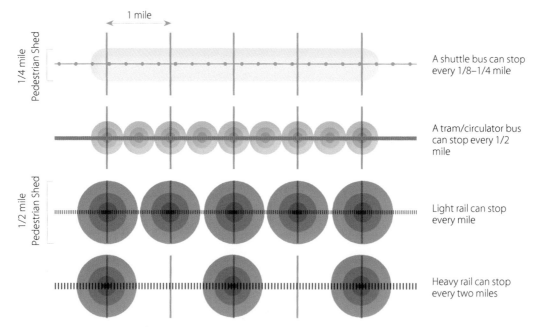

3-7. Pedestrian sheds and intervals of transit stops

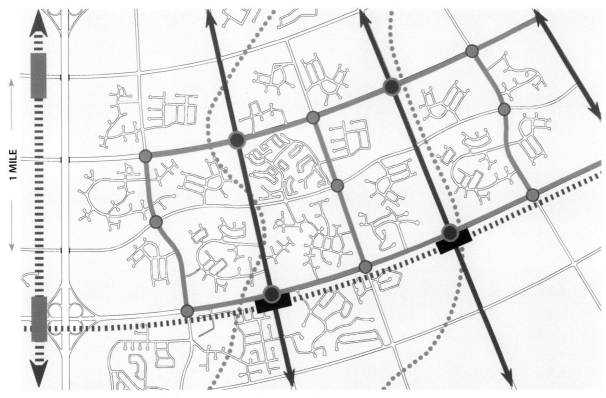

3-8. Step Four: Future transit and infrastructure networks prioritized

IIIIIIIIII	Heavy Rail Line
ıııııııııııı	Light Rail Line
▬▬▬	Rail Stop
▬▬▬	Intramodal Facility
←→	Bus Rapid Transit Route (BRT)
▬▬▬	Tram / Circulator Bus Route
●	Tram / Circulator Bus Stop / Walk-up Station
●	Shared Stop / Sub-Regional Destination
• • • • •	Trail System / Pedestrian and Bike Paths

☐ Analyze the existing thoroughfare and transit network.

☐ Propose new connections and new thoroughfares that would help to complete the sparse network and accommodate BRT and circulator buses.

☐ Propose possible routes for heavy and light rail system based on density and destinations.

☐ Propose possible routes for biking and pedestrian trail networks.

☐ Analyze and prioritize other operational infrastructure networks.

STEP FIVE: IDENTIFY THE SPRAWL REPAIR TARGETS

The next action identifies the specific locations for intervention and repair. These locations were determined in previous steps to be the best prospects for transit stops and job generation. Not all commercial nodes coincide with the spacing for transit, and not all transit stops will become full-fledged town centers. Some stops, for example, may become park-and-ride stations to serve the suburban population. The targets selected for sprawl repair are the ones where transit and job potential overlap, with the possibility for achieving residential density to support transit. They will be transformed into neighborhood centers, town centers, and regional urban cores.

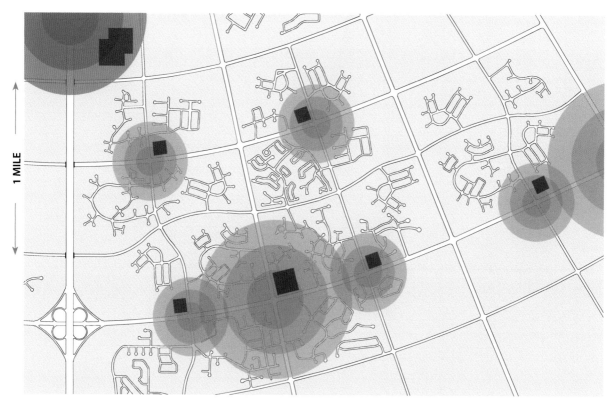

3-9. Step Five: Sprawl repair targets identified

 Neighborhood Center
 Town Center
Regional Urban Core

■ Commercial Node
▪ Employment Hub

□ Identify locations for sprawl repair targets in the form of neighborhood centers, town centers, and regional urban cores to coincide with commercial and transit nodes.

STEP SIX: IMPLEMENT TRANSFER OF DEVELOPMENT RIGHTS

The transfer of development rights (TDR) is a governmental mechanism that assigns the legal development potential allowed under zoning ordinances from an area to be protected to a property in an area slated for growth or redevelopment. In the case of sprawl repair at the regional scale, TDR could be used to transfer the right to develop land in the reservation areas to an area identified for high development priority. TDR is one tool that can be used to help ensure that the reserved areas are not developed and will join the preservation areas in perpetuity. Other tools include Purchase of Development Rights (PDRs) (in which a land bank is established to purchase development rights and hold or transfer them to designated receiving areas), and conservation

easements acquired by not-for-profit organizations or other entities.

After lands have been set aside from development, they should be assessed to see if repair is needed. These lands should receive the highest priority for repair, employing state-of-the-art principles of watershed restoration and stormwater practices. Where feasible, bodies of water should be daylighted, and impervious asphalt replaced with pervious surfaces. Stormwater facilities should be added in the form of rain gardens, depressed squares, manmade canals and lakes, and green roofs. These are all part of a green network at the community scale, but contribute to a comprehensive, regional system of environmental repair.

1 MILE

3-10. Step Six: Transfer of development rights

▨ Preservation and Reservation Areas

□ Transfer development rights from the reservation areas to the sprawl repair sector – specifically to the town centers and regional urban cores.

□ Reservation areas become preservation areas once they are protected.

STEP SEVEN: ASSEMBLE THE SECTOR MAP

The assembly of the sector map is based on the existing regional domain and is derived from the previous steps. The identified sprawl repair targets (neighborhood centers, town centers, and regional urban cores), potential transit networks, and open space areas to be preserved are combined to form the sector map. The land not targeted for repair may stay as sprawl development or devolve to natural open space or agricultural use. This will be a decision dependent on the community and their leadership, to be achieved through a public process and coordinated with the regional planning strategies. The Sprawl Repair Assessment Tool, discussed next, can assist the public in reaching consensus on how to implement sprawl repair.

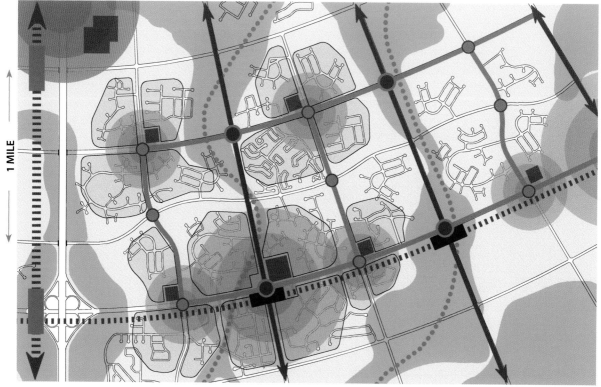

1 MILE

3-11. Step Seven: Sector map assembled

◉ Neighborhood Center	‖‖‖‖‖ Heavy Rail Line		□ Assemble the sector map with neighborhood centers, town centers, regional urban cores, transit networks, and preservation areas.
◉ Town Center	⣿⣿⣿⣿ Light Rail Line		
◉ Regional Urban Core	▬ Rail Stop		□ Set aside areas that are not designated for preservation and not targeted for repair. These may remain as sprawl or devolve into agricultural lands or natural open space.
■ Commercial Node	▬ Intramodal Facility		
■ Employment Hub	↔ Bus Rapid Transit (BRT)		
⛨ Sprawl	▬ Tram / Circulator Bus		
	● Circulator Bus Stop		
	● Sub-Regional Shared Stop		
	•••• Trail System		

SPRAWL REPAIR ASSESSMENT TOOL

As detailed in the seven steps of sprawl repair at the regional scale, the potential for repair is determined in the sector map, based on location, transit possibilities, and a variety of demographic, economic, and environmental factors.

However, the designated area or target should be further analyzed for its feasibility for successful repair. The Sprawl Repair Assessment Tool can be used to determine the potential for transformation into a complete community.

EVOLUTION OR DEVOLUTION		
POTENTIAL FOR:	**YES**	**NO**
Neighborhood Structure	☐	☐
Viable Infrastructure and Utilities	☐	☐
Environmental Performance	☐	☐
Robust Housing Stock	☐	☐
Financial Viability	☐	☐
SCORE	**THREE OR MORE?**	**THREE OR MORE?**
DECISION	**EVOLUTION**	**DEVOLUTION**
OUTCOME	Neighborhood center Town center Regional urban core	Remain as is Replace with agricultural land Revert to natural open space

3-12. Assessment tool

SPRAWL REPAIR VOID ANALYSIS

The Sprawl Repair Void Analysis facilitates the identification of the characteristics and amenities that are needed to transform sprawling places into complete communities.

The targets for sprawl repair as defined in the sector map should be vested or permitted administratively, by right. Vesting is a strong incentive for repair of sprawl. This system, however, is vulnerable to abuse by creating hybrid or incomplete neighborhoods. A checklist of criteria or void analysis can address this problem by forming a basis for acceptance. Planning officials can use it to determine whether submitted plans are likely to provide the social and environmental benefits associated with complete communities and whether they qualify for increased density allocation and other incentives such as deferral of assessment fees and vesting.

The Sprawl Repair Void Analysis can also serve developers, allowing them to analyze the deficiencies of sprawling enclaves and determine what elements need to be added and whether a retrofit is financially viable.

A target for sprawl repair has the potential for most of the following:

NEIGHBORHOOD STRUCTURE

An area targeted for repair should have a framework within which a viable neighborhood unit can be created. There should be a discernible center, with a transit stop, that can be transformed into a plaza, square, green, or memorable intersection. This center may or may not be the geographic mid-point of the neighborhood as mixed use works better at the edge if shared with other neighborhoods.

New buildings can be introduced at the center, or existing buildings can be retrofitted to be close to the sidewalk and to each other, creating a sense of spatial definition. Most other buildings in the community can retain larger setbacks and be farther apart from each other, maintaining the suburban character.

The area within a five-to-seven-minute walk from the center can be repaired by adding new buildings and repurposing existing ones.

A variety of dwelling types can be introduced, or existing buildings can be retrofitted into live-work units, duplexes, townhouses, and apartments, such that a multigenerational, diverse population can find places to live.

New businesses can be incubated and new or retrofitted workplaces can be provided in the form of office buildings or live-work units.

Sufficiently varied shops and services can be planned to supply the ordinary needs of a household. A convenience store, a post office, a teller machine, daycare, and a gym are the most important among them. It is challenging to attract shops and services to repaired enclaves; however, it will be an easier task than attracting them to brand new developments, because existing developments already have the density that will be multiplied to support transit and will be able to support shops and services.

Houses can be expanded to reduce the deep, suburban-style front setbacks to make the streets more pedestrian friendly, to introduce a mix of uses, and to provide additional density to support transit. Ancillary buildings can be permitted within the front or back yard of each house. These may be used as rental apartments or home offices. Some lots can be divided to form duplex arrangements.

An elementary school should exist or be planned, close enough that most children can walk or bike from their dwellings. This distance should not be more than one mile.

Playgrounds can be created near every dwelling. The distance from a dwelling to a playground should not be more than one-eighth of a mile. Vacant lots or leftover open space can be utilized for this purpose.

Certain prominent sites can be reserved for public buildings. A space should be provided for neighborhood meetings and civic activities.

Local food production can be introduced utilizing deep suburban-style setbacks, empty lots, defunct golf courses, and other sprawling open space. Urban agriculture should be integrated on all scales: small and large farmsteads along the edges of the neighborhood, allotment and community gardens within the community, and roof, balcony, and kitchen gardens within private lots.

It is possible, through sprawl repair, to provide independent and assisted living housing for the aging to create lifelong communities.

The community and property owners should be organized and involved in decisions relating to sprawl repair and physical evolution or devolution, maintenance, and security.

VIABLE INFRASTRUCTURE AND UTILITIES

It should be feasible to preserve and reuse most of the existing grey infrastructure and utilities, and to upgrade and expand them for higher urban intensity. Water, sewer, electricity, and communications should be upgradable to handle higher densities, as well as to incorporate new energy-saving and energy-generating technologies.

There is a potential for recovery and the creation of connections to nature and green infrastructure, such as pedestrian and biking trails, and sustainable stormwater networks.

The existing thoroughfares within the target area can be connected to form a network, providing a variety of routes and dispersing traffic. The thoroughfares should connect to those of adjacent developments as often as possible.

The existing thoroughfares can be retrofitted to calm traffic and create a comfortable environment for pedestrians and bicyclists by introducing on-street parking, wider sidewalks, medians, access lanes, and street trees, among other elements.

Open parking lots and garages can be concealed with liner buildings (thin, masking structures) or landscape. Parking lots can be reorganized and relegated to the rear of buildings, and some blocks can be retrofitted to add alleys or lanes.

ENVIRONMENTAL PERFORMANCE

Sprawl repair strategies improve the environmental performance of suburban communities. The Transect methodology can be used to provide choices of urban and rural environments and improve the overall socio-economic and natural diversity within an area (see chapter two, "The Sprawl Repair Method: Regulatory Techniques"). Allowing denser building types and mixed uses within the Transect zones will improve the total environmental performance of the place, as people will drive less, save energy, and reduce carbon emissions.

Introducing sustainable stormwater management practices calibrated along the Transect contributes to preservation and repair of regional watersheds. Stormwater should be treated on the site in the more rural zones, and off-site in urban zones. Sustainable tools such as pervious paving, channeling, storage, and filtration should be selected according to their location along the Transect. (Also see *The Light Imprint Handbook* by Thomas Low, which provides a range of sustainable alternatives to conventional stormwater practices).[2]

Open space should be connected to form networks, and environmentally sensitive areas should be protected and restored.

Additional modes of transportation can be introduced to reduce car dependence, air pollution, and energy use.

ROBUST BUILDING STOCK

Technologies for renewable and efficient energy use can be incorporated within the existing and the new building stock. Some of the techniques include retrofitting strategies to provide for natural cooling, ventilation, and daylighting, reducing the surface-to-volume ratio, adding passive solar systems, re-using grey water, and treating and recycling solid waste. Green building standards such as the ones established by the U.S. Green Building Council (Leadership in Energy and Environmental Design or LEED), Energy Star, Southface Institute, and the Florida Green Building Coalition should be integrated in the process of sprawl repair at the building scale.

FINANCIAL VIABILITY

The repair target is selected at the regional scale because it demonstrates potential for job generation and economic growth. The redevelopment should also make financial sense for the private sector. Below are some necessary conditions for economic viability of the repair (for financing sources see chapter four, "Repair at the Community Scale, Step Four: Secure Incentives for Implementation").

It should be possible to achieve the repair incrementally, in manageable phases, with smaller investments required at each stage.

In the case of multiple property owners, some parcels should be aggregated, facilitating faster and more extensive repair. The process is more feasible with commercial properties where ownership is concentrated in fewer hands, while acquisitions within residential subdivisions will be more difficult and gradual because there are multiple owners.

The higher densities and diversified uses should be adequate to expect healthy profit margins. Smart growth and New Urbanist projects in the form of complete communities have demonstrated higher real estate values and market premiums. If sprawl repair projects reach the high standards of these models, they should be able to achieve similar economic success.

Affordable housing should be included, whether through the adaptive reuse of existing structures (single-family houses converted into duplexes and multi-family units, or commercial buildings converted into residential) or in new infill buildings such as ancillary units and garage apartments.

APPLICATION: REPAIR BY DEVOLUTION

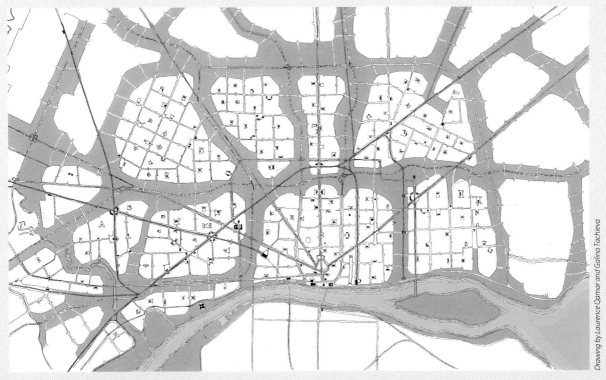

Drawing by Laurence Qamar and Galina Tachieva

4-13. Complete communities defined by agricultural greenbelts

Drawing by Laurence Qamar and Galina Tachieva

4-14. Repair of a neighborhood by contraction and densification

Detroit, which has experienced economic and population decline for decades, has long been the target of ideas for "shrinking" and devolution. A study from 1993 shows the reduction of the physical infrastructure of the city and its immediate suburbs into compact, ecologically sustainable communities (figure 3-13).

The main transportation corridors (railroads and highways) are transformed into linear greenbelts for natural drainage, habitat corridors, and local food production, but keep their mobility function. Organic gardens and open space are easily accessible from the newly restored urban fabric (figure 3-14). The denser, better preserved neighborhoods are repaired around existing clusters of civic structures, while the least populated ones are converted into low-density, agricultural settlements.

APPLICATION: COASTAL SECTOR REPAIR AND INFILL

The aerial photograph shows the existing conditions of a coastal sector dominated by sprawling development (figure 3-15). A major thoroughfare runs along the inland edge of a subdivision that is surrounded by land that has potential for infill. The predominantly single-family development is along canals, which preclude a connected thoroughfare network. Commercial uses are located in segregated pods along the main thoroughfares.

After delineating the natural zones that will be preserved using available environmental data, a neighborhood structure overlay plan is assembled (figure 3-16). It allocates the quarter-square-mile pedestrian sheds of the neighborhoods and the ten-minute center-to-edge sprawl repair sectors that will be the future town centers. The locations of the neighborhoods are selected where existing natural and manmade conditions coincide for

3-15. Sprawl at the scale of a regional sector

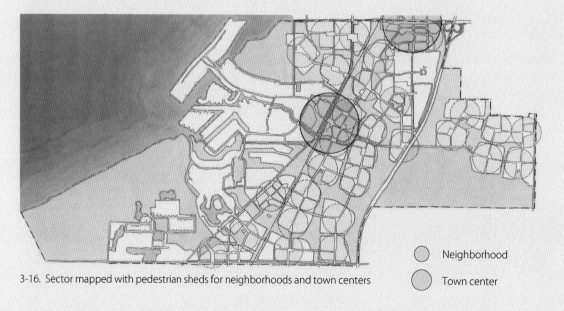

3-16. Sector mapped with pedestrian sheds for neighborhoods and town centers

○ Neighborhood

○ Town center

best connectivity and proximity, while the town centers are retrofits of existing commercial nodes into mixed-use cores serving several neighborhoods and located on projected public transportation routes.

The pedestrian sheds are further developed into urban fabric of connected, multi-modal streets (figure 3-17). The infill sector is connected to the existing suburban development across the transit corridor by multiple vehicular and pedestrian links. The Transect-based zoning overlay shows the neighborhood centers and the higher intensity town centers, in darker colors (figure 3-18). This overlay allows for a variety of building types and uses that will rebalance the collection of existing residential and commercial pods into a regional domain of connected, complete neighborhoods and town centers.

3-17. Pedestrian sheds and connected urban fabric

T1 - Natural zone
T3 - Sub-Urban zone
T4 - General Urban zone
T5 - Urban Center zone
T6 - Urban Core zone
CS - Civic Space

3-18. Transect-zoning overlay

APPLICATION: REPAIR AFTER FLOODING

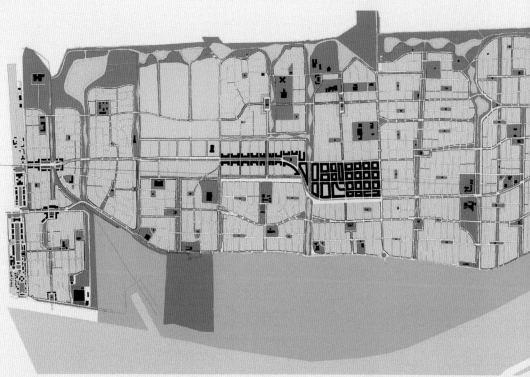

3-19. Scenario one: Full rebuilding after flooding

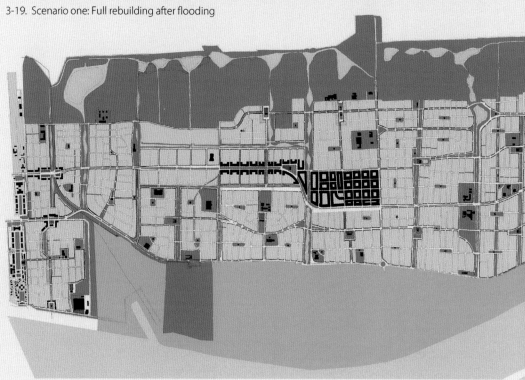

3-20. Scenario two: Partial rebuilding within smaller area

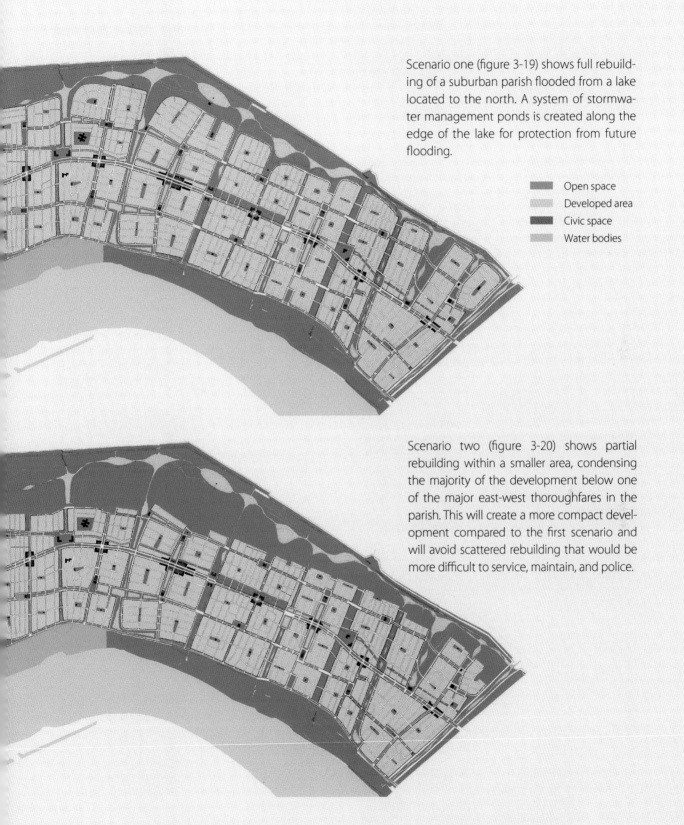

Scenario one (figure 3-19) shows full rebuilding of a suburban parish flooded from a lake located to the north. A system of stormwater management ponds is created along the edge of the lake for protection from future flooding.

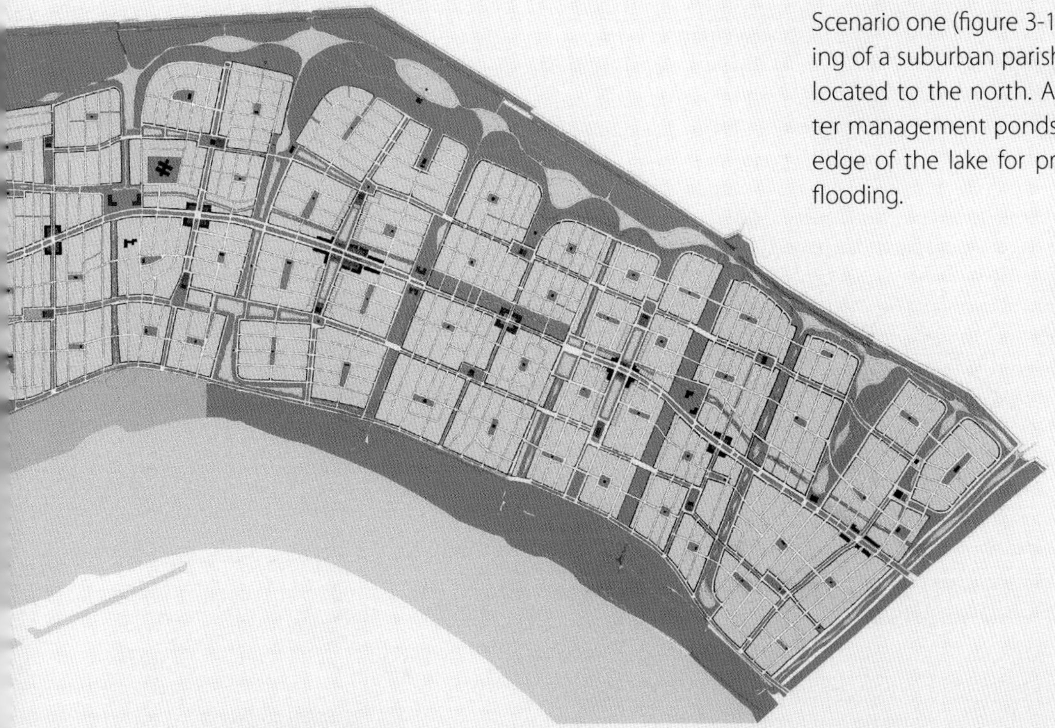
Open space
Developed area
Civic space
Water bodies

Scenario two (figure 3-20) shows partial rebuilding within a smaller area, condensing the majority of the development below one of the major east-west thoroughfares in the parish. This will create a more compact development compared to the first scenario and will avoid scattered rebuilding that would be more difficult to service, maintain, and police.

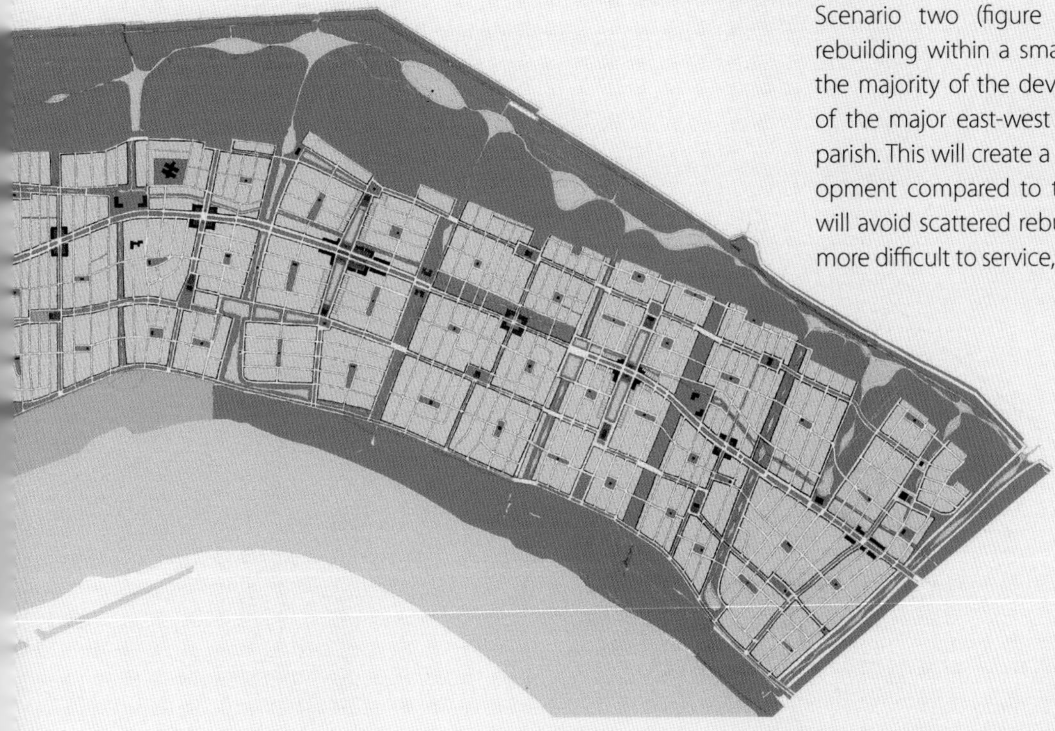

CHAPTER FOUR

REPAIR AT THE COMMUNITY SCALE

Sprawl repair at the community scale concentrates on the specific techniques used to transform the disjointed individual elements of sprawl and combine them to create complete communities that are walkable, based on the human scale, and contain a mix of uses and multi-modal transportation. The community scale is the most important in the process of sprawl repair because it makes the connection between the big picture of the region and the narrow focus of the individual street and building. It is at this scale that the crucial elements of sprawl repair – walkability and the public realm – are achieved.

The design techniques include connecting and transforming thoroughfares, creating a fabric of urban blocks, forming a variety of civic spaces, mixing uses both vertically and horizontally, introducing a variety of building types, restructuring parking, and many others. As pointed out in chapter two, "The Sprawl Repair Method," these techniques are used to create types of communities – hamlets (small villages or rural centers), neighborhood centers, town centers, and regional urban cores – that are very different from sprawl in their physical form. Strip commercial corridors are also transformed into transit corridors and commuter-oriented districts, and campuses are improved into more walkable and balanced urbanism. Sprawl-type open space is also analyzed and retrofitted at the community scale.

This chapter explains the transformation of the following typical sprawl elements:
- Rural subdivision into a hamlet,
- Single-family subdivision into a neighborhood center,
- Multifamily subdivision into a town center,
- Shopping center into a town center,
- Shopping mall into a town center,
- Commercial strip into a nodal, transit boulevard,
- Business park into a town center,
- Edge city into a regional urban core,
- Suburban campus into a traditional urban campus,
- Sprawl-type open space into various types of infill.

Throughout the country, a good number of these sprawling types of development have begun to fail. Whether because they are old and decrepit, no longer fashionable, or even brand new (sometimes not yet finished) but too far from jobs and the needs of daily life, these residential developments began to fail in record numbers in 2007–2008, and the trend is expected to continue. This is the reason such places need to be repaired, and it is important to keep this fact in mind when considering some of the radical interventions that sprawl repair entails.

Foreclosures and falling home values in failing residential subdivisions have created desperate conditions that have spread to the commercial centers the subdivisions were intended to support. Residents may react emotionally to the idea of selling or replacing their family homes, and business owners may be reluctant to lose business property, but in some cases there may be no other choice. In fact, sprawl repair offers deteriorating areas the second chance of redevelopment. In addition, none of the repair measures will be forced on communities. Ideally the goal of revitalization will foster consensus in support of the method among municipalities, property owners, and their organizations to achieve the repair.

Sprawl repair will have wide socio-economic benefits for the failing developments. The transformation of these single-use enclaves into vibrant, walkable, mixed-use communities will make them attractive for the upcoming market segments (Baby Boomers and Millennials), which may stop and even reverse the declining real estate values. Adding density will support the existing businesses, create the basis for new ones, and support mass transit.

The urbanization strategies will create affordable and varied housing options for diverse populations. The mix of uses will encourage walking, and the reduction in driving will reduce pollution and save energy and resources. The process of repair itself will support a new, green, and progressive industry that will create jobs and keep the talent in existing communities while attracting newcomers.

Another major benefit of sprawl repair projects at the community scale is the recovery of land that was previously wasted on parking lots and overscaled infrastructure but can be used to create better communities. This land is a potential tax generator for municipalities and a profit source for the private sector, and can stimulate redevelopment in adjacent sprawling areas.

Not all sprawl elements lend themselves to the same degree of repair. Residential enclaves may be the most difficult to retrofit, as they are not easily accessible and are extremely and thinly dispersed. The cost of repair – improving infrastructure or bringing in services, mixed uses, civic institutions, and the other ingredients of real neighborhoods – may be too high. Landowners may obstruct the process, and there might be no political will. As discussed in chapter three, "Repair at the Regional Scale," some areas will be left unrepaired, perhaps in hopes that they will survive as they are, or perhaps designated for devolution into agricultural or natural areas. The methodology of selective sprawl repair at the community scale will ensure that public resources will incentivize only those areas that have the potential to benefit the region.

The repair targets are identified by following priorities as defined at the regional scale. The examples analyzed in this chapter have been pre-selected for their repair potential by the public sector (municipal governments, metropolitan planning organizations, regional councils) through collaboration with the private sector (local community organizations and other bodies such as owners' associations). Use of the sector mapping sequence, the Sprawl Repair Assessment Tool, and the Void Analysis (see chapter three, "Repair at the Regional Scale") will facilitate and streamline the selection process.

Sprawl repair at the community scale includes a range of measures that are both analytical and practical, and can be performed sequentially or simultaneously.

The steps are:
- Step One: Analyze site feasibility,
- Step Two: Apply urban design techniques,
- Step Three: Introduce regulatory and management techniques,
- Step Four: Secure incentives for implementation.

STEP ONE: ANALYZE SITE FEASIBILITY

Analysis of existing conditions is done concurrently at several levels.

A survey of the ownership structure and the current tenants and their lease requirements (in the case of commercial properties) determines the extent, timing, and phasing of the repair. The length of the tenants' leases and the viability of the businesses determine the possible ownership variants for the parcel to be repaired. The ideal scenario will be a single-owner purchase of the site for full control and management of the repair process, but this is rarely achievable. Additional ownership structures can include purchase by multiple partners, lease, private-public partnership, co-operative ownership, or land trust. Eminent domain (the seizing of blighted property by a government entity) can be considered as an extreme measure if the location of the sprawl repair target is of regional importance and no other ownership transaction can be achieved.

Demographic analyses and other marketing studies provide projections for future population growth in the area and inform the mix of residential building types to include in the site. The marketing study predicts the demographic segments most likely to be attracted to the future neighborhood or town center.

A void analysis of the local and regional commercial market identifies the uses required to rebalance the existing ones – if retail is already available, office, hotel, and civic uses must be added. A void analysis also helps answer questions about the potential for additional retail in a commercial location, or for new retail in a residential area. The ideal mix will include a balance of national tenants and smaller local businesses to support the regional economy.

The potential for new job creation must be analyzed, including the need for affordable incubator space for start-up businesses. A survey of existing employment hubs and projections for job generation will inform future proposals for locations of new businesses.

Analysis of the existing building stock includes determining which buildings will be retained, renovated, and re-purposed, and which will be partially or entirely demolished. The goal should be a range of flexible and affordable building types that can easily adapt to a variety of uses and activities as the market changes. The large commercial boxes with sturdy metal structures may be easily retrofitted into civic buildings such as galleries, schools, daycares, and wellness and senior centers, while many of the repetitive, short-lifespan commercial structures may be more suitable for demolition. Residential buildings are analyzed for potential improvements in energy efficiency and possible transformation into more urban types (e.g., a McMansion transformed into multifamily) or other uses (a ranch house transformed into a live-work unit).

Thoroughfare connectivity and traffic patterns are also analyzed. Existing and potential connections will affect how a new neighborhood or town center will be created.

The available parking and the potential reduction of suburban parking requirements form the foundation for a **new parking strategy**. It will be a long time before everybody is walking or using public transit; therefore, parking needs to be provided in the meantime. It can be secured by utilizing on-street spaces, restriping and reorganizing the existing supply, reducing the parking requirements by applying shared parking ratios, or building parking structures.

Most suburban commercial sites were built under the inadequate **stormwater and conservation standards** of past decades. The excessive parking lots and roads create considerable impervious areas that alter the natural hydrologic and drainage patterns. The stormwater runoff from roads and parking lots carries contaminants downstream and pollutes nearby bodies of water. The repair of these sites requires improving the ability to handle and treat stormwater, both on-site and within the larger drainage basin. The introduction of rain gardens, depressed green squares, daylighting of buried creeks, pervious pavement, and other sustainable stormwater techniques reduce the impact of impervious areas on watershed hydrology and provide best management practices for better water quality downstream.

Suburban commercial sites usually fall under the definition of greyfield redevelopment and do not require extensive environmental remediation. However, in the case of landfill sites, gas stations, golf courses, or industrial uses involving hazardous materials, **decontamination and remediation procedures** are required. These sites are classified as brownfields, and state or federal programs may be available to support their remediation.

STEP TWO: APPLY URBAN DESIGN TECHNIQUES

The appropriate locations for the targets of sprawl repair, as well as the neighborhood structure (based on pedestrian sheds), are defined at the regional scale. Sprawl repair at the community scale deals with the capacity and dimensions of fabric, blocks, thoroughfares, and public space.

Places exhibiting a range of shared defects – such as car dependence, lack of neighborhood structure and mixed use, lack of connectivity and block organization, dendritic and overscaled thoroughfares, and scarcity of defined public realm – are characterized as sprawl development.

Below is a summary of the main deficiencies and the remedial urban-design techniques applied for their repair.

Deficiency: Single building type and use
Remedial technique: Introduce new building types to accommodate a mix of uses

The first step is to identify problems with the way the land is used in sprawl developments. The lack of mixed uses leads to car dependence and wasted energy and resources, as people are required to drive to all of their daily activities and needs. This deficiency is repaired by introducing new building types that will allow different uses to exist in close proximity within the pedestrian sheds. The precise numbers and distribution of these new buildings will vary for each site, depending on factors such as demographic growth and necessary density to support transit. Ideally such quantitative directives will come from larger regional planning efforts, with the understanding that flexibility of use will be essential to a successful repair.

The strategies for urbanization include a wide variety of types of buildings that are rarely used in sprawl. For example, large, underused parking lots can be replaced with buildings that wrap around parking garages and form perimeter blocks, creating walkable structure from the formless space and supporting the density that will sustain transit. Blank walls and parking lots can be screened with buildings that have thin footprints (liner buildings), to create pedestrian-friendly environments. These liner buildings can be used as small-business incubators. Live-work units and lofts can be added as new building types to appeal to younger buyers and perhaps active Baby Boomers. Townhouses, which in conventional suburbia are merely attached residential buildings in the middle of parking lots, can become useful infill elements of new urban streets.

Along with adding new buildings in sprawl developments, preserving, expanding, and/or reusing existing structures play an important role in introducing new uses when necessary and reusing existing materials for environmental purposes. For example, abandoned big boxes can be converted into schools, community college satellite campuses, grocery stores, offices, wellness facilities, senior centers, galleries, and other civic amenities that are often missing in sprawl. Some of the big boxes can also be used as parking garages, as they are located deep within the properties, leaving the front parking lots for redevelopment and infill. Some of these techniques are illustrated in chapter seven, "Repair at the Building Scale."

Providing workforce/affordable housing is another important aspect of sprawl repair at the community scale. Converting existing single-family houses into duplexes and multifamily buildings, and adding accessory units and apartments above shops, can increase the number of affordable units in the repaired communities (see chapter six, "Repair at the Block Scale," and chapter seven, "Repair at the Building Scale").

Deficiency: Lack of walkable block structure
Remedial technique: Connect and repair thoroughfares
Sprawl developments typically have large, uncon-

nected block structures. Large blocks should be broken down into finer-grain fabric to make walking and biking safe and easy. An internal walkable network of blocks must be knit together utilizing parking lots, driveways, and dead-end streets, and connections opened to the surrounding area. Introducing pedestrian streets and passages, as well as alleys, lanes, and mews (narrow back streets with smaller dwellings) in the back of buildings where possible, creates additional connectivity. Connecting cul-de-sacs is another tool that should be employed; the first step might include only pedestrian and bike paths, and vehicular connections can be added later. In addition, the pedestrian character and speed of movement of existing thoroughfares and intersections must be improved (see chapter five, "Repair of Thoroughfares and Parking").

Deficiency: Dispersed and exposed parking
Remedial technique: Rationalize parking
Underutilized and exposed parking is a universal defect in sprawl. These vast, paved areas make pedestrian movement unpleasant and unlikely, but they have great potential for infill and redevelopment. The parking lots should be reorganized within newly formed blocks, with on-street parking spaces added along the streets and garages inserted wherever possible. These parking options might be supported with subsidies by public-private entities or stimulus money for infrastructure. Local residents often resist the construction of parking garages, but they support the higher density needed to sustain transit and reduce impervious areas of surface parking lots. One way to reduce resistance to building and subsidizing parking garages is to design them for future conversion into office, loft, or civic use. This requires horizontal floor plates, because the sloped floors of parking garages cannot be reused as habitable space. Surface parking lots can be reserved or designated as "land banks" for future buildings after public transit becomes available (see chapter five, "Repair of Thoroughfares and Parking").

Deficiency: Residual open space/Lack of civic space
Remedial technique: Define open and civic spaces
Suburban sprawl provides a high quality and great quantity of private space in the form of spacious resi-

dential and commercial buildings, but it is infamous for the low quality of its public space. In traditional urbanism, public space (open and civic space) comprises the portions of urban fabric that are held in common: streets, squares, plazas, and parks. The quality of public space depends on the physical dimensions and character of the "outdoor rooms" that buildings create. In sprawl, public space is typically residual – leftover, an afterthought – usually taking the form of car-oriented thoroughfares, parking lots, and unusable buffers and easements. The sprawl repair design techniques include the connection of existing networks of open space for habitat corridors and natural drainage, and improving the public realm by filling in the gaps with buildings and replacing the parking lots with walkable blocks. Open space includes transitional spaces, such as courtyards and semi-public spaces (between the public and private realms) within perimeter-block buildings. Civic spaces (parks, squares, playgrounds) and civic buildings (meeting halls, markets, post offices) are added to serve as landmarks and create important views.

Deficiency: Lack of local food production
Remedial technique: Integrate local food production spaces

The sprawl repair process creates an opportunity for local food production within retrofitted commercial and residential developments. If a site will be retrofitted anyway, options for urban agriculture can be easily explored. Local food production spaces can be introduced in the form of community gardens and allotments within blocks or in public spaces, or private gardens within lots, in backyards or on the roofs of buildings. These spaces will provide many residents with access to fresh produce within walking distance, and they will become new and interesting places for socializing and educating the younger generation. The introduction of urban agriculture will also make the community more sustainable in the long run by supplying some of its food needs locally instead of having all of its food shipped from long distances.

These are the most common deficiencies and remedial techniques, many of which overlap for most of the sprawl elements. However, there are some sprawl types, such as the rural subdivisions and the suburban campuses, among others, that have some exclusive deficiencies and remedial techniques. These are described with their corresponding elements later in this chapter.

STEP THREE: INTRODUCE REGULATORY AND MANAGEMENT TECHNIQUES

As acknowledged in chapter two, "The Sprawl Repair Method," it is challenging to implement sprawl repair within the current regulatory environment, which still supports single-use, segregated zoning and policies that produce sprawl, not only in the suburbs but also within urban areas. New regulatory and management tools are needed at regional and local levels. This is likely accomplished one region or municipality at a time, by replacing existing comprehensive plans and ordinances with those that contain true incentives to create complete communities.

Model ordinances are decrees that enable the process of sprawl repair. They establish the codes as law to be followed for new infill and redevelopment construction.

Form-based codes direct how the laws should be followed to achieve a balanced public realm. Form-based codes regulate the form of buildings and their relationships to the public realm, in contrast to conventional zoning codes that regulate use.

Urban standards are guidelines within the form-based codes that prescribe the way buildings relate to the public realm: their lot occupation, disposition or placement on the lot, configuration or building height, setbacks, types of private frontages, and parking arrangements.

Regulating plans provide the visual maps for the form-based codes. They show the natural and rural zones to be preserved, the mixed-use in the form of Transect zones, civic zones, and buildings, and special districts if any. Regulating plans may also include special requirements such as mandatory retail frontages and build-to lines.

Architectural standards are adopted by the municipality or private entity developing a sprawl repair project. Their purpose is to establish a common language of tectonics, materials, and proportions between various buildings.

Thoroughfare standards will be needed for the repair of existing and proposed thoroughfares, connections, and intersections. These standards will be calibrated locally according to the principles of context-sensitive design.[1]

Main street management is crucial for sprawl repair projects. It is best to have a single managing entity that can ensure the proper operation, mix, and maintenance of retail establishments. The tenant mix should include anchors (national or regional retailers) as well as smaller local businesses. The design and maintenance of shopfronts, interiors of shops, parking, and streetscape should be coordinated in a way that is beneficial to all businesses. Signage, landscape, furnishings, and lighting are fundamental for a successful main street retail strategy; these elements should not distract from the stores.

Marketing is a necessary tool for successful sprawl repair projects. A marketing team, hired by a developer, a municipality, or a public-private partnership, should design a program emphasizing the image of a complete and healthy community and the "sense of place" that is missing from sprawl developments. Such marketing efforts can easily incorporate the numerous retrofit projects that have demonstrated high quality and economic success. By showing attractive options for repair, such programs educate the population and help developers and municipalities make the case for the mix of uses and higher densities needed in sprawl repair projects.

While the LEED Green Building Rating System encourages energy efficiency at the building level, **LEED Neighborhood Development** (LEED-ND) encourages sustainable development beyond the building, at the scale of the community.[2] Until an overhaul of the suburban regulatory system is complete, the LEED-ND standards can be used to promote targeted sprawl repair as an important option for sustainable growth. LEED-ND certifications can help developers and municipalities gain private and public support and investment for repair projects.

There are other **performance criteria** available for sustainable practices, and these can be used to provide metrics of the benefits of repairing sprawl. For example, various tools for exploring climate change mitigation strategies have been developed in recent years.[3] They can be directly applied to sprawl repair site analysis and design by using scenario modeling. Together with the qualitative urban design tools proposed in this manual, these quantitative tools can make a powerful case for policy changes to incentivize sprawl repair.

STEP FOUR: SECURE INCENTIVES FOR IMPLEMENTATION

A range of incentives, both regulatory and financial, should be used to make the implementation of sprawl repair faster and economically feasible. Regulatory incentives may include density bonuses, up-zoning, and fast permitting, while financial incentives can be direct infusions of public funding or indirect financial benefits such as tax deferrals, right to use tax money for improvements, and exemptions from fees. All of these are easier to enact or obtain when the project is a public-private partnership.

Permitting by right means a project identified as a target for sprawl repair would be approved administratively and would not need to go through a lengthy public process, saving time and money. It usually requires enabling legislation from the state.

State and federal funding for the design and construction of parking structures and transit infrastructure is one of the most useful and important incentives for the repair of large commercial sites such as regional shopping centers and malls, which will be possible only if the underutilized parking lots are urbanized to support higher-intensity, mixed-use development. Structured parking will be needed, and the investment for it can be considerable, making governmental financial support essential.

TDR (Transfer of Development Rights) See chapter three, "Repair at the Regional Scale, Step Six: Implement Transfer of Development Rights."

Tax Increment Financing (TIF)[4] is a tool to underwrite redevelopment projects. Applied to a district, TIF is typically used to pay for on-site and off-site infrastructure improvements. Bonds are issued based on the projected future increase of local taxes within a certain redevelopment area. A TIF district may be initiated by the private or the public sector and may cover several projects. The district may feature revenue sharing of generated funds so money can be distributed to the centers that most need urban intensification.

BID (Business Improvement District), also called BIA (Business Improvement Area), is an overlay area that can be funded through special assessments collected from the commercial property owners within the district or area. The funds will pay for infrastructure improvements in the process of sprawl repair. They require legislative authorization.

State and Federal Grants can be available for the redevelopment and improvement of blighted areas.

Community Development Block Grants (CDBG) may be available from the U.S. Department of Housing and Urban Development through the Neighborhood Stabilization Program (NSP), which was established for the purpose of stabilizing, through purchase and redevelopment, communities that have suffered from foreclosures and abandonment.[5] Block grants are substantial funds given by the federal government to regional governments to use at their discretion with a general purpose for the funds' allocation. Entities eligible for the NSP funds are states, local governments, non-profits, businesses, or consortiums of organizations.

The Energy Efficiency and Conservation Block Grant (EECBG) Program is funded under the American Recovery and Reinvestment Act of 2009 and administered by the U.S. Department of Energy. This program provides funds to local and state governments to develop and implement projects to improve energy efficiency and reduce energy use and fossil fuel emissions in their communities.

Sprawl repair tax credits should be considered by municipalities, which could offer the credits for projects in designated "Sprawl Repair Districts." The municipalities could keep property taxes for these districts at pre-development rates for a given number of years.

Special-Purpose Sales Taxes can be used to enable sprawl repair. In the state of Georgia, for example, any county can establish a special-purpose, local-option sales tax (SPLOST). Georgia's state sales tax is currently four percent, with the counties allowed to add up to two percent more for SPLOSTs. A SPLOST is passed by a county commission and voted up or down by residents in a referendum every five years.[6] Another technique is to allow the developer to keep the sales taxes generated on the site of the repair until the infrastructure costs are paid off, as was the case with Belmar mall redevelopment, in Lakewood, Colorado.[7]

State tax credits for workforce housing can be granted to a developer of a sprawl repair target if at least 20 percent of the units on site provide workforce housing.

Bonuses for public space creation can be given when repairing large parcels. Multiple properties may become a challenge to the coordinated master planning of a sprawl repair target. Developers can be given some incentives such as faster permitting or allowed a higher density to assemble their required open space in a specific location in order to create a larger and more meaningful public space.[8]

Federal grants for regional planning should be created. They could be given to local governments to fund planning studies, mapping processes, and master plans for sprawl repair at the regional level.

This chapter also includes protocols to assist developers with the implementation of sprawl repair. The protocols address the typical issues developers encounter on repair projects, and list practical steps for their organization and execution.[9] Certain elements of sprawl, such as the suburban campus, the edge city, and open space, exhibit idiosyncrasies related to the specifics of their type. In some cases, such as with campuses, there are differences when the implementing institution is public or private. But the main guidelines can be extrapolated from the protocols provided for the other elements. For example, the edge city implementation protocols include a combination of those used for office parks and shopping malls, as edge cities contain these elements.

RURAL SUBDIVISION

Rural sprawl occurs when natural or agricultural land is speculatively subdivided along thoroughfares. This raises real estate values along the roads, while leaving the interior properties virtually worthless. Sporadic selling off of the road frontage of large parcels leads to the systematic loss of farmland and other valuable natural resources. These resources are replaced by low-density residential development and sprawling, random infrastructure, contributing to automobile dependence and providing no civic or community amenities.

Clustering is a method of re-assembling dispersed development into smaller areas. It is often used as a way to enable a more compact form of growth for new development, but this method can also facilitate the repair of already sprawling rural subdivisions. The clustering into a hamlet or a village concentrates development into a fraction of the land otherwise consumed by residential sprawl, thus preserving farmland, woodland, and wetlands, and conserving energy and resources.

Clustering can be accomplished through the Transfer of Development Rights (TDR) or the Purchase of Development Rights (PDR), where a land bank is established to buy development rights and hold or transfer them to designated areas. The PDR can be modified so that a non-profit organization or developer purchases only a layer (approximately 400 feet) of land along the roads as a conservation easement or "legacy" view corridor. This is an important and possibly less expensive approach for the preservation of agricultural land.

A county or a municipality can incentivize clustered development by permitting by right and by up-zoning to a higher density, as well as by allowing for deferred taxation in which the up-zoned properties are taxed when the houses are built.

Another tool to be employed is a packaged sewer service within small, strategically located areas. A municipality can approve sewer districts to support small-package sewer plants servicing land less than one-quarter of a mile from certain intersections. Water and sewer services are difficult to secure for rural areas of low densities, but this strategy allows for the concentration of such services, thus incentivizing clustering.

4-1. Preservation of farmland through clustering and a variety of tract sizes

DEFICIENCIES

The following diagrams illustrate the evident defects of rural sprawl. Figure 4-2 demonstrates the large parcels platted and sold speculatively, exclusively for residential use. Figure 4-3 shows the sparse thorough-fare system, with the overscaled rural thoroughfares and the numerous vehicular driveways leading to the houses. Figure 4-4 highlights the public space, which is limited along the thoroughfares.

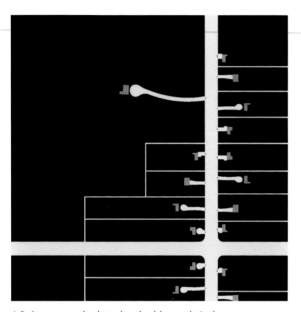

4-2. Large parcels platted and sold speculatively

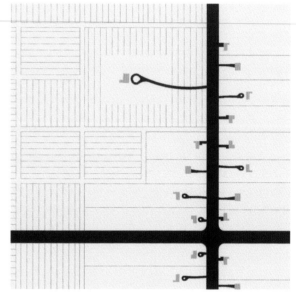

4-3. Sprawling and sporadic infrastructure

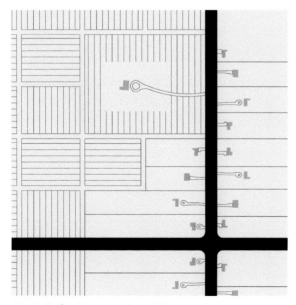

4-4. Lack of civic space and amenities

TRANSFORMATION INTO A HAMLET

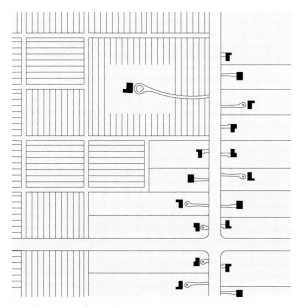

The transformation of rural sprawl into a hamlet is achieved through the repair technique of re-platting and clustering. The black footprints in figure 4-5 are existing buildings, and the red in figure 4-6 are proposed buildings.

▬▬▬ Existing buildings

4-5. Existing rural sprawl

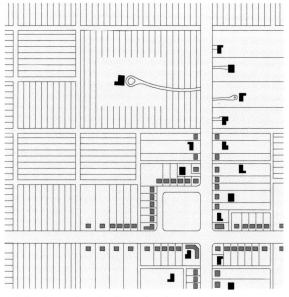

Out of 16 existing parcels, nine are subdivided into smaller lots, while only two houses need to be purchased and removed to achieve this new arrangement into a hamlet. Fifty-two new units are added, making the total number 66. This density will be able to support a hamlet (a clustered rural development with limited commercial uses) that later can grow into a village (a freestanding, complete neighborhood providing the basic daily needs).

▬▬▬ Proposed buildings
▬▬▬ Existing buildings

4-6. Rural sprawl repaired into a hamlet

4-7. Low-density rural sprawl consuming farmland and open space

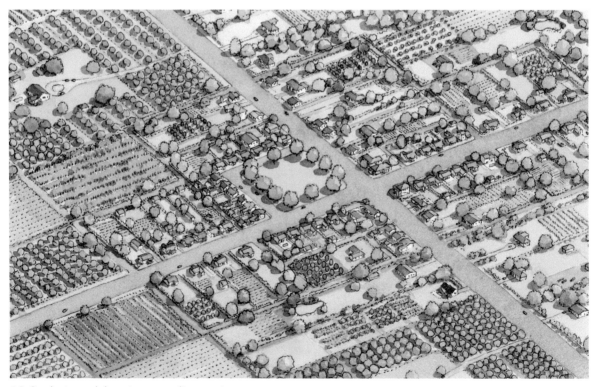

4-8. Re-platting and clustering at a rural intersection

Figures 4-7, 4-8, and 4-9 demonstrate the process of intensification and clustering. The existing condition, though quite attractive with its bucolic landscape, represents the wasteful type of land platting typical of rural sprawl.

The proposed solution shows the new green, achieved with minimal disruption of the existing pattern and structures. Only two of the houses need to be removed, while the rest are incorporated within the fabric of the hamlet. The green will be the main focal point space of the new community.

A farmers' market, small shops, businesses, or civic buildings such as a meeting hall or a chapel can be located along the edges of the green or directly within its space. Some of the preserved existing buildings can be expanded into live-work compounds by adding additional structures within the deep front setbacks.

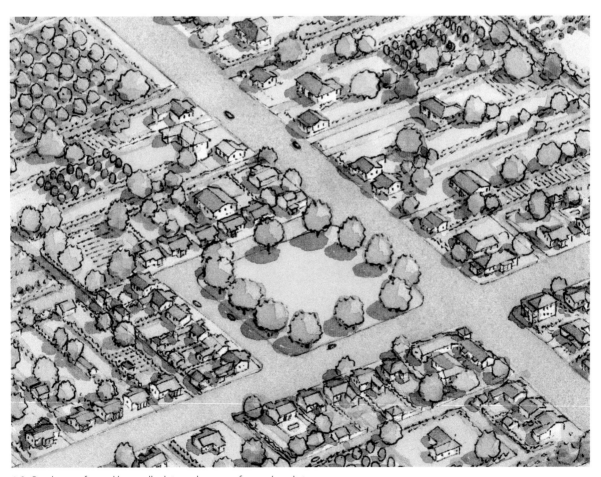

4-9. Rural green framed by smaller lots and a corner farmers' market

Cluster at intersections: Farmland is usually subdivided into smaller lots along the frontage of the roads. The key is to allow for further subdividing to create a higher density than the predominant density of one unit per one, two, or five acres of land. This technique of repair includes the preservation of the substantial farmsteads of five acres or more and re-platting at an intersection at higher density (a minimum ratio of one to five). The smaller lots are clustered around a public green, while larger lots are located on the periphery, transitioning to the farmland. Some houses need to be purchased and possibly removed to clear out the green, unless they are kept as part of its design. Flag lots (those that access a public frontage through a driveway) may also be introduced.

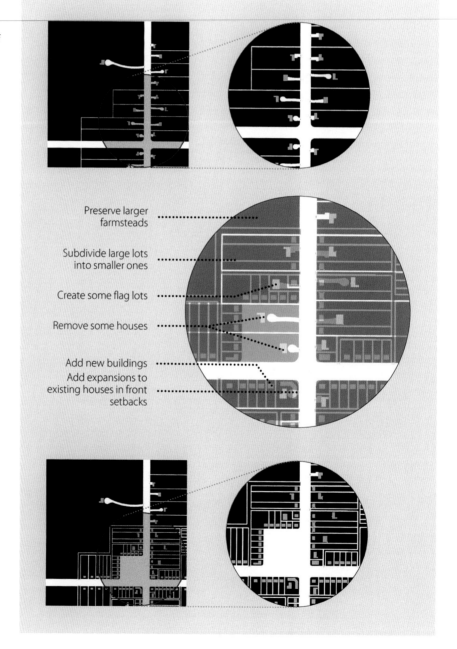

Deficiency: Large parcels held speculatively; sporadic selling off of road frontage

Remedial Techniques: Cluster at intersections through TDR, and modified PDRs

Preserve larger farmsteads

Subdivide large lots into smaller ones

Create some flag lots

Remove some houses

Add new buildings
Add expansions to existing houses in front setbacks

Outcome: Conservation of farmland, woodland, wetlands

Concentrate infrastructure: Rural subdivisions require extensive infrastructure to service limited numbers of large lots located far away from urbanized areas. The road system is overscaled in most cases, with individual driveways adding to the expanse of asphalt. By subdividing lots and clustering only around important intersections, wasteful infrastructure will be limited and concentrated into smaller areas. The cost of infrastructure per capita also will be reduced. Limited numbers of rural roads are added to create a public frontage for the rural green. Introducing back lanes (rural alleys) will help create smaller lots with buildings closer to the green and eliminate the need for driveways at the front.

Deficiency: Sprawling and sporadic infrastructure

Remedial Techniques: Concentrate infrastructure, use packaged sewer service

Eliminate some front driveways

Introduce back lanes

Add new roads

Outcome: Conservation of energy and resources

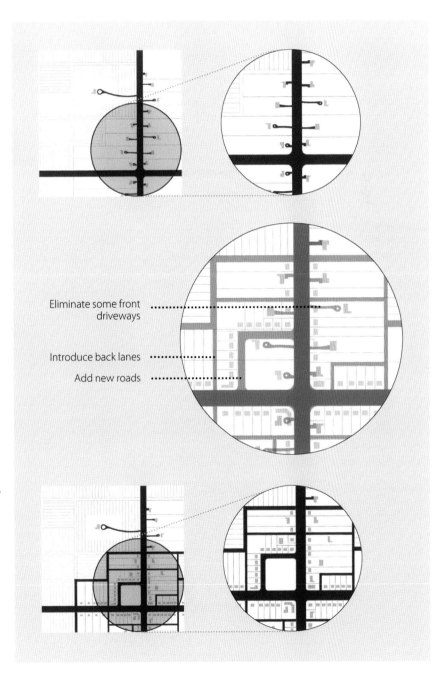

Create a rural green: Sprawling rural subdivisions typically provide few public amenities or civic space. Long-distance commutes are required for every daily need. If the large lots are subdivided into smaller ones at an intersection to form a hamlet, some community amenities become viable. A farmers' market can be held on the green, for example, and live-work units may provide services such as a small corner store or restaurant. The hamlet green should be designed as a simple square on one side of the intersection, with denser surrounding lots accessed by lanes in the back. The hamlet can grow into a village the size of a pedestrian shed or a quarter of a square mile.

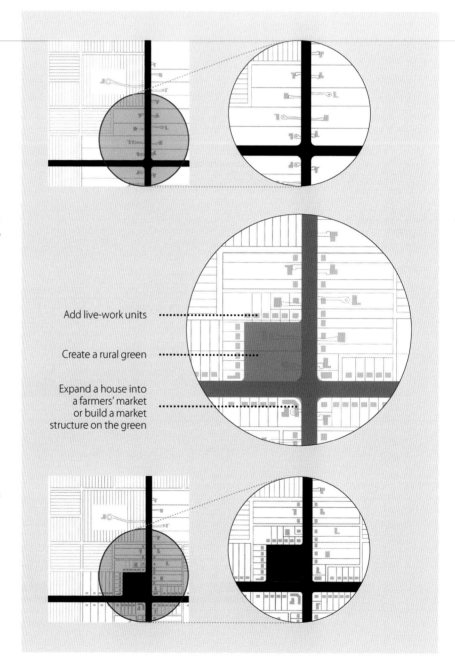

Deficiency: Lack of civic space and amenities

Remedial Techniques: Create a rural green; introduce live-works, farmers' market

Add live-work units

Create a rural green

Expand a house into a farmers' market or build a market structure on the green

Outcome: A hamlet with a variety of building types and mix of uses

IMPLEMENTATION PROTOCOL

1. Analyze the rural subdivision within its regional context according to the Sprawl Repair Assessment Tool and Void Analysis (see chapter three, "Repair at the Regional Scale"). If there is potential for successful repair, proceed to the next step.

2. Reach out to the appropriate regional entity (a council or the county) in the area. Formulate a regional strategy for the transformation of the rural subdivision, focusing on its potential for redevelopment into a hamlet that will benefit several nearby subdivisions and has the potential to grow into a complete neighborhood or village. Public support and potential investment will be more easily obtained if the developer can demonstrate that the project has regional significance and can contribute to long-term sustainability.

3. Initiate and facilitate the adoption of a new form-based code that will legalize the transformation of the rural subdivision into a clustered development or hamlet (see chapter four, "Repair at the Community Scale, Step Three: Introduce Regulatory and Management Techniques"). This can be done through a comprehensive rezoning ordinance that replaces the existing municipal code and allows clustering and repair of rural subdivisions, or through an overlay district applied specifically to one or a group of rural subdivisions.

4. Evaluate the needs of the surrounding rural community in relation to services, and consider how those needs might be met. For example, explore the potential for reuse of some existing single-family houses to incubate a farmers' market or other local businesses.

5. Explore public incentives for infrastructure improvements at the clustering location (see chapter four, "Repair at the Community Scale, Step Four: Secure Incentives for Implementation").

6. Select a strategy for partial or complete acquisition of the rural subdivision. Secure contracts and/or options to purchase (with extendable contract limits) from individual owners. During due diligence, start discussions with county government and key decision makers about the feasibility of the project. If the feedback is positive, proceed to the next step.

7. Start preparations for a public process and a possible collaborative design and planning session (charrette). Engage the regional government as well as adjacent subdivisions and their associations. Ideally a regional planning strategy will be created to allocate the locations for hamlets while assessing their effect on the preservation of agricultural and natural land.

8. Complete a charrette (public or private). Engage decision makers and stakeholders to explore various scenarios and phasing options. Results must be based on consensus.

9. Start the entitlement process for the project. By this time the hamlet should be permitted under a new ordinance.

10. Start construction.

APPLICATION: PRESERVATION OF AGRICULTURAL AND NATURAL LAND THROUGH CLUSTERING

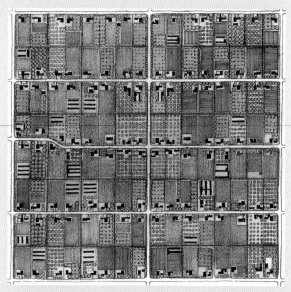

4-10. Rural sprawl at one unit per five acres shown in one square mile; 128 units total

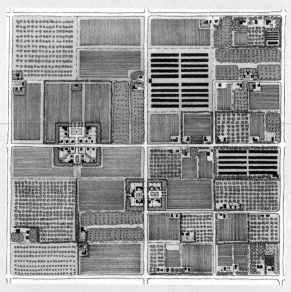

4-11. One square mile with a variety of tract sizes including clustering

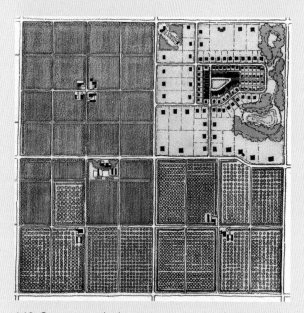

4-12. One square mile clustering into a hamlet of 128 units

These drawings illustrate a clustering technique on a square mile of land. The first drawing shows rural sprawl of 128 units at a density of one unit per five acres (figure 4-10). The second option clusters the units into a variety of tracts and small hamlets (figure 4-11), while the third concentrates all development into a village occupying only a quarter of the total square mile of land (figure 4-12).

This is a technique for the preservation of farmland outside of the urban boundary. Later in the manual, the retrofits of other sprawl elements will be addressed such as the introduction of food production within the urban boundary and its integration into the existing fabric.

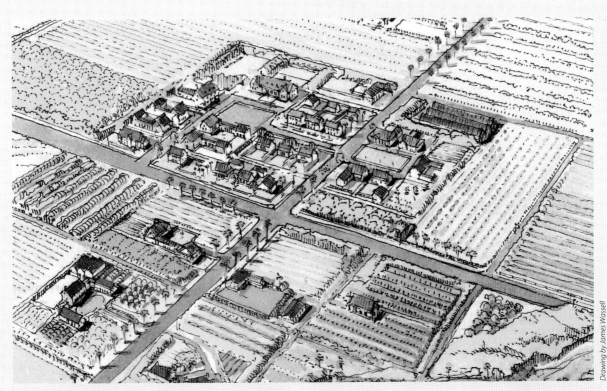

Drawing by James Wassell

4-13. Clustering at a rural intersection as a repair technique

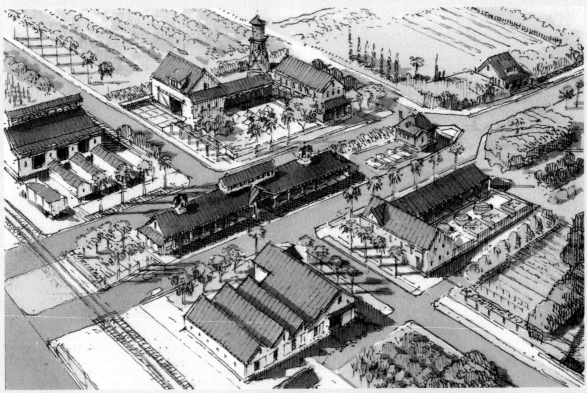

Drawing by James Wassell

4-14. A visitors' center with buildings supporting agricultural activities: a market, a school, and machinery storage

SINGLE-FAMILY SUBDIVISION

The typical single-family subdivision built in the suburbs is the antithesis of sustainable development. It is a residential-only enclave that consists of a single building type, the detached, one-family house. The layout is typically arbitrary and repetitive, with no block structure to help pedestrians orient themselves, few connections to provide convenient routes, and nothing worth going to within a walking distance. This discourages any mode of transportation other than the car.

Thoroughfares in these subdivisions are usually dendritic, over engineered, and limited to cul-de-sacs and local streets that feed into collectors. The public space is not well defined: most often it is cobbled from residual land near backyards and thoroughfares. Although many of these suburban residential developments are close to the rural edge, they do not engage in local food production. Instead, vast areas of land are used for lawns, landscaped buffers, and golf courses.

The objective of the repair of such enclaves is to re-balance their structure, land use, and composition, creating diverse and complete neighborhoods that are based on a walkable block and thoroughfare network and open and civic space hierarchy.

These goals can be achieved by a series of interventions, some of which are radical. The introduction of new building types and uses, such as row-houses, live-work units, apartments, and offices above shops, makes the community diverse; the redesign and connection of thoroughfares, and the addition of sidewalks and bike paths, make the community pedestrian- and bike-friendly. The entrance to the enclave is transformed into a square with a meeting hall and a transit stop. Portions of the residual open space are retrofitted into community gardens and allotment gardens (tended individually or by families) for local food production.

Existing incentives to tackle such a substantial transformation may be quite weak, unless there is a dramatic circumstance such as the collapse of property values within the single-family subdivision. The 2007 – 2008 crisis of the mortgage system created incentives due to the massive decline in real estate prices and a deluge of foreclosures, not only in aging, deteriorating subdivi-

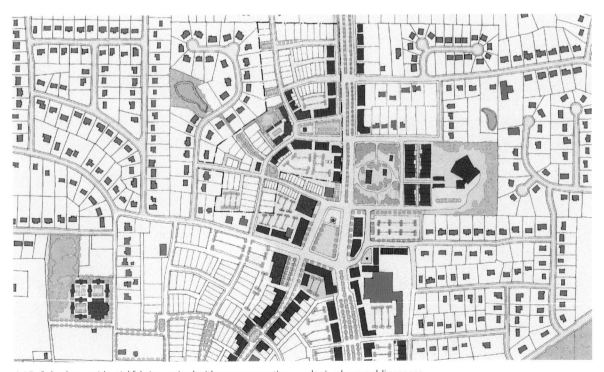

4-15. Suburban residential fabric repaired with new connections and mixed-use public spaces

sions, but also in brand new ones, some of which were still under construction.

In the best-case scenario, the homeowners' associations will initiate the retrofitting process, but in all cases they should be engaged from the beginning. The association may decide to sell off certain portions of the subdivision or negotiate the entire redevelopment with interested parties. It is the responsibility of this governing body to convince the individual property owners that the retrofitting efforts, which may even include the removal or relocation of their homes, will be for the larger good, for the establishment of a more livable, sustainable neighborhood. Landowners affected by a retrofit need to be fairly compensated, perhaps by receiving comparable property in the redeveloped project. The acquisition of foreclosed properties should happen more easily, particularly with the consensus of the association and the community at large.

Incentives for the developers who would undertake such retrofits include the possibility for faster permitting, vesting of higher density, and additional developable space in the form of new commercial and mixed-use buildings. Some incentives for infrastructure improvements may be possible if the location of the neighborhood is of regional importance, particularly if together with adjacent developments they achieve sufficient density to support a transit stop (see chapter four, "Repair at the Community Scale, Step Four: Secure Incentives for Implementation").

Where the repair of a residential enclave (blighted or not) affects a wider area, but recalcitrant property owners resist the repair, the tools of eminent domain can be applied, though condemnation of property should be the last option. This can be justified in the case of large-scale blight in a community or if the location is appropriate for a transit-oriented development. The wider community should be engaged in a public process to explore the most feasible scenarios and build consensus. Physical and financial factors such as the number and locations of foreclosures, delinquent taxes, vacancies, potential sellers, and decrease in value should be carefully analyzed. Several levels of repair – from a minimal intervention to a comprehensive restructuring – should be organized in a phasing plan and form the basis for the decision-making process.

DEFICIENCIES

The following diagrams highlight the key deficiencies of the single-family subdivision. These are the features that need to be repaired to create complete communities.

Figure 4-16 shows the monotony of the existing houses. The lots are similar in size, as are the deep setbacks in front of the buildings. There is only one type of building, and only one use. Figure 4-17 outlines the random pattern of the streets, with dead ends and limited connectivity. Figure 4-18 demonstrates the unstructured, ambiguous, and unusable character of the open space.

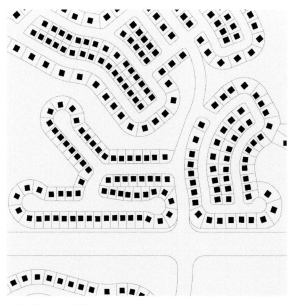

4-16. Single building type and use

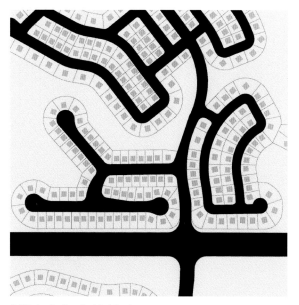

4-17. Lack of walkable block structure

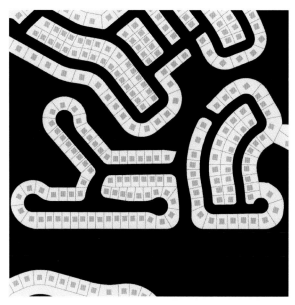

4-18. Residual open space

4-19. Existing subdivision

Suburban residential developments are planned without consideration of pedestrians. The circle overlaid on figure 4-19 represents a pedestrian shed and shows that there are no destinations, other than other residences, within walking distance in this development. The circle also shows the potential location of the mixed-use square proposed for the repair of the subdivision. After the retrofit, certain areas of this enclave will remain outside of the pedestrian shed. However, there will be secondary public spaces reachable on foot or by bike, with the potential to provide additional neighborhood amenities such as playgrounds, live-work units, and community gardens.

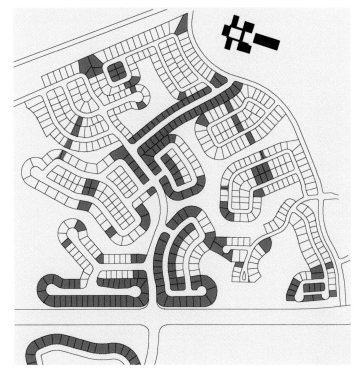

4-20. Areas of intervention

The highlighted areas in figure 4-20 show the lots and structures affected by the retrofit. This is a case of radical intervention, where almost half of the properties in the development will participate in the repair process. This intervention is deliberately amplified to demonstrate that transforming a single-family residential pod into a complete neighborhood will require substantial efforts and resources. In the larger regional context, repairing existing sprawling subdivisions, even if ambitious in scope, will be more sustainable than expanding the suburban infrastructure for new sprawl developments.

4-21. Outcome

The most important interventions include a new, mixed-use square and multiple new connections to the arterial, which is converted into a boulevard. (The square can be replicated on the other side of the boulevard to activate the repair of the other subdivision.)

The main spine of the subdivision, a former collector, has been made into an avenue with a tree-lined median leading to the square. A secondary road has also been made over by adding density to it and having it lead to a new green that connects the neighborhood to the existing school.

1. New square
2. Green
3. Main spine
4. New connections
5. Arterial repaired into boulevard

TRANSFORMATION INTO A NEIGHBORHOOD CENTER

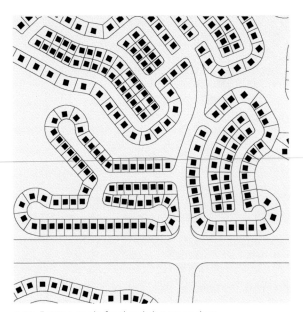

Figure 4-22 shows the existing condition of a portion of the residential enclave and figure 4-23 is its proposed transformation into a diverse and balanced neighborhood, which will become the center for other suburban enclaves adjacent to the subdivision. The existing structures are shown in black, the new infill in red.

■ Existing buildings

4-22. Existing single-family subdivision enclave

Increasing density significantly, combined with other actions at the larger regional context, is required to make transit viable for this area. Houses that are removed are replaced with denser building types such as townhouses, live-work units, and those that will accommodate apartments or offices above shops. The precise location and number of these infill buildings will depend on the local market projections for both the residential and commercial uses. The intention of this repair is not only to transform the development into a neighborhood, but also to provide amenities and create a center for the surrounding developments.

■ Proposed buildings
■ Existing buildings

4-23. Subdivision repaired into a neighborhood center

4-24. Repetitive pattern of single-family houses and cul-de-sacs

4-25. A new neighborhood center for the surrounding residential sprawl

The existing conditions of the single-family subdivision (figure 4-24) differ greatly from the final result, where the suburban structure has been substantially modified (figure 4-25). Where a repetitive cul-de-sac pattern existed before, there are now blocks with defined frontages. The meandering collector bisecting the subdivision that was a channel for speeding cars is transformed into a pedestrian-friendly avenue leading from the new square to the existing school. It becomes the main organizational spine of the community, with numerous new connections.

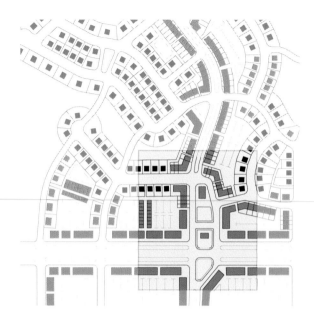

The detail in figure 4-26 focuses on the most important sprawl repair intervention in the residential subdivision – the entry square. It creates a gateway to the neighborhood and serves as an amenity – a gathering place that provides goods and services for residents of this neighborhood and nearby subdivisions. A small formal plaza marks the entrance, followed by a green square with a market structure. A meeting hall or a church can also be embedded in the fabric surrounding the square.

4-26. Entry square with a bus stop, defined by mixed-use buildings and townhouses

Introduce new building types and mixed uses:
A portion of the single-family subdivision is transformed into a neighborhood center. The houses in the existing cluster are similar in size and lot configuration. The platting follows the logic of maximum number of lots within an area, without consideration of public space or mix of uses. The diagram of the remedial technique shows newly proposed buildings superimposed over the existing condition. Townhouses, apartments, live-work units, and shops are introduced, and a substantial number of the single-family houses are preserved. Some of them are adapted to multifamily units (see chapter seven, "Repair at the Building Scale"). A civic structure that can be used as a farmers' market or community hall is proposed for the square.

Deficiency: Single building type and use

Remedial Techniques:
Introduce new building types and mix of uses: retail, office, and civic

Add townhouses

Add market structure

Adapt houses into duplexes or multifamily

Add mews units

Add apartment villas

Add office buildings

Add mixed-use buildings

Remove single-family houses

Outcome: Variety of building types and mix of uses to support neighborhood center

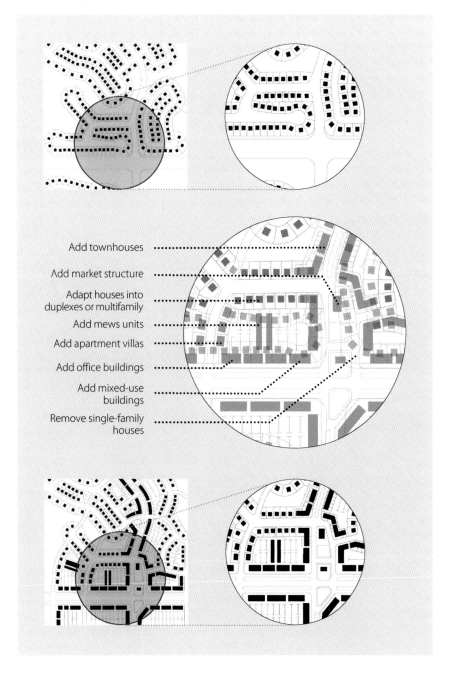

Connect and repair thoroughfares: One of the more serious inadequacies of suburban subdivisions is the absence of connectivity and block structure. A group of typical cul-de-sacs are hooked onto a local road, which then adjoins a collector. The technique requires the removal of several houses and the connection of the existing streets to form a network. The collec- tor is retrofitted into an avenue, and the arterial into a boulevard, by widening sidewalks, reducing pavement widths, and introducing parallel parking. The final result is a repaired sector of the subdivision, with a clear block structure that provides multiple routes for pedestrians and bicyclists as well as drivers.

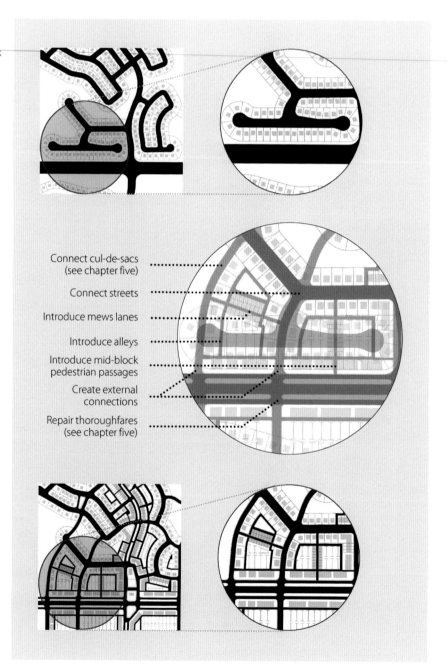

Deficiency: Lack of walkable block structure

Remedial Techniques: Connect and repair thoroughfares

Connect cul-de-sacs (see chapter five)

Connect streets

Introduce mews lanes

Introduce alleys

Introduce mid-block pedestrian passages

Create external connections

Repair thoroughfares (see chapter five)

Outcome: Walkable network and block structure

Define open and civic space: The underused open space of the single-family subdivision is transformed into a hierarchy of civic spaces. The entrance of the community, which consists of a wide intersection and a gate, is reconfigured into a formal square, with a transit stop at the edge. Extending the newly formed space across the arterial creates a point of arrival and a destination at this intersection. The outcome is a spatial definition of the square, which is complemented by additional civic spaces, such as attached greens and playgrounds, formed by the new connections between streets.

Deficiency: Residual open space

Remedial Techniques: Define open and civic space

Create a neighborhood green/playground

Repair the collector into an avenue

Create a market square

Locate a bus stop coordinated with municipality

Outcome: Hierarchy and spatial definition of public realm

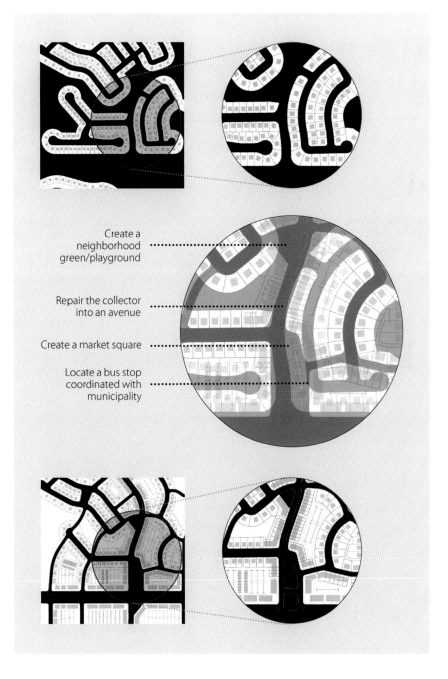

Integrate local food production: A layer of urban agriculture is superimposed over the existing subdivision. The leftover space in the middle of the blocks is subdivided into allotment gardens that can be leased to residents or managed by one custodian. This sce-nario is possible for land between lots that is not environmentally sensitive. Community gardens can be located within public squares or attached greens, and can successfully contribute to the formation of the civic realm of the newly repaired neighborhood.

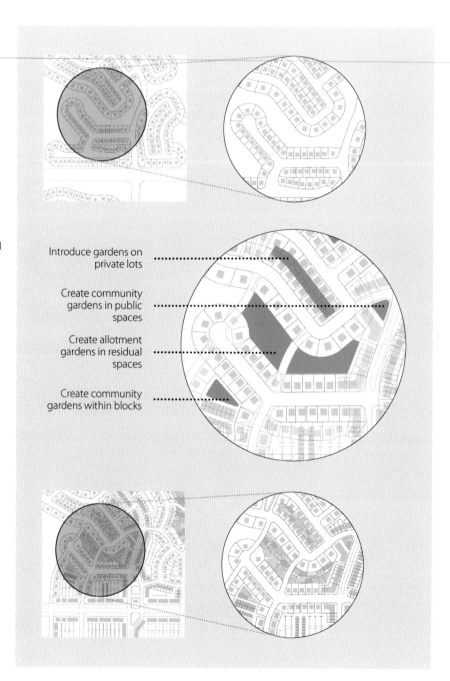

Deficiency: Lack of local food production

Remedial Techniques: Integrate local food production spaces in all urban scales

Introduce gardens on private lots

Create community gardens in public spaces

Create allotment gardens in residual spaces

Create community gardens within blocks

Outcome: A variety of local food production options

REZONING

There is a sharp contrast between the conventional zoning map of an existing subdivision (figure 4-27) and the proposed Transect-based regulating plan (figure 4-28), which is part of a form-based code. The existing zoning shows only one color, as there is only one use allowed – the single-family residence on a defined minimum lot size. This is an outdated, coarse, and inflexible type of zoning.

The proposed zoning diagram is based on different principles – maximum flexibility, mix of uses, and inclusion of the full range of human environments, from rural to the most urban. Transect-based zoning allows for different uses to co-exist within walking distance from each other and be accommodated in building types that form harmonious street frontages. The new regulating plan shows several Transect zones that include a range/hierarchy of building types according to their urban qualities. The most urban buildings – shops, apartments, lofts, and offices – are in T5, the Urban Center zone. Townhouses, live-work units and smaller houses are in T4, the General Urban zone, and the larger houses, together with the existing ones, form the T3, or Sub-Urban zone.

The newly created public spaces are organized under CS (Civic Space), while the existing green spaces, together with the newly introduced agricultural lands, are grouped within the T2, Rural zone.

The designation of Transect zones within the plan will be defined by a process of local adjustment based on an understanding of existing conditions and the need to reach densities necessary for transit.

4-27. Conventional single-use zoning

Open Space
R1 - Single-family Residential
Existing buildings

4-28. Transect-based zoning

T1 - Natural zone
T3 - Sub-Urban zone
T4 - General Urban zone
T5 - Urban Center zone
CS - Civic Space
CB- Civic Building
Existing and proposed buildings

PHASING

4-29. Existing single-family subdivision

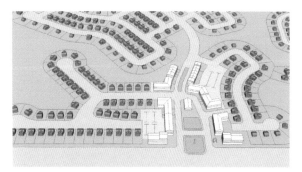

4-30. Short-term repair: Creating an entry square

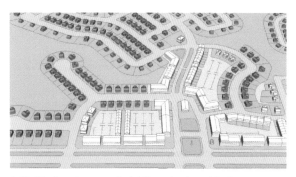

4-31. Medium-term repair: Adding mixed-use blocks

4-32. Long-term repair: Completing the urban fabric

This sequence of diagrams (figures 4-30, 4-31, and 4-32) shows a proposed phasing process for repairing a single-family subdivision.

Phase one is limited to the entrance, where a new square is proposed (figure 4-30). Only a few existing buildings are affected in the process of creating frontages along the entry road. This phase presents a rapid repair opportunity in which, with minimal means, a small-scale change can be introduced to improve the quality of life in the community by providing some of the daily needs within walking distance.

Phase two gradually adds new buildings and connections, forming the first urban, mixed-use blocks in the neighborhood (figure 4-31). The collector at the periphery of these blocks is retrofitted with access lanes and transformed into a boulevard with medians.

Phase three expands the interventions to the edges of the subdivision, adding more new connections, buildings, and public spaces, as well as redevelopment in the adjacent subdivision across the arterial road (figure 4-32).

Each of the initial two phases can also be considered possible final scenarios with no further steps taken toward repair. In this case the repair will be limited in scope, adding only the entry square and some mixed uses. The process of phasing and timing will depend on a variety of factors, the most important of which will be the regional significance of the repaired subdivision, its proximity to employment, and its potential – together with other adjacent subdivisions – to support transit. The local government, if the area is incorporated, will need to facilitate rezoning for mixed uses.

In addition, the homeowners' association will need to understand and embrace the repair of the residential enclave and dramatically change its bylaws to encourage mixed uses, new building types, shallower setbacks, and civic spaces and buildings, among other things.

IMPLEMENTATION PROTOCOL

1. Analyze the single-family subdivision within its regional context according to the Sprawl Repair Assessment Tool and Void Analysis (see chapter three, "Repair at the Regional Scale"). If there is potential for successful repair, proceed to the next step.

2. Analyze the site feasibility (see chapter four, "Repair at the Community Scale, Step One: Analyze Site Feasibility").

3. Reach out to the appropriate regional entity (a council or the county) in the area. Formulate a regional strategy for the repair of the single-family subdivision, focusing on its potential for transformation into a neighborhood center, shared by several subdivisions. Transit should be provided between the subdivisions, connecting them to a regional employment destination. Public support and potential investment will be more easily obtained if the developer can demonstrate that the project has regional significance and can contribute to long-term sustainability.

4. Initiate and facilitate the adoption of a new form-based code that will legalize the transformation of the single-family subdivision into a neighborhood center. (See chapter four, "Repair at the Community Scale, Step Three: Introduce Regulatory and Management Techniques.") This can be done through a comprehensive rezoning ordinance that replaces the existing municipal code and allows repair of single-family subdivisions, or through an overlay district applied specifically to one or a group of subdivisions.

5. Evaluate the needs of the surrounding community in relation to existing retail, office, and residential space. If the market is weak, explore the potential for reuse of some existing single-family houses to incubate local businesses.

6. Evaluate the possibilities of converting existing single-family houses into senior or student housing or multifamily units.

7. Explore the possibility of locating a civic building in the subdivision to serve as a catalyst for place making and provide community identity. A library, a market, or a meeting hall can serve this role. A daycare or a senior living facility can also become strong anchors for the redevelopment.

8. Explore public incentives for infrastructure improvements along adjoining thoroughfares and within the subdivision (see chapter four, "Repair at the Community Scale, Step Four: Secure Incentives for Implementation").

9. Select a strategy for partial or complete acquisition of the subdivision. Secure contracts and/or options to purchase (with extendable contract limits) from individual owners. During due diligence, start discussions with county government and key decision makers about the feasibility of the project. If the feedback is positive, proceed to the next step.

10. Start preparations for a public process and a possible collaborative design and planning session (charrette). Engage the regional government as well as adjacent subdivisions and their associations, the local business community, chamber of commerce, school board, and not-for-profit organizations.

11. Complete a public charrette, preferably at the project site. Engage decision makers and stakeholders to explore various scenarios and phasing options. Results must be based on consensus.

12. Start the entitlement process for the project. By this time the new neighborhood center should be permitted under a new ordinance.

13. Start construction.

APPLICATION: STRATEGIC REPLACEMENT OF SINGLE-FAMILY HOUSES WITH ATTACHED BUILDINGS

This sequence shows several strategic interventions in a single-family subdivision (figures 4-34 and 4-35). The urban structure is improved in three areas chosen for their locations, which are the best for creating identifi-

able public spaces and providing commercial services within walking distance of most homes. Live-work units define the new neighborhood greens, while townhouses line avenues that lead to the water views.

4-33. Suburban single-family development lacking neighborhood structure

4-34. Areas of sprawl repair

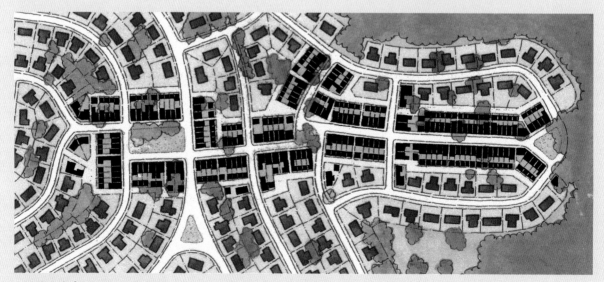

4-35. Detail of intervention includes townhouses, live-works, and public spaces

APPLICATION: REWEAVING AND INFILLING THE SUBURBAN FABRIC

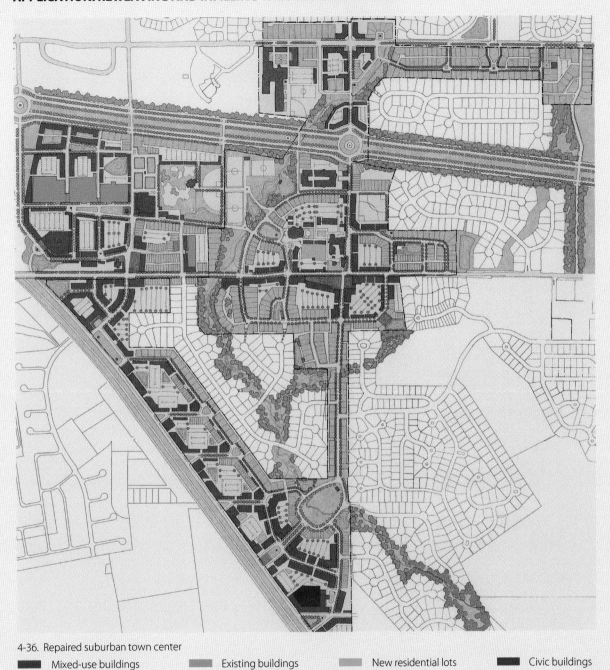

4-36. Repaired suburban town center

■ Mixed-use buildings   ■ Existing buildings   ■ New residential lots   ■ Civic buildings

Figure 4-36 shows an example of a third-generation suburb on the rural fringe of a big city transformed into a mixed-use town center for the surrounding communities. The area has a historic intersection with a church, baseball field, and some empty land that has potential for infill development. These elements formed the armature for a new, mixed-use fabric of small, walkable blocks that were connected to the existing cul-de-sacs by pedestrian and bike lanes. The town's government used creative approaches to obtain stimulus money to implement elements of its master plan.

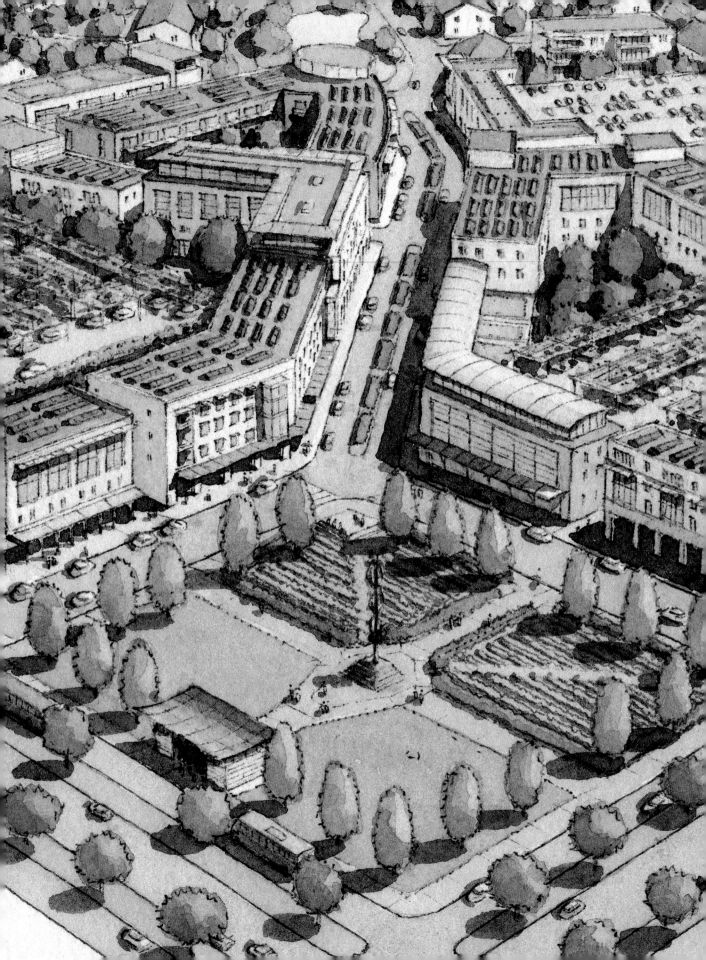

MULTIFAMILY SUBDIVISION

Similar to single-family subdivisions, multifamily enclaves consist of a limited number of building types – townhouses, garden apartments, and multi-story apartment or condominium buildings.

These types of buildings are essential as residential choices, but they are typically built in isolated, gated pods, lacking diversity of uses and walkability. Rather than using a rational block structure, they are composed of dead-end streets and cul-de-sacs, oversized and underutilized parking lots in front of randomly placed buildings.

The tools for transforming a multifamily subdivision into a complete and diverse neighborhood are similar to the ones used in the repair of single-family enclaves. They include the introduction of additional building types: shops, live-work units, offices, and possibly hotel and civic uses. The streets and cul-de-sacs need to be connected, and the surface parking lots better utilized through the addition of garage struc-tures, to allow greater flexibility, density, and mixed uses. A gathering place that adds to community identity must also be created.

These developments are often located at the intersections of arterials, which make ideal locations for urban squares and regional transit stops. The squares can also reverse the odd way in which these developments presently turn their backs to the surrounding community. By allowing the repaired community to face the arterials with useful shops, cafés, and offices, the square provides visibility to passing traffic and announces the existence of the new mixed-use village.

A developer who chooses to repair a multifamily suburban pod will need a series of incentives. They include, but are not limited to, additional development potential, permitting by right, and financial incentives for transit infrastructure and garage structures (see chapter four, "Repair at the Community Scale, Step Four: Secure Incentives for Implementation").

4-37. Apartment villas as infill buildings for multifamily subdivisions

DEFICIENCIES

The diagrams highlight the main shortcomings of the multifamily subdivision. Figure 4-38 shows structures that are in two different shapes, but they are the same building type – garden apartments, freestanding within parking lots, in a random pattern. There is no distinction between the buildings' backs and fronts. The single-use zoning limits the introduction of other building types and uses. Figure 4-39 highlights the lack of block structure that discourages walking and channels cars onto the few streets that connect, increasing congestion. Figure 4-40 shows the unconcealed parking lots that further make walking and biking unpleasant. Figure 4-41 demonstrates that there is abundant open space; there is no civic space or gathering place.

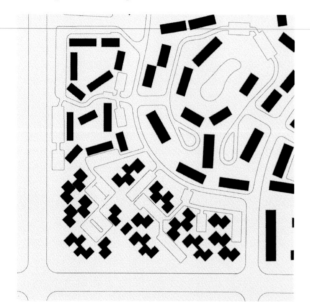

4-38. Single building type and use

4-39. Lack of walkable block structure

4-40. Dispersed and exposed parking

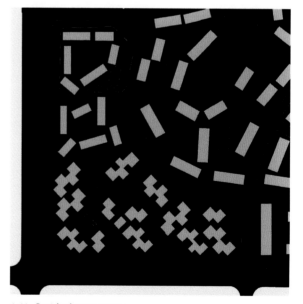

4-41. Residual open space

TRANSFORMATION INTO A TOWN CENTER

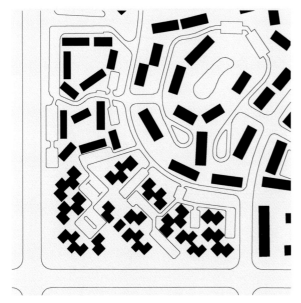

Figures 4-42 and 4-43 show a typical multifamily subdivision before and after repair. Its transformation into a mixed-use and transit-ready town center requires a radical intervention.

███ Existing buildings

4-42. Existing multifamily subdivision

The overall urban structure of the subdivision is reorganized. A new square is formed at the intersection of the bordering arterial roads, and a main street is created, leading from the square to the existing lake, which becomes a public amenity. Four- and five-story buildings are added (new buildings are shown in red, existing in black) to support mixed uses.

███ Proposed buildings
███ Existing buildings

4-43. Multifamily subdivision repaired into a town center

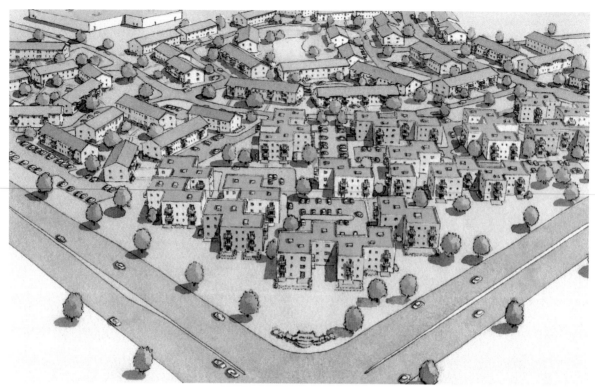

4-44. Dispersed and unstructured disposition of buildings in a multifamily subdivision

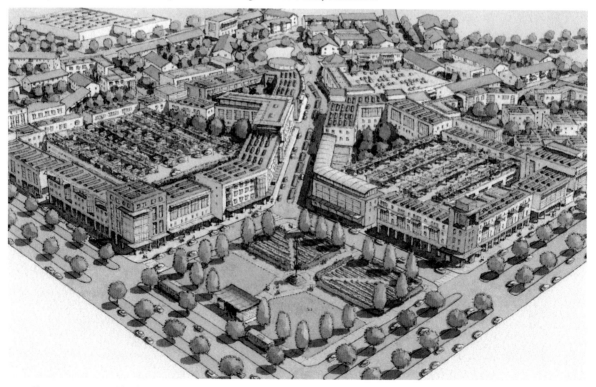

4-45. The transit-oriented, high-density town center will be used by the surrounding communities

Figures 4-44 and 4-45 show the comprehensive transformation of the multifamily subdivision into a town center. A number of the existing apartments are preserved and embedded within the new fabric of neighborhood blocks. Wide sidewalks and spaces for cafés, restaurants, and stores replace the leftover, underutilized space in the backs of the apartment buildings, spurring a new urban vitality. As a town center, the neighborhood offers the surrounding area a place for working, shopping, and socializing.

Figures 4-46 and 4-47 highlight the relationship of a lake to the existing and proposed buildings. Before the repair, the lake was an amenity to only a few, hidden behind apartment buildings. The repair opens access to the lake, creating a main street that leads to it and making it an amenity for the whole community.

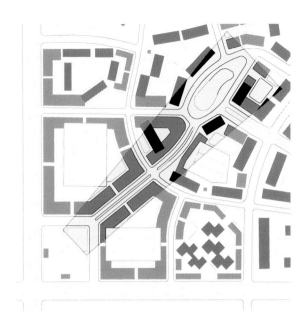

4-46. Existing lake as a private amenity to only a few

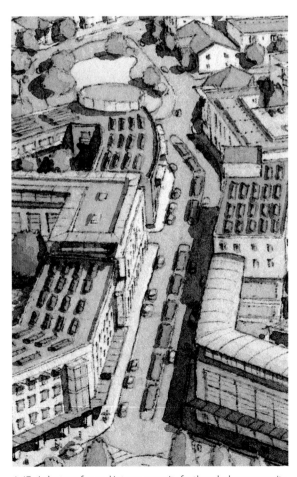

4-47. Lake transformed into an amenity for the whole community

Introduce new building types and mixed uses: The limitations of the garden apartment subdivision include incoherent fabric and restricted, singular use. The repair techniques include the removal of some buildings (the most outdated ones), expansion of others (to accommodate additional uses), and additions of liner buildings. The final goal is to create a balance of uses and building types. The monoculture of garden apartments is diversified by developing perimeter-block buildings that can accommodate shops, live-work units, and offices (when the zoning is changed to allow it). This expands the housing options, with residential units such as lofts, condominiums, and apartments on the upper floors, and allows greater density, making transit viable. Liner buildings supply affordable units and small business incubators.

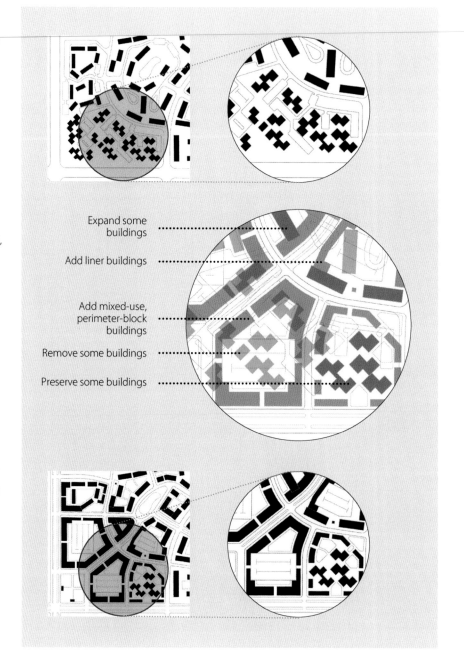

Deficiency: Single building type and use

Remedial Techniques:
Introduce new building types and mix of uses: residential, retail, office, lodging, and civic

Expand some buildings

Add liner buildings

Add mixed-use, perimeter-block buildings

Remove some buildings

Preserve some buildings

Outcome: Variety of building types and mix of uses to support a town center

Connect and repair thoroughfares: The streets in a multifamily subdivision are typically overscaled and non-hierarchical. The irrational layout is confusing and disorienting, and leads to congestion along the collector. The remedy requires removal of some buildings to connect thoroughfares and create a walkable block structure. Where the streets are retained, traffic calming is used to contribute to a comfortable pedestrian environment. Parallel parking and bike lanes are introduced, and pavement widths are reduced to provide wider sidewalks. The final result is a network that accommodates existing and new buildings and allows for multiple pedestrian and vehicular routes, reducing congestion and providing a better pedestrian environment.

Deficiency: Lack of walkable block structure

Remedial Techniques: Connect and repair thoroughfares

Repair existing thoroughfares (see chapter five)

Create a main street

Connect existing thoroughfares

Create external connections

Outcome: Walkable network and block structure

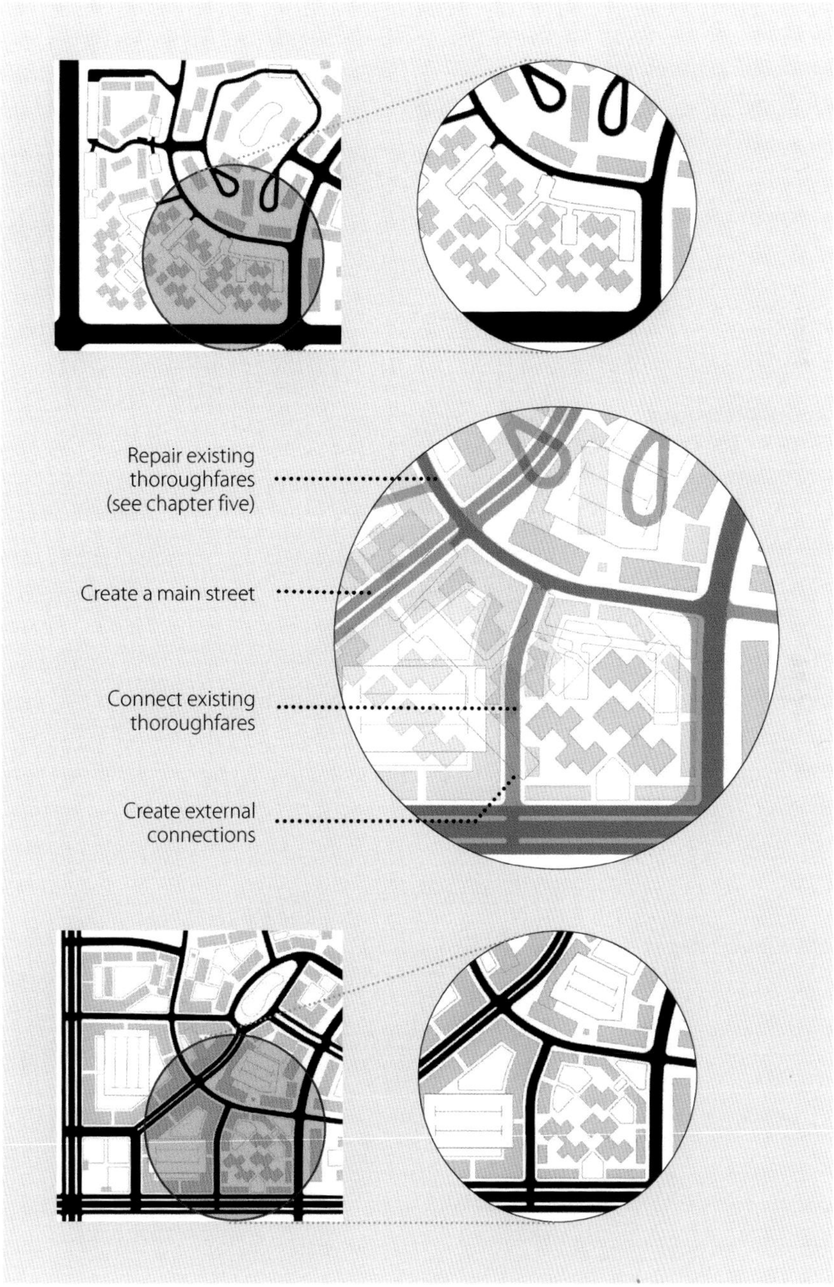

Rationalize parking: The parking lot is the ubiquitous element in multifamily suburban complexes. The lots are exposed along the building frontages, making the area less appealing and safe for pedestrians because the buildings' windows are too far from the street for residents to monitor activity. The repair includes reorganizing the parking lots in the backs of buildings where possible, providing on-street, parallel parking, and replacing some of the surface lots with parking structures. Adding garages may seem to be a radical approach, but it is often necessary because the redevelopment of a multifamily enclave makes economic sense only when replaced by higher density and a mix of uses. The parking garages allow the replacement of the parking lots with buildings that accommodate other uses.

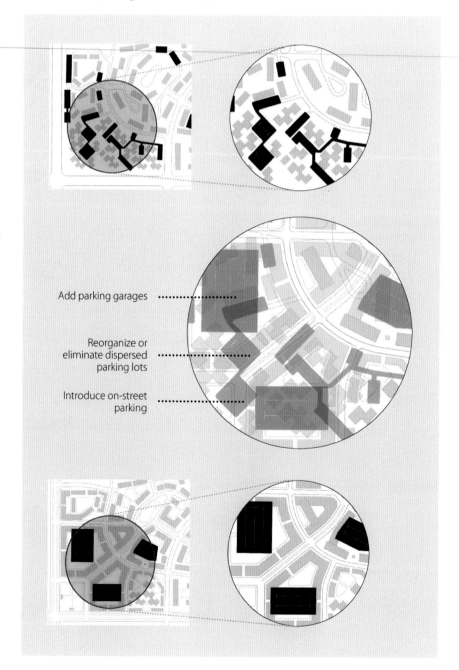

Deficiency: Dispersed and exposed parking

Remedial Techniques: Rationalize parking; add garages

Add parking garages

Reorganize or eliminate dispersed parking lots

Introduce on-street parking

Outcome: Parking strategy to support higher density and mixed use

Define open and civic spaces: The typical multifamily subdivision has a surplus of unstructured space between buildings, yet no usable public realm. Developers often try to create park-like settings by placing the buildings randomly for a "picturesque" effect, but they don't provide actual parks or greens. The development needs a center to provide a gathering space. The ideal location for the center is at the corner of the two arterials, where a new square can be created and connected with a new main street. This replaces the arbitrary building dispositions with a strong public space. Another important function of the square is to reverse the relationship of the development to the exterior thoroughfares by creating useful frontages that can be filled with shops and cafés visible to the passing pedestrian and car traffic.

Deficiency: Residual open space

Remedial Techniques: Define open and civic spaces

Define semi-public interior block spaces

Create a main street

Create an entry square

Outcome: Hierarchy and spatial definition of public realm

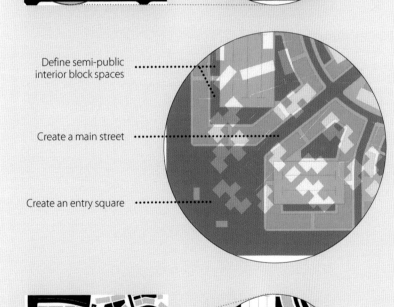

Integrate local food production: Another possibility for the underutilized open space in multifamily subdivisions is to restructure it for urban agricultural use. The newly formed blocks can accommodate individually owned or community gardens; even the new main square and other larger public spaces can hold urban orchards combined with smaller plants. A layer of urban agriculture can be added onto the existing subdivision. The space in the middle of a newly formed perimeter block is subdivided into allotment gardens that can be leased to the residents around it or managed by a custodian. The roofs of buildings and parking garages can also be used for gardening in raised beds or pots.

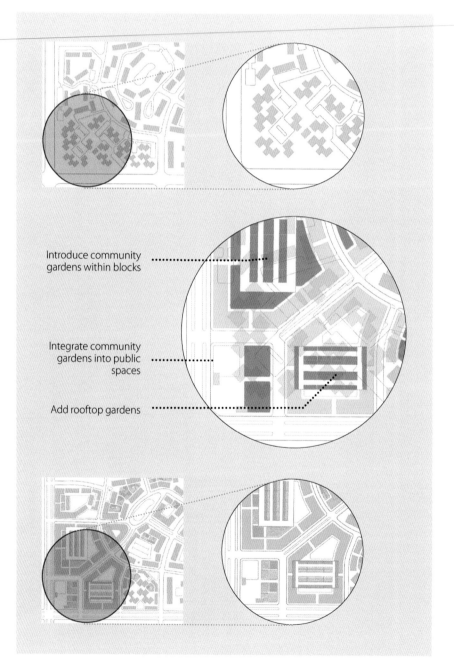

Deficiency: Lack of local food production

Remedial Techniques: Integrate local food production

Introduce community gardens within blocks

Integrate community gardens into public spaces

Add rooftop gardens

Outcome: A variety of local food production options

REZONING

Conventional zoning for multifamily subdivisions allows only one type of building and use: apartments clustered in an enclave. To transform these subdivisions into complete communities, this zoning must be changed to allow a variety of building types and uses.

Similar to the single-family zoning map, the map for the multifamily development shows only one type of building allowed (figure 4-48). The proposed Transect-based map shows several different zones of the rural-to-urban Transect (figure 4-49). The Transect is used as an organizational method to incorporate maximum flexibility, mix of uses, and inclusion of a wider range of human environments, from rural to urban. Transect-based zoning allows for different uses to co-exist within walking distance of each other and be accommodated in buildings that form harmonious environments.

In the case of the multifamily subdivision, rezoning allows denser urban ranges to transform the enclave into a transit-ready town center. The T6, or Urban Core zone, includes perimeter-block buildings with structured parking, which can significantly increase the density while creating a high-quality public space. These blocks can accommodate shops, apartments, lofts, and offices. The T5, or Urban Center zone, includes new smaller apartment buildings, townhouses, and live-work units, while T4, or General Urban zone, incorporates some of the existing buildings and their expansions. The newly created public places are labeled under CS, Civic Space, including the park around the lake, which becomes an important public amenity.

The designation of Transect zones within the plan will be defined by a process of local adjustment based on an understanding of existing conditions and the need to reach necessary densities for transit. The ratios of Transect zones vary according to the location of the subdivision within its regional context.

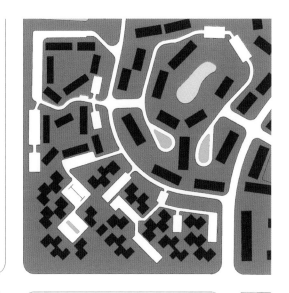

4-48. Conventional single-use zoning

- Open Space
- R3 - Multifamily Residential
- Existing buildings

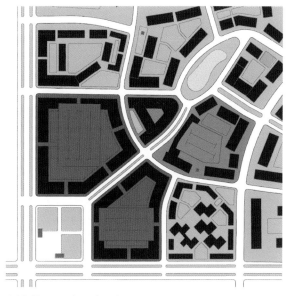

4-49. Transect-based zoning

- T4 - General Urban zone
- T5 - Urban Center zone
- T6 - Urban Core zone
- CS - Civic Space
- CB - Civic Building
- Existing and proposed buildings

IMPLEMENTATION PROTOCOL

1. Analyze the multifamily subdivision within its regional context according to the Sprawl Repair Assessment Tool and Void Analysis (see chapter three, "Repair at the Regional Scale"). If there is potential for successful repair, proceed to the next step.

2. Analyze the site feasibility (see chapter four, "Repair at the Community Scale, Step One: Analyze Site Feasibility").

3. Reach out to the appropriate regional entity (a council or the county) in the area. Formulate a regional strategy for the repair of the multifamily subdivision, focusing on its potential for transformation into a town center, shared by several subdivisions. Transit should be provided between the new town center and other nodes, connecting them to a regional employment destination. Public support and potential investment will be more easily obtained if the developer can demonstrate that the project has regional significance and can contribute to long-term sustainability.

4. Initiate and facilitate the adoption of a new form-based code that will legalize the transformation of the multifamily subdivision into a town center (see chapter four, "Repair at the Community Scale, Step Three: Introduce Regulatory and Management Techniques"). This can be done through a comprehensive rezoning ordinance that replaces the existing municipal code and allows repair of multifamily subdivisions, or through an overlay district applied specifically to one or a group of subdivisions.

5. Evaluate the needs of the surrounding community in relation to existing retail, office, and residential space. If the market is weak, explore the potential for reuse of some existing multifamily buildings to incubate local businesses.

6. Evaluate the possibilities of preserving and expanding some buildings, removing others, adding mixed-use perimeter-block and liner buildings.

7. Explore the possibility of locating a civic building in the subdivision to serve as a catalyst for place making and provide community identity. A library, a market, a religious building, or a meeting hall can serve this role. A daycare or a senior living facility can also become strong anchors for the redevelopment.

8. Explore public incentives for infrastructure improvements along adjoining thoroughfares and within the subdivision (see chapter four, "Repair at the Community Scale, Step Four: Secure Incentives for Implementation").

9. Select a strategy for partial or complete acquisition of the subdivision. Secure contracts and/or options to purchase (with extendable contract limits) from individual owners. During due diligence, start discussions with county government and key decision makers about the feasibility of the project. If the feedback is positive, proceed to the next step.

10. Start preparations for a public process and a possible collaborative design and planning session (charrette). Engage the regional government as well as adjacent subdivisions and their associations, the local business community, chamber of commerce, school board, and not-for-profit organizations.

11. Complete a public charrette, preferably at the project site. Engage decision makers and stakeholders to explore various scenarios and phasing options. Results must be based on consensus.

12. Start the entitlement process for the project. By this time the new town center should be permitted under a new ordinance.

13. Start construction.

APPLICATION: TRANSFORMING AN AGE-RESTRICTED COMPLEX INTO A LIFELONG COMMUNITY

This illustrative case study shows the repair of a 1960s, age-restricted apartment complex. The site contains a park, a recently built library, and a lifelong learning center, and is embedded in a larger area that is designated by the municipality to become a mixed-use town center for the surrounding older, single-family neighborhoods (figure 4-50).

The site is close to a university and a hospital, which – because of their amenities and the potential for connectivity, convenience, and transit – makes it an ideal location for a lifelong community where seniors will want to live, even without specific age requirements.

The new plan removes most of the inadequate apartment buildings and replaces them with a variety of townhouses, small apartment villas, and courtyard blocks, as well as buildings that can house retail and offices, creating the intensity of urbanism necessary to support the evolving town center (figure 4-51).

4-50. Suburban multifamily subdivision with outdated housing stock

A new hierarchy of streets is superimposed on the suburban megablocks, creating a porous and walkable network that results in views of and public access to the park. A new square organizes several existing and new civic structures and connects to the repaired apartment complex and shopping centers.

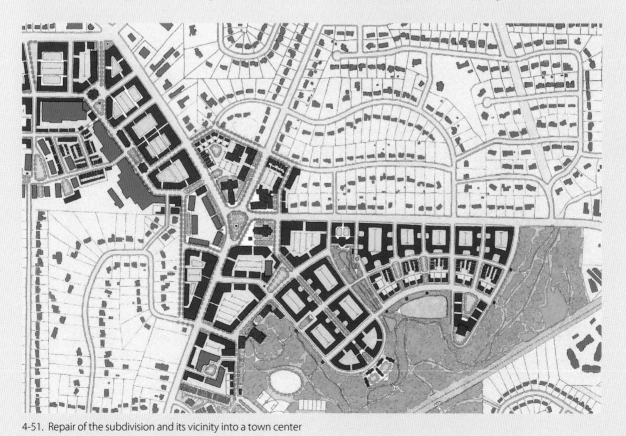

4-51. Repair of the subdivision and its vicinity into a town center

■ Existing buildings ■ Proposed buildings ■ Park ■ Civic buildings

APPLICATION: REDEVELOPMENT OF APARTMENTS AND PRESERVATION OF EXISTING VEGETATION

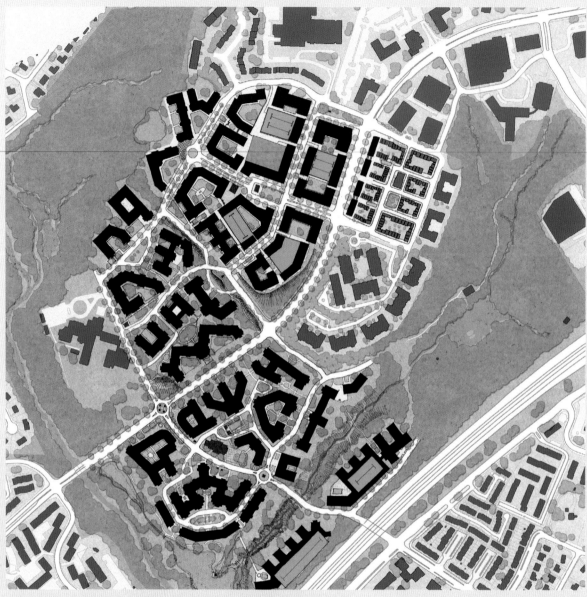

Drawing in collaboration with Dover Kohl and Partners

4-52.   Redevelopment of a multifamily subdivision preserving existing trees

■ Existing buildings   ■ Proposed buildings   ■ Civic buildings

This is an example of repair of a multifamily enclave on a sloping site in a forest of mature trees. New construction is largely limited to existing foundations in order to preserve the trees and to craft a more complete neighborhood out of a repetitive and arbitrary layout of apartment slabs. Additional streets and pedestrian paths are introduced for better connectivity, but their location is carefully selected for minimal disturbance of vegetation. The detail on figure 4-53 shows the new plan superimposed with the existing layout. The new and remodeled buildings are arranged in a campus-like fashion with a picturesque sequence of better defined quadrangles, squares, greens, and pathways (figure 4-54).

4-53. Superimposing of existing and proposed buildings

☐ Existing buildings

4-54. New buildings forming urban blocks and new public spaces

■ Proposed buildings

Drawing in collaboration with Dover Kohl and Partners

APPLICATION: TOWNHOUSE ENCLAVE REDEVELOPMENT

4-55. Existing enclave of townhouses, shopping center, and cul-de-sacs

Townhouse development in the U.S. typically consists of attached building clusters in parking lots. The example shown is in a British New Town, where townhouses have sizable private yards and a certain mix of uses. Parking lots are mostly associated with commercial uses. Most of the fabric consists of dead-end streets forming megablocks that encourage car speeding and discourage walking (figure 4-55). The existing commercial center, which the townhouses surround, consists of a one-story dilapidated structure fronted by a large, under-landscaped pedestrian plaza and a parking lot. A stand-alone building blocks views of the retail from the street, contributing to its blight. A church occupies one end of the plaza, but lacks civic presence (figure 4-57).

4-56. Cul-de-sacs transformed into green closes and parking lots transformed into public space

The proposed plan is to redevelop the site with new townhouses and mixed-use buildings but within a better-connected, more pedestrian-friendly fabric (figure 4-56). The dead-end streets are connected, alleys are introduced in the backs of lots, and the buildings are pushed to the front of the lots to better define the street frontage. Paved cul-de-sacs are transformed into rational and useful green pockets. The square is redesigned with three-story mixed-use buildings, vehicular circulation close to the new shops, and a civic green in front of the church, which is architecturally improved with a detached bell tower (figure 4-58).

Drawing by Max von Trott

4-57. Lack of walkable block structure and public space

Drawing by Max von Trott

4-58.   Introduction of blocks, alleys, and hierarchy of public spaces

SHOPPING CENTER

"Shopping center" is a generic term for a group of commercial establishments that are developed, owned, and managed as one entity and are related to the trade area in location, size, and types of shops

On-site parking is provided at the front of buildings, as required by suburban parking regulations. The shopping center has evolved into several types; there are multiple definitions and classifications of these types, including those by the Urban Land Institute and the International Council of Shopping Centers (ICSC). Some of the most frequently used terms are: convenience store, convenience center, neighborhood center, community center, regional center, power center, and lifestyle center. These range in size from 1,500 square feet to more than 800,000 square feet, and in service areas from a quarter-mile radius to more than 15 miles.

Convenience stores are usually located at the intersections of local and collector roads, and consist of a gas station or a store like 7-Eleven offering food and everyday items.[10] In a sprawl repair scenario, a convenience store

can be transformed into a corner store in a repaired neighborhood (see chapter seven, "Repair at the Building Scale: Drive-through and Gas Station").

Convenience centers are usually anchored by a small food market, and offer a limited range of food and personal services. If located adjacent to residential enclaves at intersections of collectors and arterial roads, a convenience center can be retrofitted into a mixed-use neighborhood center.

Neighborhood centers are anchored by a full-size supermarket and/or a pharmacy, and offer a more complete range of goods and services than the convenience centers.

Community centers have multiple anchors and often include discount department stores, apparel stores, bookstores, supermarkets, and restaurants. Within the metropolitan region, "neighborhood centers" and community centers can be repaired into transit-oriented town centers (see chapter three, "Repair at the Regional Scale").

Regional centers usually take the form of enclosed shopping malls anchored by multiple department stores. In this chapter, malls are reviewed

4-59. Liner buildings masking a shopping strip to create a main street

as a separate type, following this one, as they represent a unique opportunity for sprawl repair, especially in light of their current blight.

Power centers are even larger agglomerations of category-dominant anchors, usually a collection of "big-box" retailers. Power centers sometimes exceed a million square feet in gross leasable area (GLA).

Lifestyle centers are the trendiest retail type, offering upscale fashion and home furnishings in an open-air setting that the developers hope will make shoppers think of a main-street environment. This type is too new and well managed to become a target for sprawl repair, especially when office and residential uses are incorporated in these centers, making them relatively self-sufficient.

Stores are necessary and valuable components of neighborhoods and cities when they are woven into the urban fabric and easily accessible. Indeed, shopfronts are among the most interesting elements of a street. But when they are conceived in high concentrations, isolated from residences and workplaces, they contribute to sprawl. The repair of such sprawl elements remediates the lack of block structure and connectivity to the surrounding context, the over-scaled parking lots at the fronts of buildings, the lack of civic and green space, and, most importantly, the full dominance of a single use.

Following the exodus of residents from urban areas, shopping centers multiplied and flourished, primarily in the decades of federal incentives between 1954 and the Tax Reform Act of 1986. In hopes of stimulating the economy, the federal government granted tax breaks to cheap, new construction through accelerated depreciation. Most commercial development in suburbia was financed as a seven- to 15-year asset class, meaning that developers built cheaply and with no concern for the long-term viability of their projects. Shopping centers appeared at almost every intersection and along endless strips, cannibalizing each other, while fast becoming prone to obsolescence and decay. These were abandoned as replacements were built farther out. Today we are faced with hundreds of thousands of square feet of such shopping centers in need of demolition, renovation, or reuse.

According to the ICSC, there are 23.1 square feet of retail space per person in the U.S., amounting to 7 billion square feet of gross leasable area.[11] It is difficult to imagine the retail industry growing any time soon, especially after the meltdown of 2007–2009, when the largest players in the business suffered tremendous losses and bankruptcies. The image of boarded-up, dilapidated storefronts in shopping centers has become a common sight in the suburbs.

On the other hand, Bulmash Real Estate Advisors predicts the end of the mega-projects; they say there will be more activity in existing places, as lenders require more equity and tighter standards. Public subsidies will become very important as real estate investment trusts (REITs) continue to deleverage, Bulmash asserts.[12] Distressed retail properties have potential for redevelopment for less than the cost of new construction, and if they have good location, at important intersections, relative integration within communities, and not too much competition in close vicinity, such repairs can be successful. Crucial factors are current job availability and the prospect for incubating new businesses within the retrofit. The repair of shopping centers should employ strategies for offering cheap workspace by using the existing structures, temporary structures, inexpensive liner buildings, or outdoor space for farmers' markets.

The repair of shopping centers has a range of social benefits. By introducing apartments above commercial premises, it provides affordable housing for workers and for senior citizens, who will be able to walk to their daily needs and continue living independently. The area will be inhabited 24 hours a day, which will increase safety through continuous informal supervision. Less parking will be necessary because parking will serve commercial and residential uses at different times. Less driving will be required because more trips will be taken on foot.

For incentives, see chapter four, "Repair at the Community Scale, Step Four: Secure Incentives for Implementation."

DEFICIENCIES

This sequence illustrates the deficiencies of shopping centers as elements of sprawl. Figure 4-60 shows the lack of variety of building types (and therefore uses), and figure 4-61 shows the lack of walkable block structure. Figure 4-62 demonstrates the vast, underutilized areas of surface parking, and figure 4-63 highlights the surplus of residual, underutilized space.

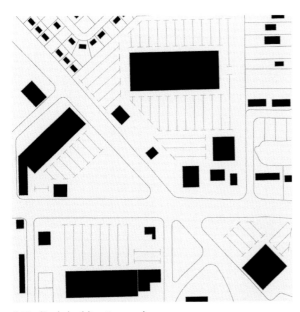

4-60. Single building type and use

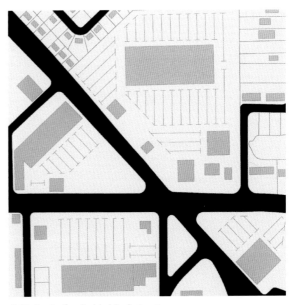

4-61. Lack of walkable block structure

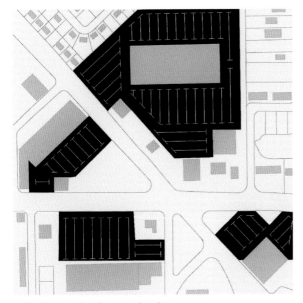

4-62. Dispersed and exposed parking

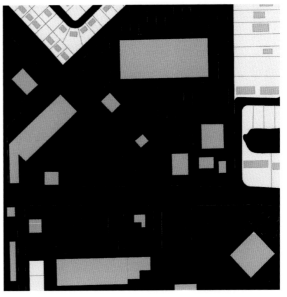

4-63. Lack of civic space

TRANSFORMATION INTO A TOWN CENTER

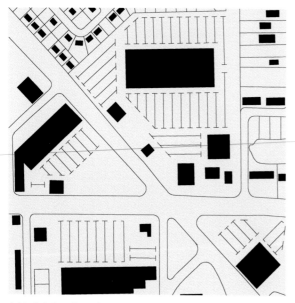

The typical suburban intersection, with strip development on all corners, is transformed into a mixed-use, compact, and well-connected town center that will serve the surrounding area. The purpose of this example is to challenge the limits for this type of sprawl repair and provide the urban design tools for their implementation.

■ Existing buildings

4-64. Existing shopping center

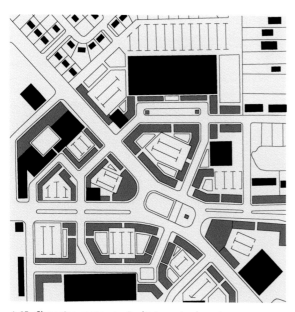

The intervention demonstrated in figure 4-65 is radical and idealized to show the full redevelopment potential of a site. All buildings with substantial footprints are preserved and included in the urban fabric. The intersection is transformed from a confusing and dangerous junction of overscaled traffic "channels" into a civic square defined by urban, mixed-use buildings.

■ Proposed buildings
■ Existing buildings

4-65. Shopping center repaired into a mixed-use town center

4-66. Parking lots dominating the public realm

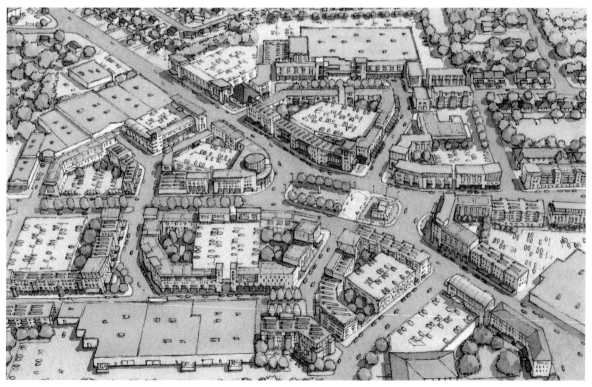

4-67. Parking lots redeveloped into mixed-use, walkable fabric

The repair of this agglomeration of strip shopping centers will ideally happen on all corners of the existing suburban intersection. However, the same approach can be applied to only one or two of the corners, if necessary because of the ownership pattern and growth dynamics of the area. The critical task is the retrofit of the intersection, which currently is confusing, completely car oriented, and prone to accidents. Repairing it into a square will calm the traffic, create a real focus and landmark for the surrounding community, and add developable real estate for new mixed-use buildings (figure 4-68).

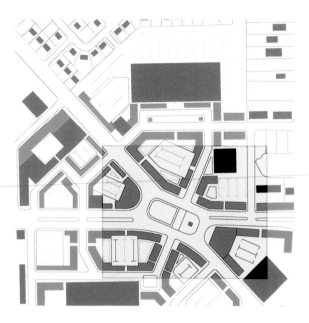

This repair case study demonstrates how most of the existing buildings can be preserved and embedded in the future town center, including some of the smaller structures in the outparcels. The urban fabric forms a retail loop, which connects the main clusters of shops, including the grocery store at the top of figure 4-67. The existing buildings can be renovated and used for retail, or they can be repurposed into civic institutions (schools, galleries, libraries), office space, or senior or wellness facilities.

In some cases the structures may be converted into garages, creating the conditions for development of the fronting parking lots without the need to build new parking garages.

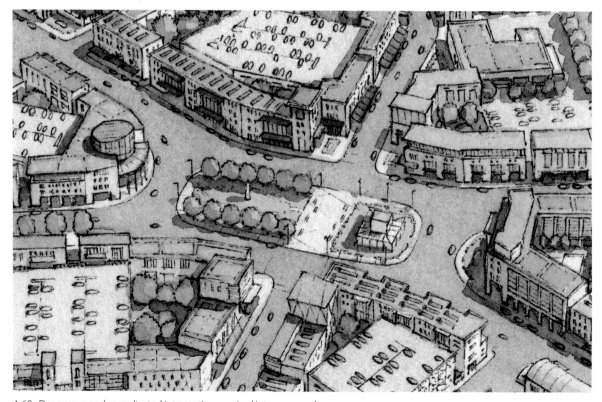

4-68. Dangerous and complicated intersection repaired into a new, urban square

Introduce new building types and mixed uses: This shopping center consists of several big boxes, including a grocery store. The buildings are surrounded by parking lots and outparcels with drive-through establishments. The repair starts with the introduction of other building types such as liner structures for incubator businesses and perimeter block buildings for residential and office uses. The intensification of the site also requires parking structures. The big boxes are embedded in new fabric and remain as shopping anchors. If the retail fails, they can be converted to other uses such as galleries, museums, senior centers, or college satellite campuses.

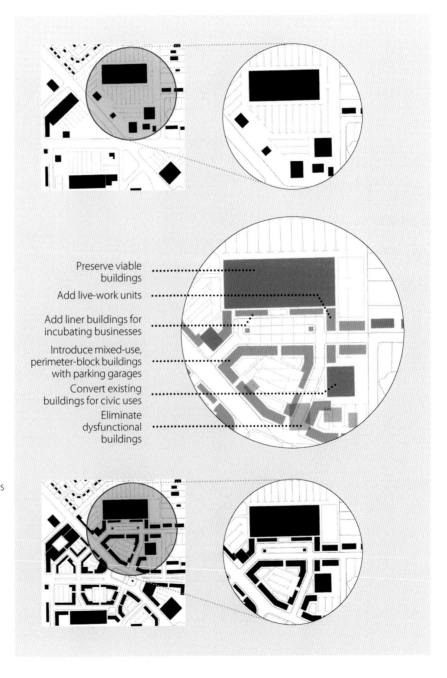

Deficiency: Single building type and use

Remedial Techniques:
Introduce new building types and mixed uses: residential, office, lodging, and civic

Preserve viable buildings

Add live-work units

Add liner buildings for incubating businesses

Introduce mixed-use, perimeter-block buildings with parking garages

Convert existing buildings for civic uses

Eliminate dysfunctional buildings

Outcome: Variety of building types and mix of uses to support a town center

Connect and repair thoroughfares: Shopping centers rarely have block structure. Most of the surface in front of the stores is paved for parking lots. The repair starts with adding streets in front of the stores and connecting them with a pedestrian-friendly retail loop. The newly formed blocks should have perimeters no longer than 1,200 to 1,500 feet to make walking pleasant. The larger blocks need to be broken up by pedestrian passages. Complicated intersections should be simplified, avoiding extensive pavement. A square easily connects a multitude of intersecting streets and creates substantial developable real estate along its perimeter.

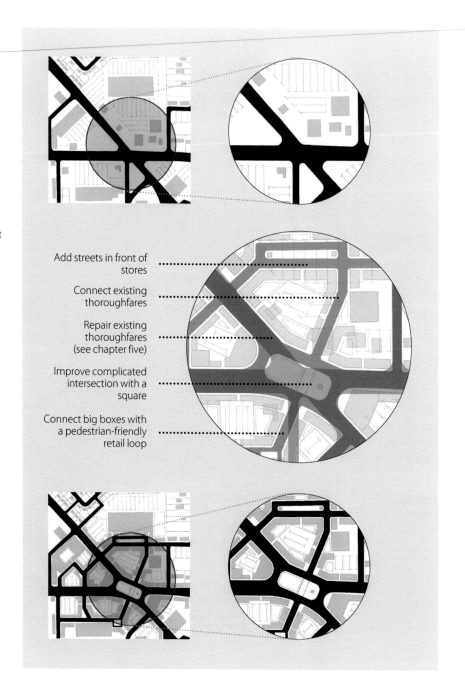

Deficiency: Lack of walkable block structure

Remedial Techniques: Connect and repair thoroughfares; add streets in front of stores

Add streets in front of stores

Connect existing thoroughfares

Repair existing thoroughfares (see chapter five)

Improve complicated intersection with a square

Connect big boxes with a pedestrian-friendly retail loop

Outcome: Walkable network and block structure

Rationalize parking: Parking lots are the most prominent feature of suburban shopping centers. In most cases they are overscaled; with the exception of one or two holidays each year, they are vastly underutilized. These parking lots have great potential to be urbanized with new, mixed-use buildings. The introduction of parking garages allows the replacement of the parking lots with buildings that accommodate other uses, such as high-density housing, office space, and civic use. Additional parking is provided along new and repaired streets.

Deficiency: Underutilized and exposed parking

Remedial Techniques: Rationalize parking; add garages

Add on-street parking

Add parking garages

Organize parking in backs of buildings

Outcome: Parking strategy to support higher density and mix of uses

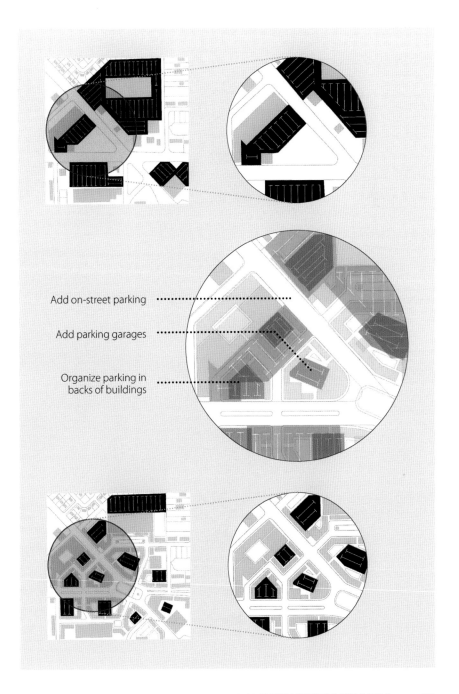

Define open and civic space: Suburban shopping centers rarely have civic space because they are intended for a single use. In recent years some have been designed to mimic main streets with restaurants and entertainment, but the majority lack any defined or useful public realm. By adding buildings that accommodate housing, office, and civic uses, these places become main streets, neigh-borhood centers, or even town centers that are active 24 hours a day. The excessive, undefined space is to be reorganized into a range of public spaces. The focus is a new square that improves the awkward traffic intersection, creates a landmark and a sense of arrival, slows the traffic, and distributes the car flow to the streets leading to the shops.

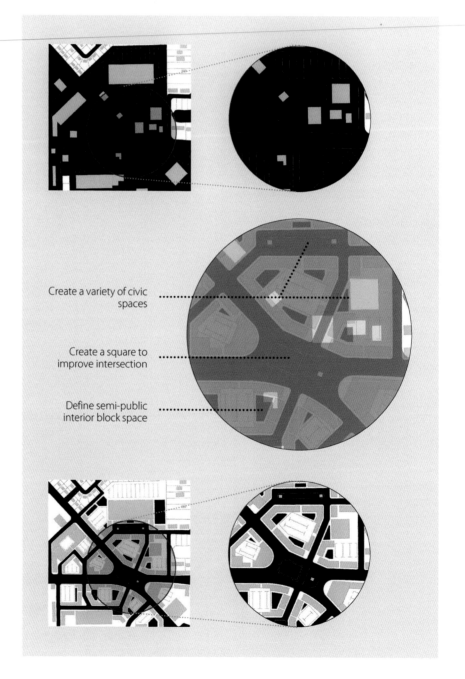

Deficiency: Lack of civic space

Remedial Techniques: Define open and civic spaces

Create a variety of civic spaces

Create a square to improve intersection

Define semi-public interior block space

Outcome: Hierarchy and spatial definition of public realm

REZONING

The existing zoning of shopping centers is usually limited to commercial use. The goal of the rezoning process is to allow a wide variety of mixed uses and transform the shopping center into a town center.

Transect-based zoning creates the conditions for different building types to co-exist along harmonious streetscapes. The uses are flexible and interchangeable, and parking requirements are based on shared use. For example, the newly added office space can share parking with the new residential infill and some civic uses because they need parking at different times. Parking needs will be further reduced because the local mix of uses induces fewer car trips.

The proposed regulating plan (figure 4-70) shows several different zones of the Transect. The T6, or Urban Core zone, includes perimeter-block buildings with structured parking, radically increasing the urban intensity. These perimeter blocks can accommodate shops, apartments, lofts, and offices. The T6 zone delineates the new square, creating a high-quality public realm. The T5, or Urban Center zone, adds live-works and incorporates some of the existing buildings. The T4, or General Urban zone, creates the possibility for the existing buildings at the perimeter (mostly single-family housing) to be up-zoned for better transition to the new town center. The newly created public spaces are organized under CS, Civic Space, including the new square and the plaza in front of the existing big boxes.

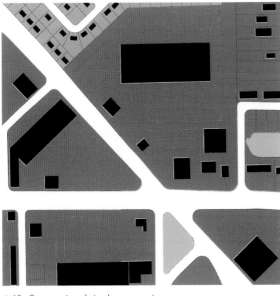

4-69. Conventional single-use zoning

Open Space
R1 - Single-family Residential
C1 - Commercial
Existing buildings

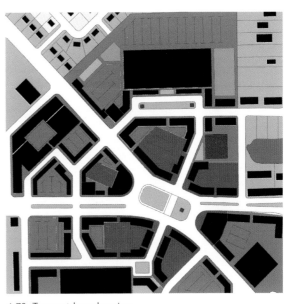

4-70. Transect-based zoning

T1 - Natural zone
T3 - Sub-Urban zone
T4 - General Urban zone
T5 - Urban Center zone
T6 - Urban Core zone
CB - Civic Building
CS - Civic Space
Existing and proposed buildings

PHASING

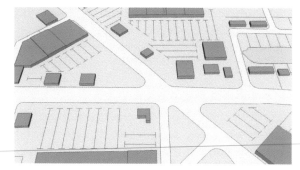

4-71. Existing shopping center

4-72. Short-term repair: Transforming the intersection into a square

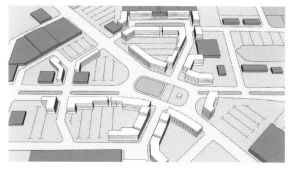

4-73. Medium-term repair: Creating a retail loop

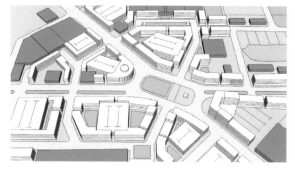

4-74. Long-term repair: Completing the urban fabric

The transformation of a shopping center into a town center is accomplished through several steps that include short-, medium-, and long-term strategies. The existing condition shows the large expanses of asphalt and the dispersion of smaller structures and big boxes (figure 4-71).

The short-term intervention includes the improvement of the intersection and the creation of a recognizable public space – a square that will serve not only as a traffic-calming device but as a focal point, an orientation landmark, and the location of the town center. The initial network connecting the big boxes is laid out as well (figure 4-72).

The next phase adds mixed-use buildings along the new streets. These structures line the loop that connects the big boxes, and the surface parking lots are kept in the back. Liner buildings mask some of the existing buildings and provide affordable commercial and residential space. This phase is the beginning of a pedestrian-friendly urban fabric (figure 4-73).

The third phase, or long-term repair, completes the urban blocks with parking structures and fully built-out perimeters. In addition to the new street network, the existing thoroughfares will be repaired to make them more pedestrian-friendly and provide better access for the surrounding suburban communities (figure 4-74).

IMPLEMENTATION PROTOCOL

1. Analyze the shopping center within its regional context according to the Sprawl Repair Assessment Tool and Void Analysis (see chapter three, "Repair at the Regional Scale"). If there is potential for successful repair, proceed to the next step.

2. Analyze the site feasibility (see chapter four, "Repair at the Community Scale, Step One: Analyze Site Feasibility").

3. Reach out to the appropriate regional entity (a council or the county) in the area. Formulate a regional strategy for the repair of the shopping center, focusing on its potential for transformation into a town center. Transit should be provided between the new town center and other nodes, connecting them to a regional employment destination. Public support and potential investment will be more easily obtained if the developer can demonstrate that the project has regional significance and can contribute to long-term sustainability.

4. Initiate and facilitate the adoption of a new form-based code that will legalize the transformation of the shopping center into a town center (see chapter four, "Repair at the Community Scale, Step Four: Introduce Regulatory and Management Techniques"). This can be done through a comprehensive rezoning ordinance that replaces the existing municipal code and allows repair of shopping centers, or through an overlay district applied specifically to one or a group of shopping centers.

5. Explore public incentives for infrastructure improvements along adjoining thoroughfares and within the shopping center (see chapter four, "Repair at the Community Scale, Step Four: Secure Incentives for Implementation").

6. Select a strategy for partial or complete acquisition of the shopping center. Secure contracts and/or options to purchase (with extendable contract limits) from individual owners. During due diligence, start discussions with county government and key decision makers about the feasibility of the project. If the feedback is positive, proceed to the next step.

7. Prepare a tenant-mix strategy that optimizes national, regional, and local retailers.

8. Create a strategy to manage the main street. Organize a single entity to coordinate tenants and property owners to ensure proper operation, balance, and maintenance of shopfronts, as well as simplicity and economy of streetscape.

9. Introduce a marketing program designed to emphasize the new town center's "sense of place."

10. Analyze the jurisdiction of the main thoroughfares adjacent to or within the shopping center, and if they are under the state DOT, work to have them relinquished to the local municipality if possible. State thoroughfare standards are more challenging to modify to create pedestrian-friendly and transit-oriented environments. Local jurisdictions are able to work directly with communities affected by sprawl.

11. Evaluate the needs of the community in relation to existing retail, office, and residential space. If the market is weak, explore the potential for reuse of the existing commercial buildings to incubate local businesses. Identify and attract struggling businesses that cannot afford the rents in more expensive locations but that provide essential services to a community – a coffee shop, dry cleaner, hairdresser, and so forth.

12. Evaluate the possibilities for preserving viable buildings, eliminating dysfunctional buildings, adding liner buildings for incubating businesses, adding live-work units, and introducing mixed-use perimeter-block buildings with parking garages.

13. Explore the possibility of locating a civic building in the transformed shopping center to serve as a catalyst for place making and to provide community identity. A post office, a library, a market, a religious building, or a meeting hall can serve this role.

14. Start preparations for a public process and a possible collaborative design and planning session (charrette). Engage the regional government as well as adjacent subdivisions and their associations, the local business community, chamber of commerce, school board, and not-for-profit organizations.

15. Complete a public charrette, preferably at the project site. Engage decision makers and stakeholders to explore various scenarios and phasing options. Results must be based on consensus.

16. Start the entitlement process for the project. By this time the new town center should be permitted under a new ordinance.

17. Start construction.

APPLICATION: RECLAIMING A SQUARE OUT OF PARKING LOTS

Drawing by James Dougherty/Dover Kohl and Partners

4-75. Car-oriented environment of a blighted shopping center

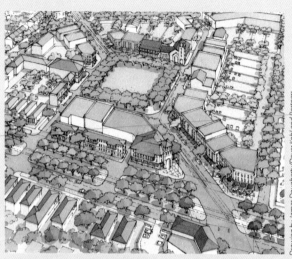

Drawing by James Dougherty/Dover Kohl and Partners

4-76. Public square as a traffic-calming and place-making device

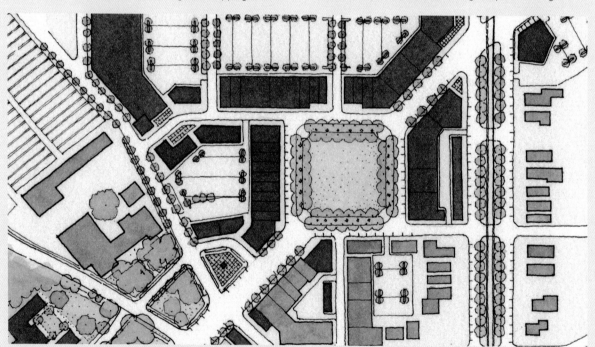

4-77. Parking lots transformed into a town center

Located in fairly urban conditions on both sides of a diagonal avenue, this shopping center exhibits all the characteristics of its suburban counterparts. The buildings are set back deeply in the parcels, leaving the frontages to large parking lots. The few existing streets meet the diagonal at odd angles, creating confusing and wasteful geometries (figure 4-75).

The proposal is to keep the location of the existing buildings (that can be gradually replaced by new ones), but to reorganize the space in front of them into a square, channeling the circulation close to the storefronts and creating a memorable civic space (figures 4-76 and 4-77).

APPLICATION: TRANSFORMING A GREYFIELD INTO A TOWN CENTER

Conceived more than twenty years ago, Mashpee Commons in Massachusetts is a pioneering transformation of a strip shopping center into a town center serving the surrounding 23 square miles of suburbia. It debuted several urban design techniques, including puncturing pedestrian passages through, and reusing, existing structures (figure 4-78), using liner buildings to mask parking lots and accommodate local tenants, and creating primary and secondary street networks (A and B streets). The A/B street technique (figure 4-79) designates the external,

vehicular-oriented thoroughfares, where the pedestrian experience is of lesser quality, as secondary, or B streets. The internal streets of excellent pedestrian quality are designated as primary, or A streets, and are required by code to maintain high standards (such as continuous, safe, and interesting building frontage). This technique has subsequently been utilized in downtown redevelopments, allowing for the inclusion of parking lots, gas stations, and other necessary elements of urban life while preserving a vibrant pedestrian network.

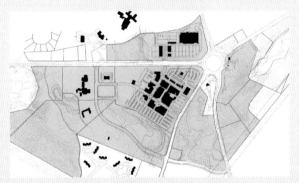

4-78. Defunct shopping center retrofitted with pedestrian passages and new thoroughfares

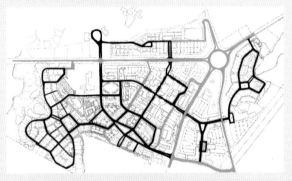

4-79. Primary (black) and secondary network (grey) of streets

4-80. Final repair of the shopping center into a town center, adjacent to new, mixed-use neighborhoods

APPLICATION: GRADUAL URBANIZATION OF HIGHWAY-FACING STRIP SHOPPING CENTER

The strategy for gradual urbanization of a shopping center facing a highway is to create a parallel main street. This approach includes three phases. The first phase incorporates the existing drive-through establishments and big boxes into a main street (figure 4-82). The restaurants remain visible from the highway through their exposed parking lots, but they are embedded in mixed-use urban frontage. A plaza is formed in front of two of the big boxes. The second step eliminates one of the big boxes, replacing it with mixed-use blocks (figure 4-83). The last step removes the second box and urbanizes the main street on both sides (figure 4-84).

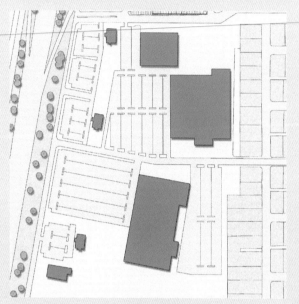

4-81. Existing conditions: Drive-throughs and big boxes

4-82. Phase One: Existing buildings incorporated into a main street

4-83. Phase Two: First big box replaced with urban blocks

4-84. Phase Three: Second big box and drive-throughs replaced with urban blocks

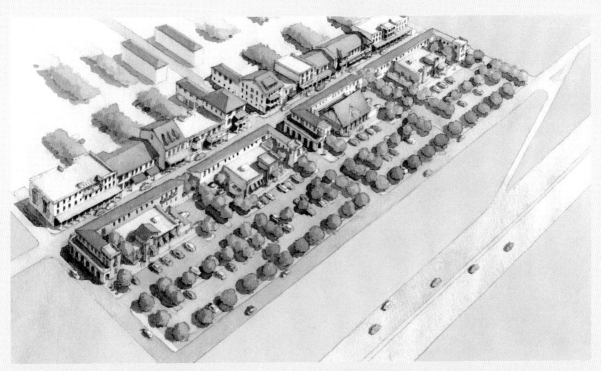

4-85. Drive-through structures, visible from the highway, are embedded into a main street

4-86. View of the new main street incorporating the existing big boxes

SHOPPING MALL

Malls are the most promising contenders for sprawl repair. Because of their location, parcel size, ownership structure, and opportunities for transit and mixed uses, they have great potential to be transformed into town centers or transit-ready urban cores.

Malls are usually located at major arterial intersections, along the paths of growth, in the vicinity of numerous residential subdivisions. This makes them ideal as centers along an integrated regional bus rapid transit network, light rail line, or other mode of public transportation. The overabundant retail space in malls can be rebalanced or replaced by complementary uses such as office, residential, hotel, civic, or institutional buildings. Because of these advantages, malls have been the most frequent targets for sprawl repair.

Examples include Mizner Park in Boca Raton, Florida; Paseo Colorado in Pasadena, California; and Belmar in Lakewood, Colorado.

To reach the full potential of the repair of a mall, it is necessary to understand its regional context – its location and its relationship to the other centers in the region. As very large structures and agglomerations of retail use, malls have the capacity to influence their surroundings – if a mall is flourishing, the surrounding strip shopping, fast food restaurants, banks, and entertainment venues also thrive. Conversely, if a mall starts to decline, it can take businesses in the region down with it. But not all malls are alike. For example, a mall embedded in suburban residential fabric may be repaired more swiftly into a town center than a mall located in the exurban fringes, where it is entirely dependent on the prospect of future growth.

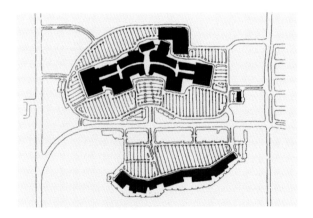
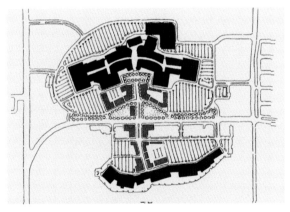

4-87. Three-phase transformation of a shopping mall keeping the main structure

To make the critical distinctions between location and type, a site analysis must be performed, and from there the nature and feasibility of the repair can be determined. When the mall is still successful, the repair should be forward looking – visionary and proactive in character – and the process of the retrofit started while the mall is still economically vital. When the shopping mall has already lost its economic momentum, the retrofit becomes post-factum or retroactive.

The repair of a mall can be achieved through a series of interventions executed as one major redevelopment or in phases implemented over the course of decades. The main structure of the mall can first be preserved and embedded in fabric, and then pieces can be disassembled step-by-step, keeping only the anchors, and creating a main street. The final stage may include the full demolition of the mall if the remaining structures become obsolete. These are separate strategies that can be employed sequentially, as phases, or partially, depending on the circumstances.

The introduction of mixed uses, together with the reconnection of thoroughfares into urban blocks, are logical steps of the transformation. However, the most important intervention will be the rationalization of parking and the addition of parking garages, because that will facilitate the high density and mixed uses necessary for a town center.

The incentives for repairing malls need to be strong, as the financial commitments of the private sector required for such redevelopments are very high. When dead or dying malls are redeveloped and intensified as complete town centers, with residential and office components to supplement the retail, transit between these intensified nodes becomes viable. Just as the federal government subsidizes the interstate highway system that advances sprawl, federal, state, and local governments should support the creation of a network of repaired commercial nodes to support regional transit.

The incentives and implementation techniques may include a range of the following: permitting by right, which requires state enabling legislation, exemption from state and federal assessments, state and federal funding for parking structures and transit, Transfer of Development Rights and Purchase of Development Rights mechanisms, Tax Increment Financing, Business Improvement Districts, and others (see chapter four, "Repair at the Community Scale, Step Four: Secure Incentives for Implementation").

DEFICIENCIES

The deficiencies of the mall are similar to those of the other commercial sprawl elements, but some of them are more extreme: the footprint is excessively large for a single-use building (figure 4-88), pedestrian circulation is hampered by the vast areas of underutilized surface parking (figures 4-89 and 4-90), and the only well-defined public space is inside the mall (figure 4-91). However, these deficiencies also present opportunities for the repair of the mall. For instance, the large parking lots can easily accommodate a new urban fabric as well as a range of public spaces, including urban gardens for local food production.

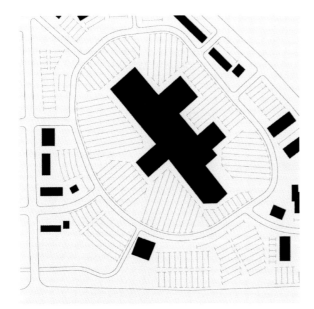

4-88. Single building type and use

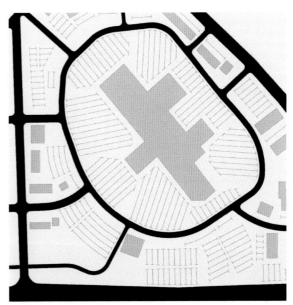

4-89. Lack of walkable block structure

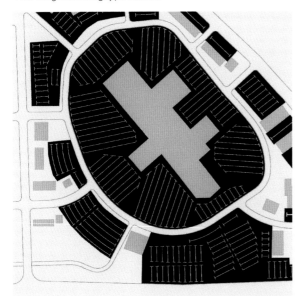

4-90. Overscaled and exposed parking

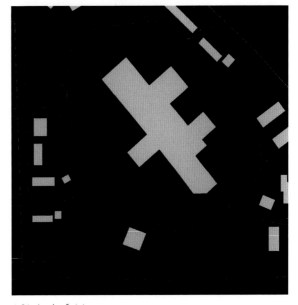

4-91. Lack of civic space

TRANSFORMATION INTO A TOWN CENTER

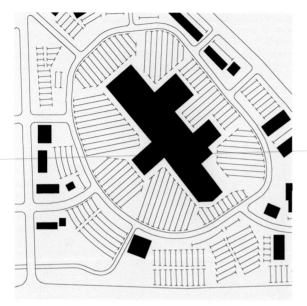

The two dominant elements within the existing site are the massive footprint of the mall structure and the overwhelming surface parking surrounding it (figure 4-92). Smaller commercial establishments mainly in the form of drive-through buildings are located along the perimeter of the parcel.

▬ Existing buildings

4-92. Existing suburban mall

Figure 4-93 shows a hypothetical infill of the parking lots with urban fabric of perimeter blocks, some of which contain parking garages. The high percentage of red color highlighting the proposed infill structures shows the dramatic nature of this remediation. This radical intervention is justified, and required, because of the importance the repaired mall will have for the re-structuring and revitalization of the region.

▬ Proposed buildings
▬ Existing buildings

4-93. Repaired town center

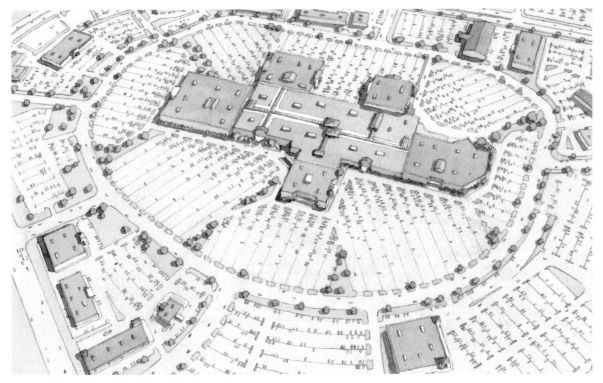

4-94. Public realm dominated by parking lots and a megastructure

4-95. One strategy for mall repair is retaining the main structure and redeveloping the parking lots

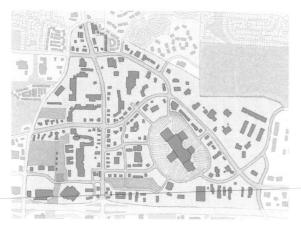

4-96. Existing context: Shopping centers, office parks, and parking lots

There are three means of proactive repair of a mall with different degrees of intervention. The existing context map (figure 4-96) shows the mall within its suburban surroundings with potential for a larger scale intervention. All three strategies engage the vicinity in a unified design of a town center, connecting to the adjacent thoroughfares. An option for the design is a stormwater management canal parallel to the loop road around the mall. This canal is not only a utilitarian device, but also a civic amenity for the community.

In the first stategy, the main structure of the mall is preserved and embedded in new fabric (figure 4-97). The structure is renovated and the roof is converted into a garden. This option is the most conservative, assuming that the mall will survive as a megastructure, though its function may change. The mall building or portions of it can be transformed into civic (college campus, daycare facilities, community center, museum, etc.) or office use. This option is analyzed through a sequence of diagrams showing the steps necessary for its transformation into a mixed-use hub.

The second strategy preserves only the anchors and incorporates a main street (figures 4-105 and 4-106). The third strategy demonstrates the transformation of the mall parcel into an agricultural village (figure 4-111 and 4-112).

4-97. Option One: Evolution of the mall with main structure preserved and embedded in mixed-used walkable fabric

Introduce new building types and mixed uses: The main characteristic of the mall is the single megastructure that contains large concentrations of retail use. The first type of repair keeps the building intact and embeds it in mixed-use fabric. This is the case when the shops and anchors are still viable or they can be adapted for other purposes. The building of the mall is preserved and treated as a grand "galleria," with new blocks forming a framework of streets, plazas, and squares around it. The large amount of retail use is balanced with apartments, lofts, townhouses, live-work units, offices, and hotels.

Deficiency: Single building type and use

Remedial Techniques:
Introduce new building types and mixed use: residential, retail, office, lodging, and civic

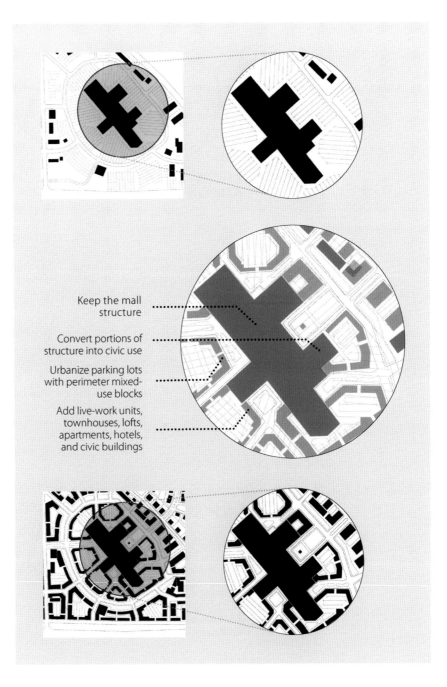

Keep the mall structure

Convert portions of structure into civic use

Urbanize parking lots with perimeter mixed-use blocks

Add live-work units, townhouses, lofts, apartments, hotels, and civic buildings

Outcome: Variety of building types and mix of uses to support a town center

Connect and repair thoroughfares: A mall usually occupies a central location, "floating" in a mega parcel as large as 50 to 100 acres and surrounded by surface parking lots. Usually positioned on one corner of a high-volume intersection, a mall site has a limited number of entrances accessed from a loop road. These diagrams show a simple technique of keeping the loop road as an organizational element and extending and connecting all existing streets into a radial fabric oriented toward the mall. The blocks formed are large enough to accommodate parking structures, but for pedestrian convenience and permeability do not exceed 1,500 feet in length.

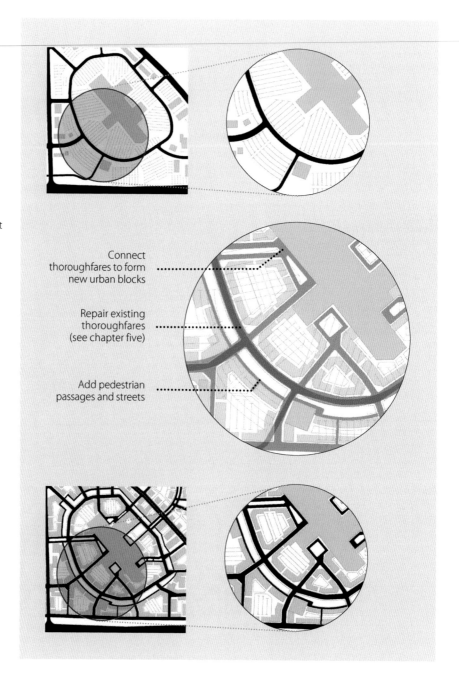

Deficiency: Lack of walkable block structure

Remedial Techniques: Connect and repair thoroughfares; create urban blocks

Connect thoroughfares to form new urban blocks

Repair existing thoroughfares (see chapter five)

Add pedestrian passages and streets

Outcome: Walkable network and block structure

Rationalize parking: The vast parking lots of suburban malls are usually overscaled and therefore underutilized, with the rare exceptions of one or two times each year. These parking lots have great potential for high-intensity development. These diagrams show a detail of the mall parking lot and how it can be transformed into a piece of urban fabric. The surface lots are replaced by garages, allowing hundreds of thousands of square feet of housing, offices, hotels, and civic uses to be created. Parking garages are crucial elements in the redevelopment of malls, and should therefore be incentivized as important public infrastructure.

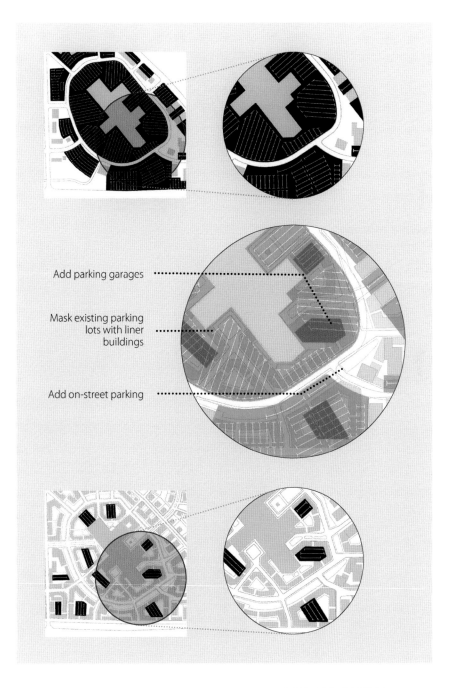

Deficiency: Dispersed and exposed parking

Remedial Techniques:
Rationalize parking; add garages

Add parking garages

Mask existing parking lots with liner buildings

Add on-street parking

Outcome: Parking strategy to support higher density and mixed use

Define open and civic spaces: Mall interiors are often the only public gathering spaces for suburban residents. One way to provide civic space is to add fabric around the existing structure, weaving plazas, playgrounds, and squares throughout. The new blocks contain semi-public spaces that are part of the pedestrian network. A canal is also added parallel to the loop road. It becomes not only a stormwater-management device, but also a civic amenity for the new community.

Deficiency: Lack of civic space

Remedial Techniques: Define open and civic spaces

Create squares and plazas

Define semi-public spaces in block interiors

Create a canal as a civic and infrastructure amenity

Outcome: Hierarchy and spatial definition of public realm

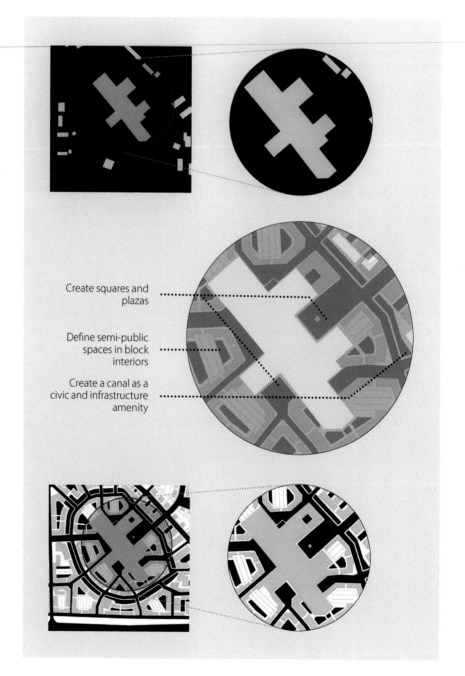

Integrate local food production: The newly created public spaces in this repaired mall site – the squares, attached green spaces, and the interiors of the mixed-use blocks – are potential sites for community gardens. Private gardens can be introduced on the roofs of buildings and parking garages. The new canal will be an ideal source for irrigation of the community gardens. Integration of urban agriculture in the new town center should be calibrated to the preferences of the market.

Deficiency: Lack of local food production

Remedial Techniques:
Introduce local food production spaces

Integrate community gardens into public spaces

Create rooftop gardens

Introduce community gardens into block interiors

Outcome: A variety of local food production options

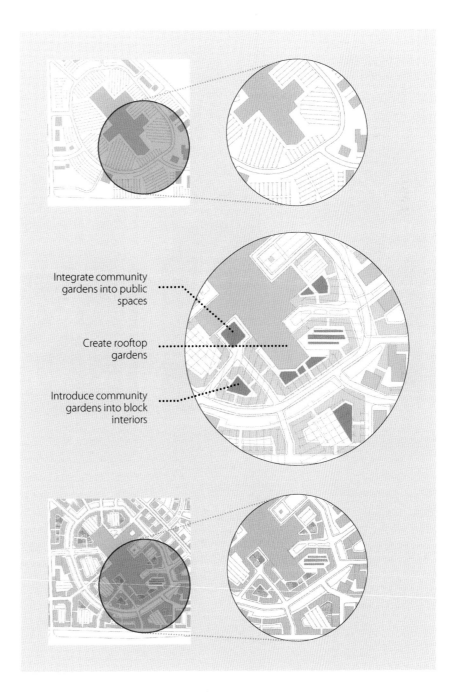

REZONING

The conventional zoning of malls allows for a very high concentration of retail use (figure 4-98). While the large square footage of shops is not problematic in itself, the lack of any other use contributes to a monocultural environment, which can blight the surrounding area if the mall fails. The goal of the rezoning process is to allow a wide variety of uses so the mall can be transformed into a town center.

The densification of the site will be accomplished by introducing perimeter-block buildings, which are very flexible urban types and can accommodate shops,

offices, lofts, and apartments in various combinations. These building types fall under the T6 Urban Core zoning.

The proposed regulating plan (figure 4-99) shows several zones of the Transect. The T6, or Urban Core zone, includes perimeter blocks; the T5, or Urban Center zone, includes live-work units and townhouses, and incorporates some of the existing buildings. The T4, or General Urban zone, includes apartment villas. The new public spaces are organized under CS, Civic Space, including squares and plazas in front of the existing mall.

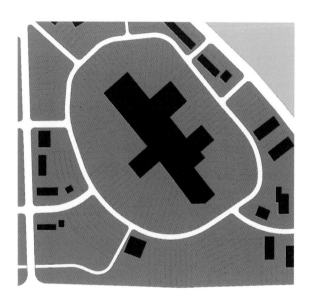

4-98. Conventional single-use zoning

- Open Space
- C - Commercial
- Existing buildings

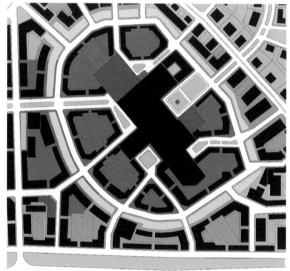

4-99. Transect-based zoning

- T4 - General Urban zone
- T5 - Urban Center zone
- T6 - Urban Core zone
- CS - Civic Space
- CB - Civic Building
- Existing and proposed buildings

PHASING

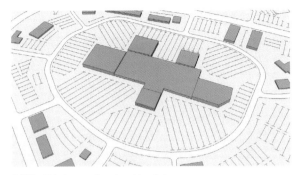

4-100. Existing mall and parking lots

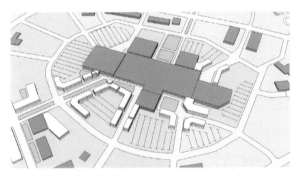

4-101. Phase One: Delineating street network and avenue to transit

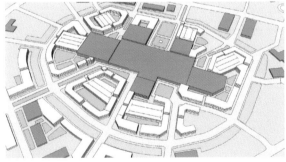

4-102. Phase Two: Building most of inner loop fabric and canal

The strategy for the mall repair includes four possible phases. The first three phases keep the mall structure intact. The repair starts with the delineation of an avenue leading from a new or proposed transit stop to the entrance of the mall (figure 4-101). The street network within the loop road is also created. Only a first layer of buildings is constructed along the frontage of the main street, keeping the existing surface parking lots behind them.

The second phase (figure 4-102) includes the build-out of most of the perimeter blocks and garage structures within the loop road and the creation of a canal parallel to the loop road to collect the stormwater runoff from the new urban fabric.

The third phase incorporates all blocks around the mall, as well as the parcels outside of the loop road (figure 4-103).

The fourth phase is a special case. It can serve as a final option, to be used if the mall becomes obsolete as a megastructure, or it can stand alone as a separate option altogether. In this phase only the anchor stores are kept and repurposed, while the rest of the mall is demolished (figure 4-104). A main street is formed between the anchors preserving the block structure from the prior phases, adding infill only where necessary to complete the street frontages.

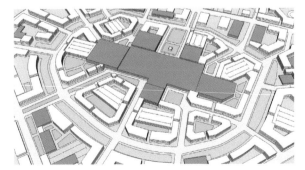

4-103. Phase Three: Finishing the build-out

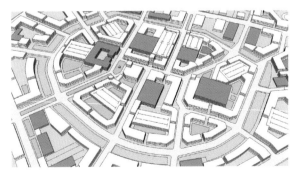

4-104. Phase Four: Proceeding to main street option if appropriate

The second strategy shows the evolution of the mall into a main street reusing the anchors. Multiple streets forming the new fabric feed the main street. The anchors may retain retail use or become civic destinations. Senior centers may also be accommodated, with courtyards carved out of the footprints.

4-105. Option Two: Evolution of the mall, keeping the anchors and creating a main street between them

4-106. The main street is fed by multiple new streets

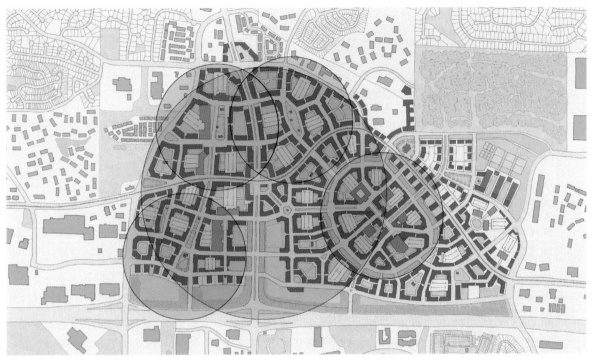

4-107. Diagram of pedestrian sheds of the town center

◯ Five-minute walk pedestrian shed   ◯ Ten-minute walk transit shed

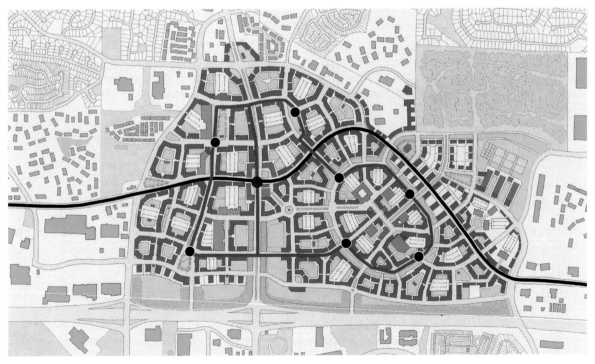

4-108. Diagram of transit organization of the new town center

━━ Light rail   ⬤ Light rail stop   ▬ Circulator   ● Circulator stop

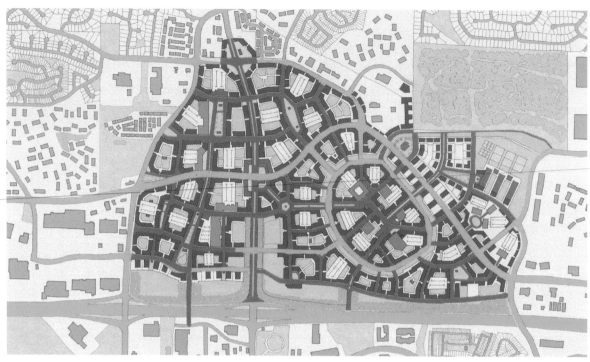

4-109. Diagram of thoroughfares showing the newly connected network

▬▬ Existing thoroughfares ▬▬ Proposed thoroughfares

4-110. Diagram of intersection density, doubled by new plan

✛ Existing intersections ✛ Proposed intersections

The third strategy is the polemic devolution of the mall into an agricultural village. The assumption is that the surrounding region has lost population and the mall is transformed into a rural settlement where gardens replace parking lots. For comparison, the plaza has the dimensions of *Piazza Del Campo* in Sienna, Italy.

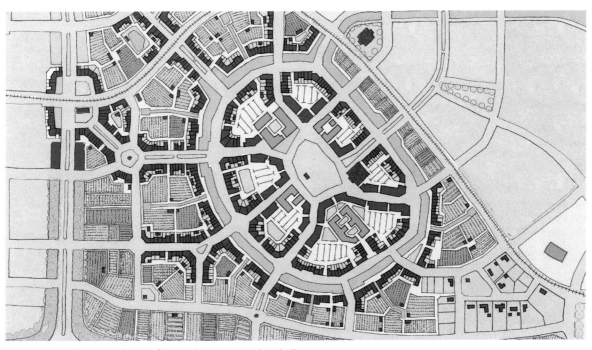

4-111. Option Three: Devolution of the mall into an agricultural village

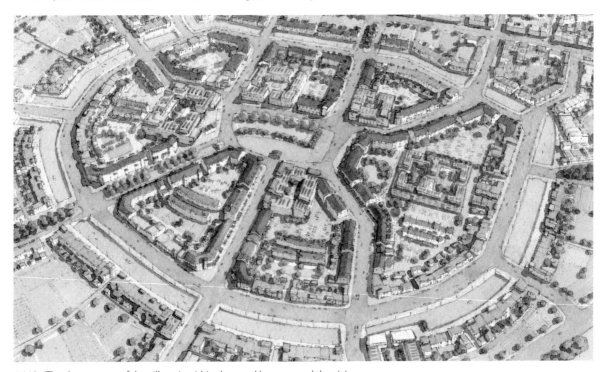

4-112. The densest part of the village is within the canal loop around the civic green

Environmental elements are incorporated into the existing mall buildings and the new infill infrastructure. The new buildings provide for natural ventilation and daylighting. Passive solar systems and gardens are introduced on existing and new roofs (figure 4-113).

The canal, which is a feature of all repair options, becomes an attractive amenity, while serving as stormwater retention and irrigation source (figure 4-114). The civic green can be used as a community garden (figure 4-115).

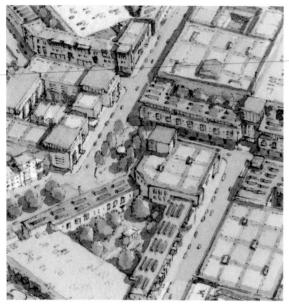

4-113. Passive solar technologies, solar panels, and rooftop gardens

4-114. Canal as stormwater and irrigation infrastructure, as well as civic amenity

4-115. Civic green used for a community garden and improved stormwater performance

IMPLEMENTATION PROTOCOL

1. Analyze the mall within its regional context, and according to the Sprawl Repair Assessment Tool and Void Analysis (see chapter three, "Repair at the Regional Scale"). If there is potential for successful repair, proceed to the next step.

2. Analyze the site feasibility (see chapter four, "Repair at the Community Scale, Step One: Analyze Site Feasibility").

3. Assess the leasing structure of the mall – identify anchors (department stores), junior anchors and aggregated national credit tenants (The Limited, The GAP, or companies that control 40,000 to 50,000 square feet of combined stores in malls or power centers), individual national credit tenants (national chains with a store or two in a given mall or power center), and local mom-and-pop tenants (typically pay high rents and require more management attention from the property owner). Identify the co-tenancy clauses typically in place for the national credit tenants (they can leave or not pay rent if any of the anchors leave).

4. Identify the type of mall repair and phasing. There are several variations of sprawl repair for malls:

- Incorporation of the existing buildings while the mall is still prosperous. This is a proactive repair, anticipating the decline of the mall and the need for transit-oriented, mixed-use town centers.
- Partial incorporation of existing structures, keeping some of the anchors and/or existing parking garages. This approach is appropriate when the mall is in a process of deterioration, but has not yet closed. A main street can be delineated where the central spine of the mall was before.
- Full replacement of the mall, or retroactive repair. This is a strategy to use when the mall has failed, the existing buildings have deteriorated beyond repair, and the parcel should be fully redeveloped.
- Devolution. If the area loses population for socio-economic reasons, a full or partial reversion to agricultural land is possible, in the form of individual and community parcels. Some of the infrastructure is utilized for streets and plazas. The mall is replaced with small-scale

buildings that form an agricultural village.

5. Reach out to the appropriate regional entity (a council or the county) in the area. Formulate a regional strategy for the repair of the shopping mall, focusing on its potential for transformation into a town center. Transit should be provided between the new town center and other nodes, connecting them to other regional destinations. Public support and potential investment will be more easily obtained if the developer can demonstrate that the project has regional significance and can contribute to long-term sustainability.

6. Initiate and facilitate the adoption of a new form-based code that will legalize the transformation of the mall into a town center (see chapter four, "Repair at the Community Scale, Step Three: Introduce Regulatory and Management Techniques"). This can be done through a comprehensive rezoning ordinance that replaces the existing municipal code and allows repair of shopping malls, or through an overlay district of the mall parcel.

7. Explore public incentives for infrastructure improvements along adjoining thoroughfares and within the shopping mall (see chapter four, "Repair at the Community Scale, Step Four: Secure Incentives for Implementation").

8. Select a strategy for partial or complete acquisition of the shopping mall. Secure contracts and/or options to purchase (with extendable contract limits). During due diligence, start discussions with county government and key decision makers about the feasibility of the project. If the feedback is positive, proceed to the next step.

9. Prepare a tenant-mix strategy that optimizes national, regional, and local retailers.

10. Create a strategy to manage the main street. Organize a single entity to coordinate tenants and property owners to ensure proper operation, balance, and maintenance of shopfronts, as well as simplicity and economy of the streetscape.

11. Introduce a marketing program designed to emphasize the new town center's "sense of place."

12. Analyze the jurisdiction of the main thoroughfares adjacent to the shopping mall, and if they are under the state DOT, work to have them relinquished to the local municipality if possible. State thoroughfare standards are more challenging to modify to create pedestrian-friendly and transit-oriented environments. Local jurisdictions are able to work directly with communities affected by sprawl.

13. Explore the possibility of locating civic institutions within the mall (if the building is reused) or within the new fabric to serve as a catalyst for place making and provide community identity. A post office, a library, a market, or a religious building can serve this role. Similarly, when large portions of the mall are repurposed, college satellite campuses, senior facilities, meeting halls, and theaters can also become strong anchors for the redevelopment.

14. Start preparations for a public process and a possible collaborative design and planning session (charrette). Engage the regional government as well as adjacent subdivisions and their associations, the local business community, chamber of commerce, school board, and not-for-profit organizations.

15. Complete a public charrette, preferably at the project site. Engage decision makers and stakeholders to explore various scenarios and phasing options. Results must be based on consensus.

16. Start the entitlement process for the project. By this time the new town center should be permitted under a new ordinance.

17. Start construction.

APPLICATION: CREATING A MAIN STREET BY KEEPING AN ANCHOR

This case study of the re-urbanization of an obsolete mall into a main street and a town center uses one of the anchors, a Macy's store, as a termination and a landmark (figures 4-116 and 4-117).

The strategy is to create multiple internal and external connections and a full range of environments, transitioning from an urban core to the surrounding suburban community. The creek, covered by a parking lot, is daylighted and transformed into a linear park.

4-116. Existing mall to be repaired into a town center keeping one anchor building

4-117. A main street of mixed-use buildings organizes the urban structure of the new town center

■ Existing anchor ■ New mixed-use buildings ☐ New townhouses, live-works, and single-family units

COMMERCIAL STRIP

Commercial strips began as rural roads connecting cities and towns, but later became the main spines for suburban growth. They became explicitly commercial in the late 1950s and early '60s to support the nearby residential developments.

These corridors consist predominantly of car-oriented retail uses, shopping centers, big boxes, drive-through restaurants, banks, and occasional places of worship. Their relentless similarity is due to their cheap design and construction. Businesses invest as little as possible in these properties because most expect to move to a farther location in only a few years (15 years or less). Because they are all identical, and because there

is always more land to develop farther out, commercial strips are viewed as disposable commodities and therefore susceptible to overdevelopment and wastefulness.

One of the primary deficiencies of the commercial strip is the lack of a walkable, compact, neighborhood structure. This precludes the efficient use of transit, which works only when stops are in walkable environments. The remedy is to identify important intersections along the corridor and create mixed-use, compact, well-connected neighborhoods at those sites.

Repair of a commercial strip begins only after regional analysis identifies the corridor as having potential for new or expanded transit. The strip is then designated as a transit boulevard to be gradually redeveloped

City of Miami Planning Department

4-118. Lack of spatial definition along a commercial strip

City of Miami Planning Department

4-119. Sprawl repair of the strip into a walkable street

into a string of transit-oriented, high-density, mixed-use nodes. A transit-oriented node has a nucleus of higher-intensity development covering a five-minute walk from the center to the edge. That pedestrian shed can be extended to a half-mile radius, if desired, as people are willing to walk farther to a transit stop.

The techniques for repair include the introduction of a variety of building types, the most versatile of which is the perimeter urban block. Consisting of buildings at the reasonable heights of four or five stories, the perimeter urban block can accommodate transit-supportive urban densities of more than 50 units per acre and accommodate a variety of uses.

As with all elements in sprawl, the commercial strip is characterized by underutilized space. These expanses of parking lots, landscaped buffers, and driveways are ideal real estate for infill development. Civic spaces should also be included as part of the repair strategy, and existing streets should be connected to provide more choices for pedestrian and vehicular movement.

Incentives for repair projects along commercial strips are similar to those for regional shopping centers and malls, including permitting by right (which will require state enabling legislation), exemption from state and federal assessments, state and federal funding for parking structures and transit, Transfer of Development Rights and Purchase of Development Rights, Tax Increment Financing, Business Improvement Districts, and state and federal grants for improvement of blighted areas (see chapter four, "Repair at the Community Scale, Step Four: Secure Incentives for Implementation").

DEFICIENCIES

The three most important deficiencies of a strip corridor are the lack of neighborhood structure (figure 4-120), no variety of uses (figure 4-121), and underutilized open space (figure 4-122). The inefficient use of the land makes redevelopment efforts challenging.

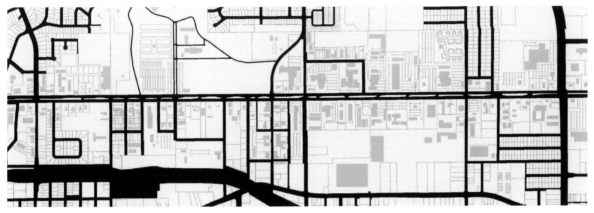

4-120. Lack of neighborhood structure and transit

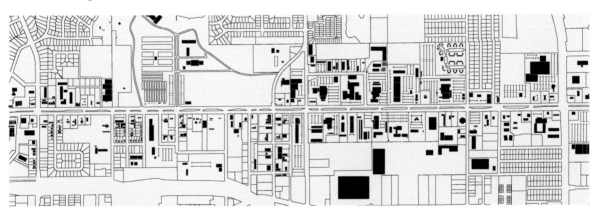

4-121. Lack of urban building types and mixed uses

4-122. Underutilized open space

TRANSFORMATION INTO A NODAL TRANSIT BOULEVARD

The goal for the repair of the strip corridor is to transform it into an urban thoroughfare that supports transit. The distances between the transit nodes will depend on the type of transportation: light rail, bus, or trolley. This par- ticular repair demonstrates the introduction of light rail. The interventions occur at every mile, each encompassing an area centered on a pedestrian shed, which is five to ten minutes' walking distance from center to edge.

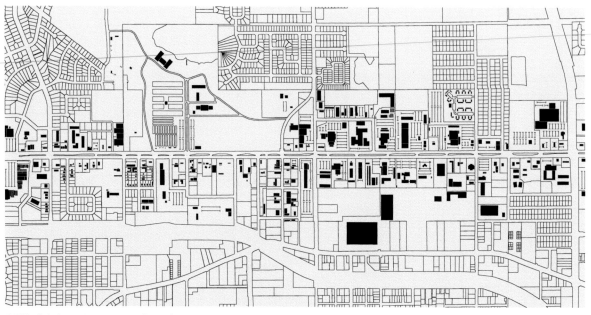

4-123. Existing strip commercial corridor

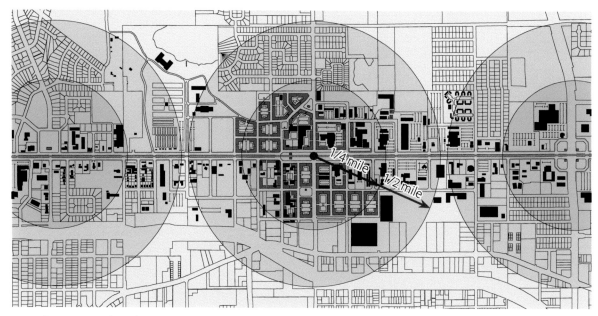

4-124. Interventions along the commercial strip. The circles show the transit nodes, located every mile, with quarter-mile pedestrian sheds

Connect thoroughfares and accommodate transit:
The commercial strip usually commands a very wide right-of-way, which is good for the introduction of transit. Light rail lines can be built along a median in the middle, or rapid bus lanes can be designated on both sides of the corridor, along one-way access lanes. New intersections should be introduced as the existing streets are connected to form urban block fabric. It is rare that the existing infrastructure coincides with a rational block structure at a given location. In most cases, substantial readjustments of utilities will be necessary. Parallel parking is also added to shield pedestrians on the sidewalks.

Deficiency: Lack of neighborhood structure and transit

Remedial Techniques: Connect thoroughfares and accommodate light rail line at mile intervals

Connect existing thoroughfares

Introduce transit along corridor

Create smaller urban blocks

Introduce alleys and lanes

Outcome: Walkable network of streets and blocks; easy access to transit

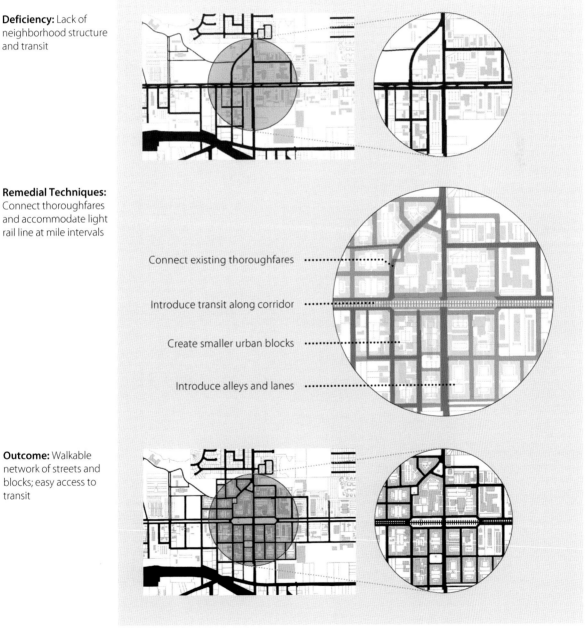

Introduce urban building types and mixed uses: The predominant building types along the strip are repetitive, single-use, freestanding building types. They support the daily needs of suburban residents but these buildings are not welcome in close proximity to residential areas because of their appearance and overwhelming parking lots. Repair includes the introduction of parking garages to support density and a variety of building types accommodating a mix of uses: residential, hotel, office, with shops and restaurants along the ground floors.

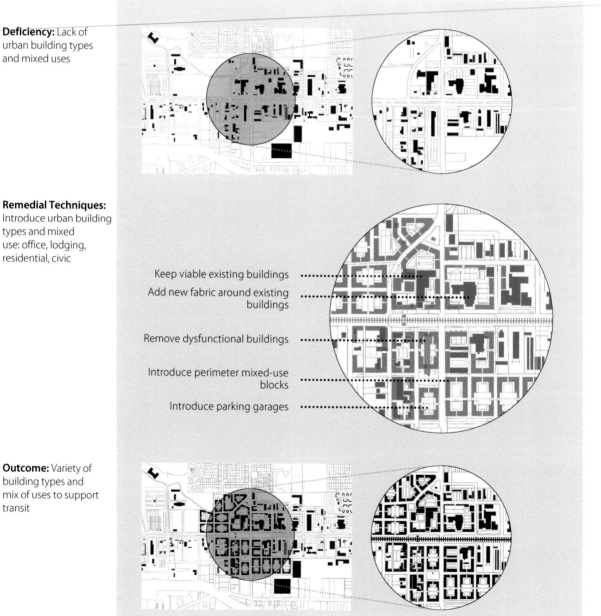

Deficiency: Lack of urban building types and mixed uses

Remedial Techniques: Introduce urban building types and mixed use: office, lodging, residential, civic

Keep viable existing buildings
Add new fabric around existing buildings
Remove dysfunctional buildings
Introduce perimeter mixed-use blocks
Introduce parking garages

Outcome: Variety of building types and mix of uses to support transit

Define open and civic space: Public space along commercial strips is dominated by parking lots. An explicit network of public spaces, including squares, transit plazas, playgrounds, and smaller greens, should be designed at locations designated as transit nodes. Transit stops should be comfortable, shielded from the elements, and ideally in the vicinity of cafés, corner stores, or newsstands. Light rail stops should be more prominent than bus stops, perhaps requiring separate structures in the medians, while bus stops can be incorporated in the wide sidewalks in front of the mixed-use buildings.

Deficiency:
Underutilized open space

Remedial Techniques:
Define open and civic spaces

Create small civic spaces, greens, and playgrounds

Create transit stop plazas

Create squares

Define semi-public space in block interiors

Outcome: Mixed-use corridor of urban nodes and a variety of civic spaces

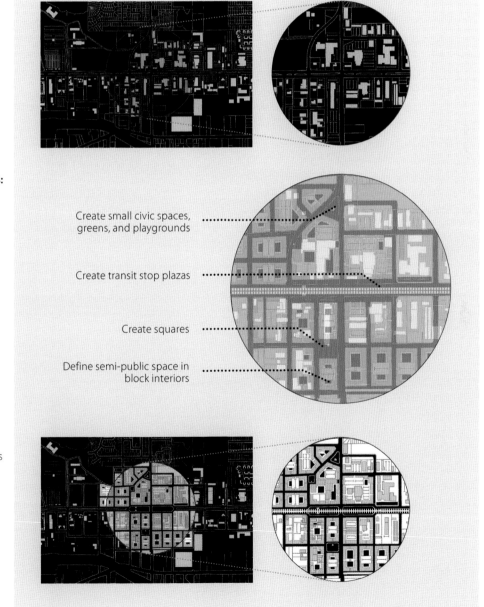

IMPLEMENTATION PROTOCOL

1. Analyze the commercial strip within its regional context according to the Sprawl Repair Assessment Tool and Void Analysis (see chapter three, "Repair at the Regional Scale"). If there is potential for successful repair, proceed to the next step.

2. Analyze the site feasibility (see chapter four, "Repair at the Community Scale, Step One: Analyze Site Feasibility").

3. Reach out to the appropriate regional entity (a council or the county) in the area. Formulate a regional strategy for the repair of the strip commercial corridor, focusing on its potential for transformation into a transit boulevard. Transit should be provided between the nodes, connecting them to other regional destinations. Public support and potential investment will be more easily obtained if the developer can demonstrate that the project has regional significance and can contribute to long-term sustainability.

4. Initiate and facilitate the adoption of a new form-based code that will legalize the transformation of the strip commercial corridor into a transit boulevard (see chapter four, "Repair at the Community Scale, Step Three: Introduce Regulatory and Management Techniques"). This can be done through a comprehensive rezoning ordinance that replaces the existing municipal code and allows repair of strip commercial corridors, or through an overlay district along the corridor.

5. Analyze the jurisdiction of the corridor, and if it is under the state DOT, work to have it relinquished to the local municipality if possible. State thoroughfare standards are more challenging to modify to create pedestrian-friendly and transit-oriented environments. Local jurisdictions are able to work directly with communities affected by sprawl.

6. Evaluate the needs of the community in relation to existing retail, office, and residential space. If the market is weak, explore the potential for reuse of the existing commercial buildings to incubate local businesses.

Identify and attract struggling businesses that cannot afford the rents in more expensive locations but that provide essential services to a community – a coffee shop, dry cleaner, hairdresser, and so forth.

7. Explore the possibility of locating a civic building at one or more of the nodes along the corridor to serve as a catalyst for place making and provide community identity. A post office, a library, a market, a religious building, or a meeting hall can serve this role. A college satellite campus, a school, or a senior living facility can also become strong anchors for the redevelopment.

8. Explore public incentives for infrastructure improvements along the corridor (see chapter four, "Repair at the Community Scale, Step Four: Secure Incentives for Implementation").

9. Select some parcels and secure contracts and/or options to purchase (with extendable contract limits) from individual owners. During due diligence, start discussions with county government and key decision makers about the feasibility of the project. If the feedback is positive, proceed to the next step.

10. Start preparations for a public process and a possible collaborative design and planning session (charrette). Engage the regional government as well as adjacent subdivisions and their associations, the local business community, chamber of commerce, school board, and not-for-profit organizations.

11. Complete a public charrette, preferably at the project site. Engage decision makers and stakeholders to explore various scenarios and phasing options. Results must be based on consensus.

12. Start the entitlement process for the project. By this time the new transit boulevard should be permitted under a new ordinance. A simultaneous process is also possible, using a specific project as a model for the rest of the nodes. As a pilot project, it should be permitted in an expedited manner.

13. Start construction.

APPLICATION: INTRODUCING A NODAL DEVELOPMENT PATTERN

The evolution of a city from a sprawling suburban environment to transit-supportive urbanism requires a transformation from the linear, vehicle-dependent pattern to a nodal, compact organization of land use.

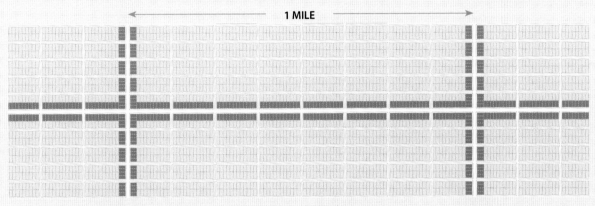

4-125. Linear commercial corridors that encourage uncontrolled strip development

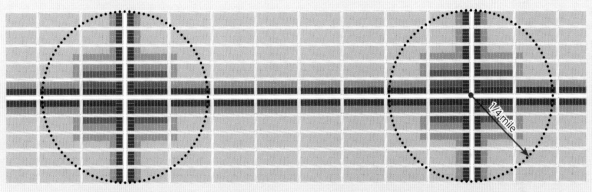

4-126. Higher density at the intersections form transit-oriented nodes at every one-mile intersection

4-127. The transition between the higher density and the single-family fabric requires a special strategy of introducing transitional building types, such as mid-rise, townhouses, and live-works

APPLICATION: PREPARING THE CORRIDOR FOR SUCCESSIONAL GROWTH

The existing commercial corridor has unpredictable development and improper parking arrangements. Growth requires parking accommodations that negatively affect adjacent residential neighborhoods, especially if denser buildings such as mid- and high-rise with parking garages are introduced. Remediation strategies include the introduction of alleys for parking access, liner buildings to mask the parking lots and garages, and transitional building types to be harmonious with the residential fabric.

4-128. Historic conditions: Commercial and residential development are adjacent

4-129. Existing conditions: Commercial development encroaches into residential fabric, with garages facing houses

4-130. Phase One: The initial stage of repair includes townhouses lining parking structures for a gradual transition

4-131. Phase Two: Townhouses on both sides of the street ease the transition to denser redevelopment

APPLICATION: REBUILDING THE COMMERCIAL STRIP

This is a case study of a typical suburban highway in need of rebuilding after a natural disaster. Three different scenarios are possible. The first is to rebuild the roadside strip developments as they had been before, with new buildings following the same pattern (figure 4-132). The second is to rebuild a more aesthetically pleasing commercial strip in a hybrid manner, following tighter design regulations, including landscape and signage. The look will improve, but the overall neighborhood structure will not (figure 4-133). The third scenario is to rebuild into a transit corridor with mixed-use buildings shielding rows of parking. Extra space is designed into squares and greenways (figure 4-134).

4-132. Rebuilding according to the previous model

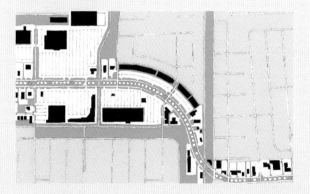

Drawing by James Wassell

4-133. Rebuilding with better aesthetics

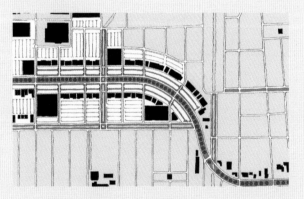

Drawing by James Wassell

4-134. Rebuilding scenario as a transit corridor

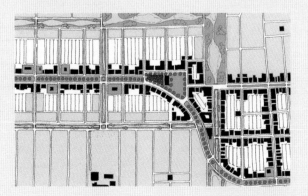

BUSINESS PARK

The business park is the predominant type of workplace in suburbia. Heavy manufacturing has declined in the past five decades and has been replaced by clean technologies and knowledge-based industries. Today the greatest workforce concentrations in suburbia can be found in corporate campuses in "edge cities."

The typical suburban business park contains clusters of freestanding buildings dedicated exclusively to office and/or warehouse use. The arrangement of buildings tends to be arbitrary, without an identifiable block structure or connectivity to the surroundings. The parking lots are underutilized and overscaled, dominating the building frontages. The business park typically includes only a single use, requiring office workers to drive to other places for lunch and errands.

When business parks have multiple tenants, repair efforts are more difficult. Repair is most feasible when a business park is located close to dense residential development or concentrations of retail and other commercial space. Rebalancing it with mixed uses and increased density can transform it into a town center that combines offices, housing, shopping, and civic activities. This is a practical possibility when large concentrations of office space are available in one place, thus attracting a portion of the workforce to live there.

According to retail expert Robert Gibbs, two hundred square feet of office space can support five square feet of restaurants and four square feet of retail.[13] This symbiosis between office and other commercial space can sustain a variety of uses within a walkable network and block structure. The parking lots can be reorganized and masked by liner buildings, with garages inserted where possible. Existing buildings, especially Class A office space, should be retained and included in the newly connected fabric of blocks and civic spaces.

The conditions for retrofitting office parks may not be good, particularly for the small pockets of offices dispersed along highways and interchanges. However, in cases where more substantial concentrations of good-quality office buildings exist close to transit hubs or corridors, or have the potential for future transit, their repair makes sense for the long run. The main incentive for such repair is the extra development potential for infill of the underutilized parking lots. Municipalities can create additional incentives such as permitting of office park repair by right, and Tax Increment Financing or Business Improvement District tax credits for workforce housing, if possible. At the state and federal level, funding may be available for public parking and transit infrastructure (see chapter four, "Repair at the Community Scale, Step Four: Secure Incentives for Implementation").

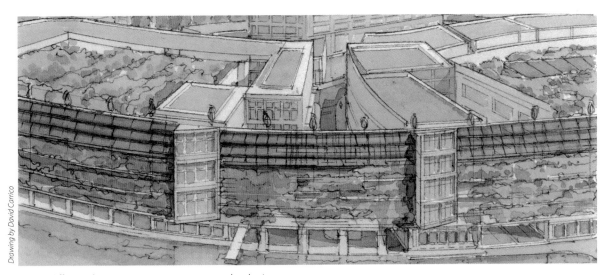

Drawing by David Carrico

4-135. Office park repair incorporating green technologies

DEFICIENCIES

The diagrams below show the deficiencies of a typical suburban office park: limited, segregated uses in free-standing buildings (figure 4-136), the lack of walkable streets and block structure (figure 4-137), the large, exposed parking lots that discourage walking (figure 4-138), and the lack of structured civic space and well-defined public realm (figure 4-139).

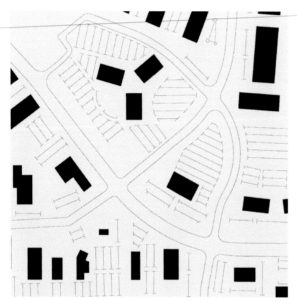

4-136. Single building type and use

4-137. Lack of walkable block structure

4-138. Dispersed and exposed parking

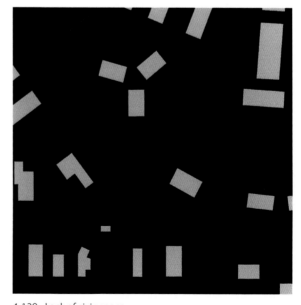

4-139. Lack of civic space

TRANSFORMATION INTO A TOWN CENTER

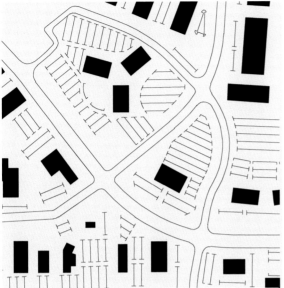

Figure 4-140 shows a typical suburban office park consisting of clusters of office buildings and some adjacent warehouse structures surrounded by parking lots. These are located on both sides of an arterial, in segregated pods, not easily accessible for pedestrians and drivers.

█ Existing buildings

4-140. Existing suburban business park

The plan for repair includes an aggressive infill and transformation into a transit-ready town center. The higher-intensity urbanism will support the light rail line proposed along the arterial. The new town center will become a regional generator of economic activity.

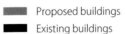

Proposed buildings
Existing buildings

4-141. Business park repaired into a town center

4-142. Dispersed building and parking layout in existing office park

4-143. Office park repaired into a transit-oriented town center

These illustrations show an ambitious intervention covering two office parks, the adjoining arterial, and the warehouses across from it (figures 4-142 and 4-143).

The existing buildings are embedded seamlessly within the newly created fabric; liner buildings are built around some and others are incorporated within a courtyard. Another strategy is to replace the dead-end drop offs of the office buildings with useful public spaces delineated by new structures.

The new fabric consists mainly of perimeter blocks with structured parking. The assumption is that this intersection will become the transit hub for the surrounding area. The square accommodates a light rail stop, as well as a generous public green that can be used for a community garden (figure 4-144).

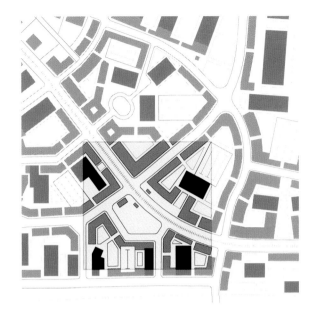

4-144. New square organized around a transit stop, incorporating mixed-use buildings and a community garden

Introduce new building types and mixed use: The predominant – often only – building type in a business park is the freestanding office building. Buildings are clustered, but they do not form defined blocks or fabric. Parking usually surrounds them on all sides. The repair of an office park starts with the re-balance of uses. Housing, shopping, and lodging are inserted to create a place that is occupied 24 hours a day. Together with the other interventions the radical infill of dense, mixed-use blocks makes transit viable.

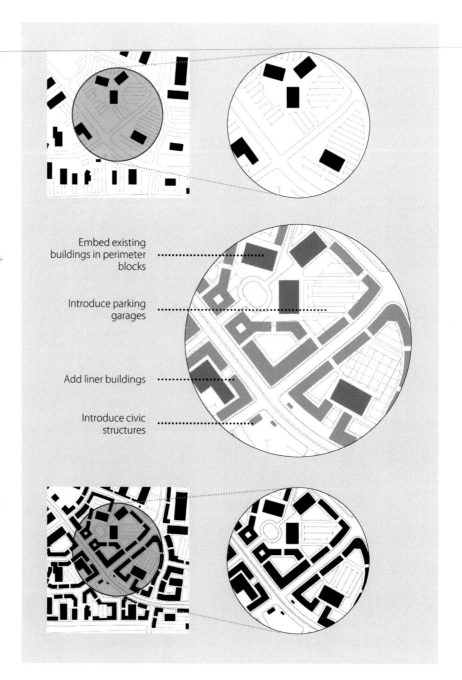

Deficiency: Single building type and use

Remedial Techniques:
Introduce new building types and mix of uses: residential, retail, lodging, and civic

Embed existing buildings in perimeter blocks

Introduce parking garages

Add liner buildings

Introduce civic structures

Outcome: Variety of building types and mix of uses to support a town center

Connect and repair thoroughfares: The business park has a sporadic thoroughfare network and lacks pedestrian-friendly block structure. The oversized blocks can easily accommodate parking garages with residential and retail buildings wrapped around their perimeters. Creating a denser network of streets will calm the traffic and encourage pedestrian circulation. Additional repair techniques include the reduction of lane widths by adding parallel parking and sidewalks, reducing curb radii for easier pedestrian crossings, and adding medians and access lanes.

Deficiency: Lack of walkable block structure

Remedial Techniques: Connect and repair thoroughfares; create urban blocks

Repair existing thoroughfares (see chapter five)

Connect existing thoroughfares

Add new streets

Outcome: Walkable network and block structure

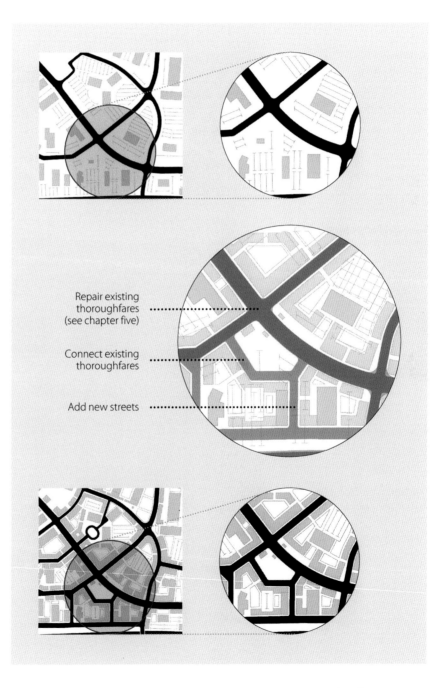

Rationalize parking: The suburban parking require-ments for office uses are extreme, in the range of three to four cars per 1,000 square feet. This requirement produces vast parking lots that are empty after business hours. The introduction of parking garages allows the replacement of the parking lots with buildings that accommodate other uses. Concurrently, a portion of the parking spaces can become shared. Offices can share parking with housing. Additional parking will be available on and off the streets. The garages can be built every other block, as one garage serves two blocks (when the average build-ing height is four stories). The total number of parking spaces is increased, but there is additional density, and these spaces support new buildings.

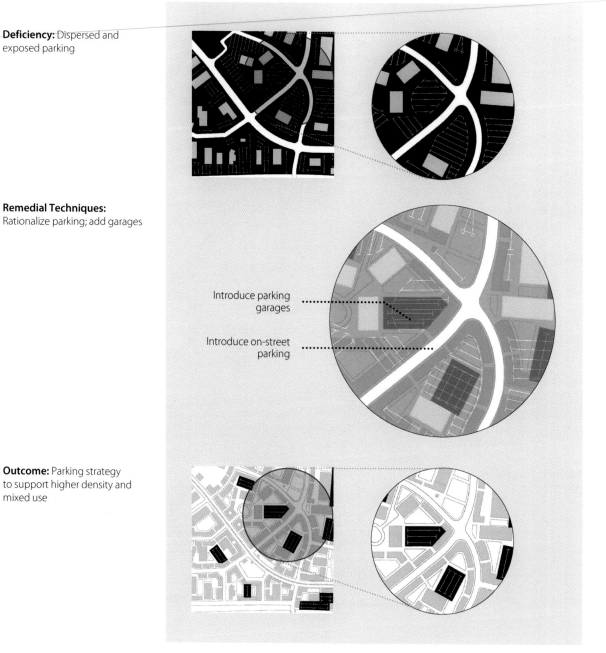

Deficiency: Dispersed and exposed parking

Remedial Techniques: Rationalize parking; add garages

Introduce parking garages

Introduce on-street parking

Outcome: Parking strategy to support higher density and mixed use

Define open and civic space: Suburban business parks, like shopping centers and housing subdivisions, are devoid of meaningful civic space. The assembly of a new block structure allows for the design and conscious, hierarchical allocation of civic spaces. A large square, which will accommodate a future transit stop, becomes a focal point. It consists of two parts – one delineated by streets, and the other attached to the fabric, forming a small plaza for outdoor cafés. It will be the landmark of the community, its gateway, as well as its gathering place. Smaller civic spaces are added, such as plazas and greens.

Deficiency: Lack of civic space

Remedial Techniques: Define open and civic space

Redefine drop-off areas as civic spaces

Create a civic square with a transit stop

Define semi-public space within blocks

Outcome: Hierarchy and spatial definition of public realm

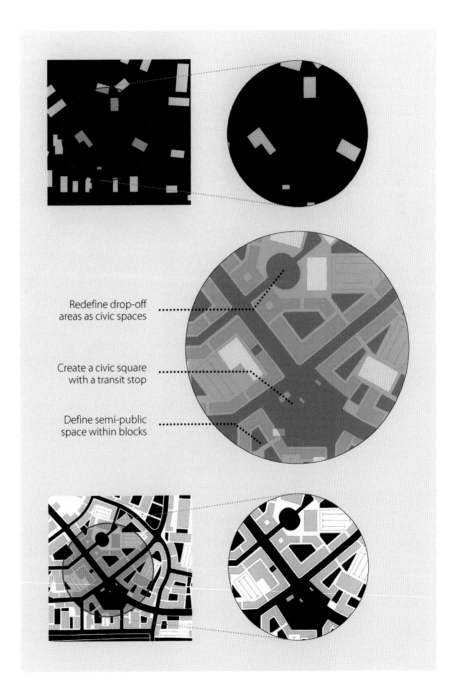

REZONING

The conventional zoning of a business park is exclusively for offices, with the occasional addition of warehouses (figure 4-145). Transect-based zoning creates the flexibility needed to transform a business park into a mixed-use environment.

The existing office use and the main square will be zoned under T6, or Urban Core zone, with parking garages added to support high-density residential infill and retail (figure 4-146). T5, Urban Center zone, will include the next tier of urban intensity that will incorporate live-work units, lofts, and townhouses.

A variety of civic spaces will be zoned CS to accommodate civic structures such as a transit stop and farmers' market. The mix of uses can also be accomplished vertically, in the new buildings, as the ground floors can be used for shops, daycare facilities, and so forth, with the upper floors used for residences and offices.

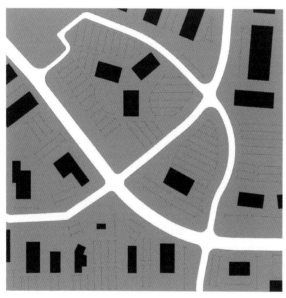

4-145. Conventional single-use zoning

 Open Space
C - Commercial
Existing buildings

4-146. Transect-based zoning

T4 - General Urban zone
T5 - Urban Center zone
T6 - Urban Core zone
CS - Civic Space
CB - Civic Building
Existing and proposed buildings

IMPLEMENTATION PROTOCOL

1. Analyze the business park within its regional context according to the Sprawl Repair Assessment Tool and Void Analysis (see chapter three, "Repair at the Regional Scale"). If there is potential for successful repair, proceed to the next step.

2. Analyze the site feasibility (see chapter four, "Repair at the Community Scale, Step One: Analyze Site Feasibility").

3. Reach out to the appropriate regional entity (a council or the county) in the area. Formulate a regional strategy for the repair of the business park, focusing on its potential for transformation into a town center. Transit should be provided between the new town center and other nodes, connecting them to other regional destinations. Public support and potential investment will be more easily obtained if the developer can demonstrate that the project has regional significance and can contribute to long-term sustainability.

4. Initiate and facilitate the adoption of a new form-based code that will legalize the transformation of the business park into a town center (see chapter four, "Repair at the Community Scale, Step Three: Introduce Regulatory and Management Techniques"). This can be done through a comprehensive rezoning ordinance that replaces the existing municipal code and allows repair of office parks, or through an overlay district of the office park and its vicinity.

5. Analyze the jurisdiction of the main thoroughfares adjacent to the business park, and if they are under the state DOT, work to have it relinquished to the local municipality if possible. State thoroughfare standards are more challenging to modify to create pedestrian-friendly and transit-oriented environments. Local jurisdictions are able to work directly with communities affected by sprawl.

6. Evaluate the needs of the community in relation to existing retail, lodging, and residential space. If the market is weak for new construction, explore the potential for reuse of the existing office buildings to convert into residential lofts and live-work units.

7. Evaluate the possibilities for preserving viable buildings, eliminating dysfunctional buildings, adding liner buildings for incubating businesses, adding live-work units, and introducing mixed-use perimeter-block buildings with parking garages.

8. Explore the possibility of locating a civic building in the transformed shopping center to serve as a catalyst for place making and provide community identity. A post office, a library, a market, a religious building, or a meeting hall can serve this role. A college satellite campus, a school, or a senior living facility can also become strong anchors for the redevelopment.

9. Explore public incentives for infrastructure improvements along adjoining thoroughfares and within the business park (see chapter four, "Repair at the Community Scale, Step Four: Secure Incentives for Implementation").

10. Select a strategy for partial or complete acquisition of the business park. Secure contracts and/or options to purchase (with extendable contract limits). During due diligence, start discussions with county government and key decision makers about the feasibility of the project. If the feedback is positive, proceed to the next step.

11. Start preparations for a public process and a possible collaborative design and planning session (charrette). Engage the regional government as well as adjacent subdivisions and their associations, the local business community, chamber of commerce, school board, and not-for-profit organizations.

12. Complete a public charrette, preferably at the project site. Engage decision makers and stakeholders to explore various scenarios and phasing options. Results must be based on consensus.

13. Start the entitlement process for the project. By this time the new town center should be permitted under a new ordinance.

14. Start construction.

APPLICATION: OFFICE PARK REPAIR INTO A TRANSIT-ORIENTED CORE USING GREEN TECHNIQUES

A master plan was prepared with two detailed alternatives for the first phase of the redevelopment (figures 4-147 and 4-148). In both schemes, the existing office buildings are seamlessly integrated into new blocks and lined by smaller structures that form pedestrian-scale civic spaces, including a covered market. Both embrace techniques of green architecture, such as roof gardens, energy-producing sound walls, solar collectors, and wind harvesters. Both support varied uses such as lofts, live-work buildings, affordable retail, moderately

Image by Steve Price

4-147. Existing buildings in the office park

Image by Steve Price

4-148. Green buildings and green urbanism in the new town center

4-149. Option One: The first phase with orthogonal fabric

■■■ Existing buildings ☐ Proposed buildings

4-150. Option Two: The first phase with organic fabric

▥▥ Future transit way (light rail line)

priced dwellings, and senior housing. But they differ in their approach to urban pattern, exploring block structure, spatial definition, and climatic response in different ways. The first has an orthogonal grid of more angularly defined buildings, streets, and squares, while the second emphasizes the environmental benefits of urban design. It employs the historically tested techniques of a fluid, medieval fabric and organic geometry to facilitate air circulation and natural ventilation, while also incorporating the modern technologies.

Drawing by David Carrico

4-151. Energy-producing sound wall viewed from the highway

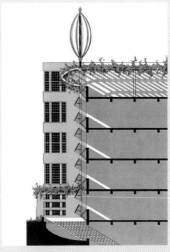

4-152. Section of wall through garage

Image by Steve Price

4-153. Existing office buildings and parking lots

Image by Steve Price

4-154. Office buildings converted into lofts

Image by Steve Price

4-155. Parking lot converted into a pedestrian-friendly street with buildings on both sides, parallel parking, and wide sidewalks

APPLICATION: INFILL REPAIR STRATEGY FOR CORPORATE CAMPUSES

Urban infill can be used as a repair technique for master-planned corporate office campuses. In this case study, an empty site adjacent to a sprawling campus is developed as a transit-ready, mixed-use town center with thousands of residences, a hotel, a movie theater, a manmade lake, and numerous shops, restaurants, and cafés. Comparing the existing megablocks of the office campus with the compact fabric of the infill shows the radical shift from a car-oriented environment to a walkable and complete community that becomes an amenity and a walkable destination for the surrounding developments.

1. Retail
2. Office
3. Hotel
4. Residential

4-156. Infill repair of a corporate campus

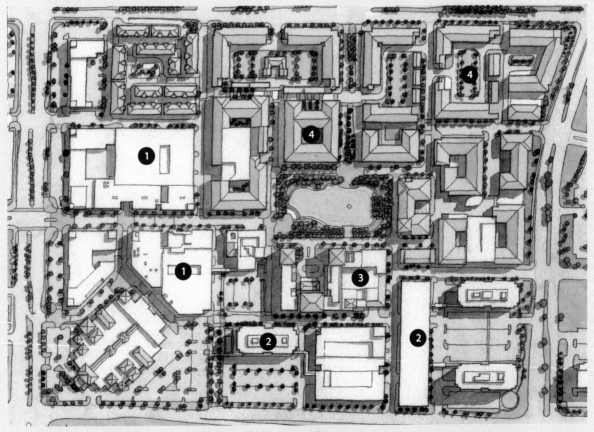

4-157. New mixed-use fabric with shops, apartments, townhouses, and civic uses

EDGE CITY

The edge city is an American phenomenon of high-intensity, auto-dependent development outside of the traditional urban core. Conceived as new downtowns for polycentric metropolises, edge cities never fulfilled their great expectations.

Most started as agglomerations of high-intensity office use, mainly Class A office towers, and later were joined by additional commercial establishments, high-density residences, and hotels. Edge cities contain the individual components of traditional urban cores, including high concentrations of retail, offices, hospitality, entertainment, and in some cases, residential uses, but all are located in separate enclaves, keeping the edge cities from becoming functional equals to real downtowns. Offices, condominium towers, hotels, and malls are surrounded by vast parking lots, reachable by overscaled collectors and arterials, and a web of interchanges. Insufficient block structure, pedestrian convenience, and civic space are typical deficiencies found in other sprawl elements, but in edge cities they achieve the most intense manifestation.

Based on the vast financial, real estate, and infrastructure investments already poured into them, and the fact that they are employment hubs for hundreds of thousands of people, edge cities should be repaired into more balanced places. On the other hand, their underlying framework is so dramatically suburban and car-dominated that their retrofit may require prohibitive amounts of resources and coordination. These retrofits will likely depend on public-private initiatives and political leadership to implement such ambitious plans.

In most cases additional infill, in the form of smaller-scale building types such as townhouses, mixed-use perimeter block buildings, and live-work units, will be necessary. Structured parking should be introduced to utilize the vast fields of asphalt, to support the added density, and create a walkable network and block structure. The street network should include the full variety of complete, context-sensitive roads and streets, and possibly a main street and a hierarchy of civic spaces.

The incentives for the repair of an edge city must be very strong, as the financial commitments to redevelop it into a true, mixed-use urban core are very high. The rationalizing of overscaled infrastructure and underutilized space will open acres of additional real estate for new development and infill, which can attract the attention of developers and investors while creating leverage for municipal governments. The formation of public-private partnerships, in combina-

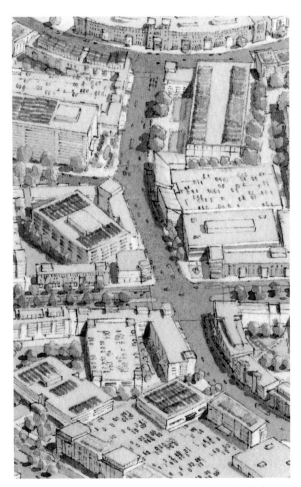

4-158. Freestanding buildings incorporated into high-density urban fabric

tion with incentives crafted to benefit and expedite these specific retrofits, will be crucial for repair on a regional scale. The benefits for the surrounding suburban communities will be substantial, as the newly enhanced urban cores will provide them with a wide range of amenities such as increased housing options, community gathering places, and the basis for public transportation. Transit will become viable between (and around) the regional urban cores, which for many people will shorten or even eliminate their commutes, reduce air pollution, and improve the overall environ-

mental and sustainability performance of the region.

Similar to the mall redevelopments, the incentives and implementation techniques for retrofitting edge cities may include permitting by right (requiring state enabling legislation), exemption from state and federal assessments, state and federal funding for parking structures and transit, Transfer of Development Rights and Purchase of Development Rights mechanisms, Tax Increment Financing, Business Improvement Districts, and others (see chapter four, "Repair at the Community Scale, Step Four: Secure Incentives for Implementation").

DEFICIENCIES

The deficiencies of the edge city are similar to those of other commercial sprawl elements, but they are amplified by the extensive infrastructure and the millions of square feet of development in segregated agglomerations (figure 4-159). The formation of walkable block structure and the shaping of public space are especially challenging, as the spatial connections require tremendous redevelopment and investment. Yet the challenges also present opportunities to reuse some of the existing infrastructure and fill the parking lots with mixed-use fabric incorporating the existing megastructures and a range of public spaces.

4-159. Agglomerations of high-intensity segregated uses

4-160. Lack of walkable block structure

4-161. Dispersed and exposed parking

4-162. Lack of civic space

TRANSFORMATION INTO A REGIONAL URBAN CORE

Figures 4-163 and 4-164 show the existing conditions and the retrofit of an edge city. Only a portion of the development is shown, but the techniques and the repair should apply to the entire edge city. Most of the existing buildings are preserved and embedded in a fabric of perimeter blocks that hide interior surface parking and garages.

■ Existing buildings

4-163. Existing edge city

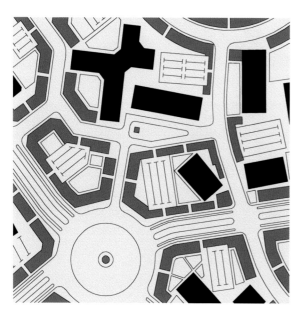

The most substantial intervention is the elimination of the highway interchange, which currently disconnects the elements of this suburban enclave. The interchange is replaced by a parkway roundabout, which, along with the new street network, pulls together all parts of this sector and opens up a substantial amount of land for new development. The roundabout becomes a landmark civic space, which can be used for a monument and/or energy-producing technologies such as windmills.

▨ Proposed buildings
■ Existing buildings

4-164. Repaired regional urban core

4-165. View dominated by highway interchange and parking lots

4-166. Edge city repaired into a regional urban core

Figures 4-165 and 4-166 illustrate the radical transformation of the edge city into a portion of a complete community. A monumental roundabout replaces the interchange and becomes a gateway and focus of the new urban core. Mixed-use buildings and wide sidewalks shape the edges of the roundabout, creating a safe and interesting experience for pedestrians.

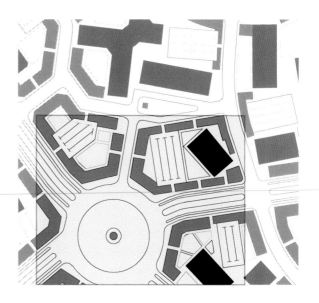

High-capacity avenues merge into the roundabout, but multiple medians and crosswalks create safe and pleasant conditions for walkers and bicyclists (figure 4-167). An important strategy for this type of repair is the formation of public space that respects the current entrances of existing buildings. The challenge comes in determining how to engage the usually arbitrary disposition of buildings into a system of blocks and public space.

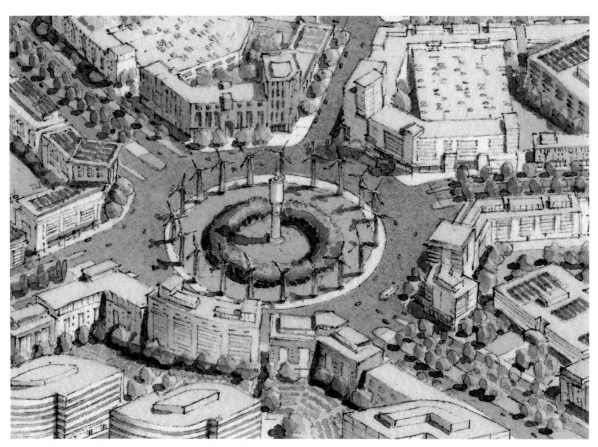

4-167. Urban roundabout as a gateway and a landmark

Introduce new building types and mixed uses: A finer fabric of smaller buildings is introduced to delineate public spaces and a street network. The perimeter block building is appropriate for filling in the expansive parking lots common to edge cities, as it can easily accommodate the irregular geometries. Liner buildings can be used to mask undesirable blank walls and parking lots. The existing buildings are seamlessly inserted within a new urban fabric that organizes the disconnected pods into a walkable and better-connected environment.

Deficiency: Agglomerations of high-intensity segregated uses

Remedial Techniques:
Introduce new building types and mix of uses: residential, retail, office, lodging, and civic

Keep most existing buildings

Add civic structures

Mitigate geometries with liner buildings and perimeter mixed-use blocks

Outcome: Variety of building types and mix of uses to support a regional urban core

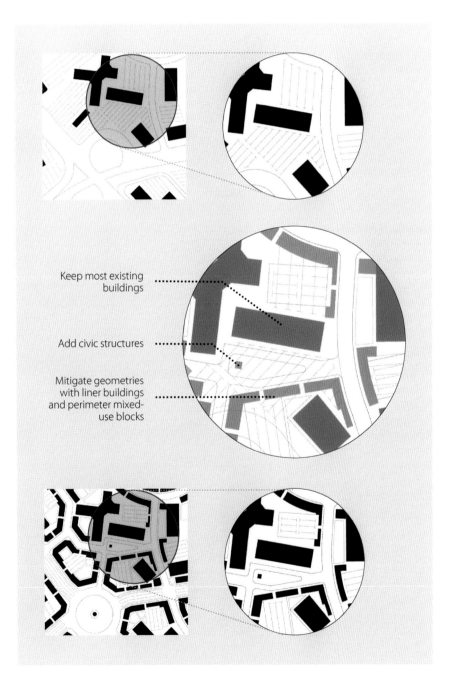

Connect and repair thoroughfares: Land use in edge cities is wasteful and unstructured. By rationalizing parking and connecting thoroughfares, a new block structure can be established. The re-configuration of the interchange into an urban roundabout in the tradition of Place De L'Etoile in Paris or Dupont Circle in Washington, DC, creates additional real estate as an incentive for such a radical intervention. The roundabout handles the vehicular flow and also creates a memorable urban space at the pedestrian level, where buildings located close to the street help calm traffic. The building facades define the public space of the roundabout, which has a presence as a landmark and a gateway, even when shared by cars along its periphery.

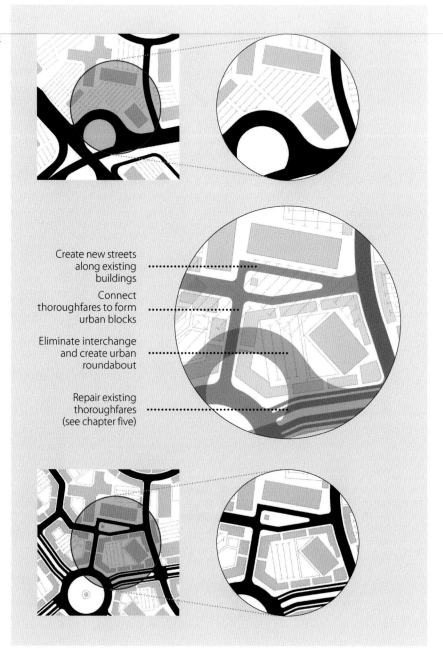

Deficiency: Lack of walkable block structure

Remedial Techniques: Connect thoroughfares; create urban blocks

Create new streets along existing buildings

Connect thoroughfares to form urban blocks

Eliminate interchange and create urban roundabout

Repair existing thoroughfares (see chapter five)

Outcome: Walkable network and block structure

Rationalize parking: The edge city has an overwhelming amount of parking. With parking on all sides, fronts and backs of buildings are indistinguishable, which further discourages walking. The diagrams show how parking garages are embedded within the newly delineated perimeter blocks and unnecessary parking lots are redeveloped. The garages accommodate the parking requirements of the existing buildings and provide sufficient capacity for new development, both residential and commercial.

Deficiency: Dispersed and exposed parking

Remedial Techniques: Rationalize parking; add garages

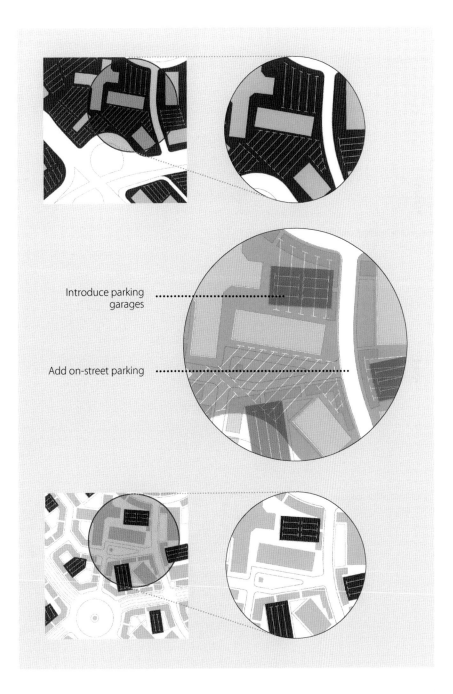

Introduce parking garages

Add on-street parking

Outcome: Parking strategy to support higher density and mixed use

Define open and civic space: The public realm of the edge city is dominated by parking lots, with every destination reached only by car. The technique demonstrated here is the reorganization of the superblocks into a walkable network that yields a hierarchy of private, semi-public, and public spaces. The interiors of the perimeter blocks are private and semi-public courtyards.

The public realm is formed and enhanced by the streets and the squares dispersed throughout the fabric. The goal is to create continuity between destinations, which is challenging, as the distances are not of pedestrian scale. Nevertheless, without a radical advance toward restoring walkability and incorporating well-defined civic space, the retrofit cannot be successful.

Deficiency: Lack of civic space

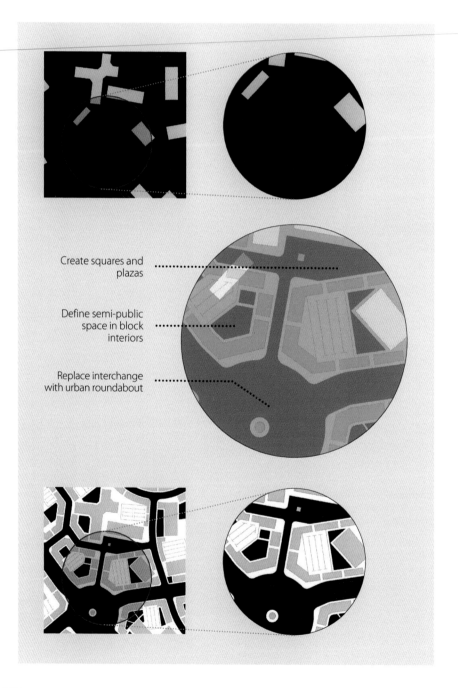

Remedial Techniques: Define open and civic space

Create squares and plazas

Define semi-public space in block interiors

Replace interchange with urban roundabout

Outcome: Hierarchy and spatial definition of public realm

APPLICATION: REPAIRING AN EDGE CITY BY URBANIZATION AROUND A FUNCTIONING MALL

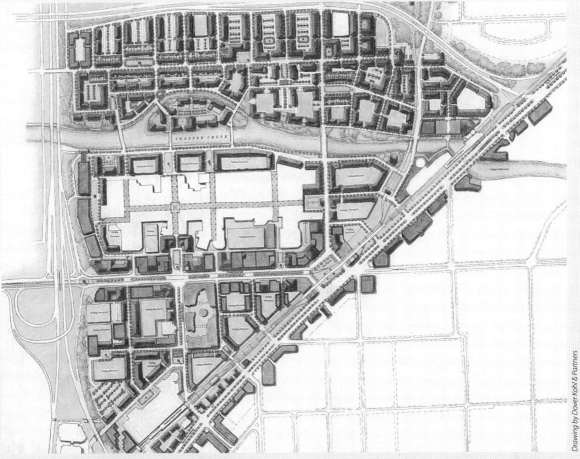

Drawing by Dover Kohl & Partners

4-168. Located between three major thoroughfares, this edge city includes a still viable mall and a regional transit hub; the repair incorporates walkable, mixed-use fabric and public spaces coordinated by a new code

Dillon-Reynolds Aerial Photography, Inc.

4-169. Edge city surrounded by suburban fabric

Drawing by Dover Kohl & Partners/James Dougherty

4-170. Transformation into a transit-oriented, regional urban core

SUBURBAN CAMPUS

The American university campus has not been spared from suburbanization. Though it is an assembly of academic, institutional, or civic buildings, the suburban campus exhibits the same spatial, social, and environmental deficiencies as the rest of sprawl.

Historically, campuses were part of the urban fabric, embedded within towns and cities or clustered as independent, self-sustaining entities. They were either anchors within the city cores or destinations of strong civic presence along the edges. Formally or informally composed, academic campuses consistently exhibited synergy with their context.

The designs conceived by Thomas Jefferson for the University of Virginia and later by Frederick Law Olmsted for Stanford University became exemplars of order and balance in campus building. Detached buildings were united in larger compositions – by colonnades, balustrades, and landscaping – forming main axes or malls and cross axes. The campus could grow organically by multiplying the sequences of quadrangles and courts, but always supporting "interrelation, balance, and symmetry" between buildings.[14]

The competence of university campus design, which was considered one of the most important American contributions to the history of urbanism, was stifled with the ascent of suburbia. Campuses became dependent on the car as sprawl became the main pattern of growth. Campuses morphed into segregated enclaves, with their fabric distorted by the fashion of "landmark" buildings and overscaled parking lots to accommodate commuting students and faculty.

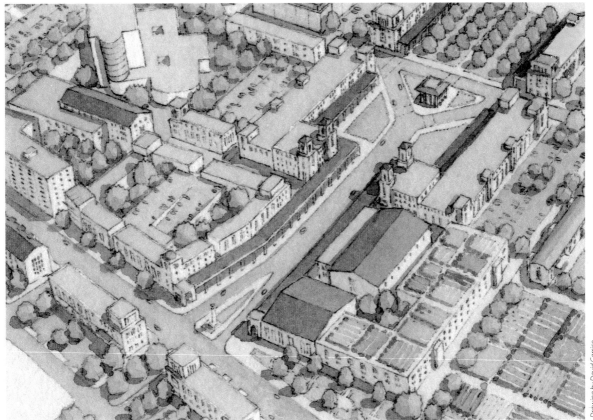

Drawing by David Carrico

4-171. Transformation of a suburban campus into balanced, walkable urbanism

A low-grade physical environment typifies academic campus design of the 1960s and '70s. The campus is disconnected from its surrounding community, and its layout is arbitrary, consisting of freestanding structures lacking the discipline of the traditional axial relationships. The landscape may be lush, but vast areas of the campus are dominated by surface parking lots. Although many have pedestrian-only environments within their boundaries, they have lost the clarity of composition, the hierarchy of public space, and the compactness typical of the classical American campus.

The main goal for the retrofit of a typical suburban academic campus is to establish an ordering system of first-rate spaces. This new structure seeks principal axes that visually and physically connect important buildings on the campus, as well as relate the campus to its surroundings. Gaps are filled with new buildings, combining with existing ones to form courtyards; liner buildings are introduced to define pedestrian-friendly frontages; structured parking is embedded within blocks; and lots are hidden behind buildings or relegated to the edges.

DEFICIENCIES

These diagrams illustrate the most evident deficiencies of the suburban campus. Freestanding buildings follow no hierarchy or pattern (figure 4-172). The pedestrian experience is downgraded by megablocks, large gaps between buildings, and excessive, exposed parking lots (figures 4-173 and 4-174). There are no strong axial relationships to organize the expanse of open space (figure 4-175).

4-172. Freestanding building layout

4-173. Lack of walkable block structure

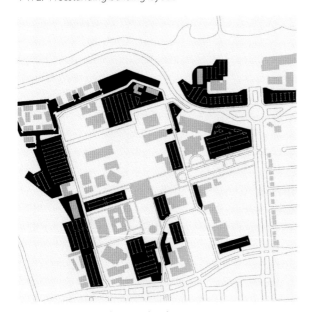

4-174. Dispersed and exposed parking

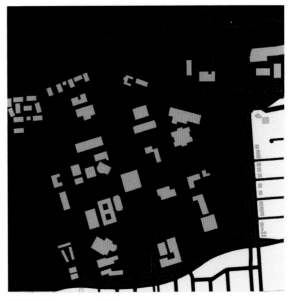

4-175. Unstructured civic space

TRANSFORMATION INTO A TRADITIONAL URBAN CAMPUS

These drawings show the transformation of a typical suburban university campus into a well-structured, walkable urban fabric. The campus is adjacent to existing development and faces a waterfront to the north. The campus character is defined by buildings dispersed among leftover open space and parking lots (figure 4-176).

■ Existing buildings

4-176. Existing suburban campus

Drawing in collaboration with Dhiru Thadani

The repair is based on the recovery and strengthening of the main axial relationships, traces of which are observed in north-south and east-west directions. By introducing new buildings, structured parking, landscaping, and colonnades, the proposed repair achieves spatial organization and a walkable environment along newly connected streets and pathways. Most buildings front on streets designated as primary, with parking on secondary streets. The main academic buildings are linked together by arcades that become important organizational elements and gathering places for the campus (figure 4-177).

■ Proposed buildings
■ Existing buildings

4-177. Repaired suburban campus

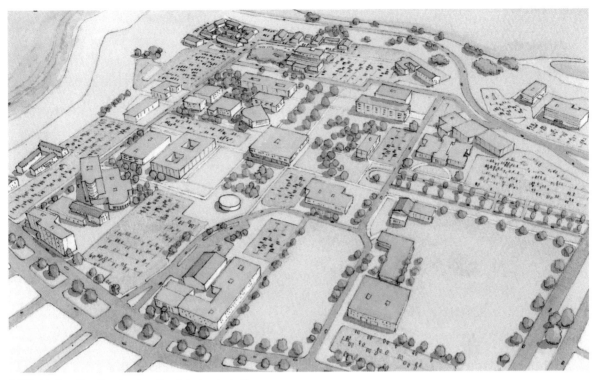

4-178. Underutilized land and parking lots dominate the campus

4-179. New organization of campus with enhanced principal axes

The illustrations in figures 4-178, 4-179, and 4-180 further demonstrate the process of repairing a suburban college campus. The existing conditions show the lack of spatial organization and axial relationships on the campus.

The proposed repair reconstructs the fabric in the tradition of the classical American university campus. The main axes are recovered and strengthened by adding new buildings along their edges and at their ends. The residual open space has been restructured along the axes and/or utilized for campus gardens. Along the eastern boundaries of the campus, where it interfaces with an existing residential development, U-shaped and L-shaped student residences are proposed, with courtyards facing the single-family housing without overwhelming it.

4-180. Some buildings are renovated and new buildings, arcades, and landscape are added to complete the campus

Introduce new buildings: The locations of the buildings in the suburban university campus are arbitrary and dispersed. The buildings are objects in green space or parking lots rather than elements of a community. New buildings are needed to delineate clear public spaces and pedestrian networks, and to provide space for academics, administration, or student housing. Liner buildings mask unsightly facades and parking lots. The continuous frontage of arcades becomes a unifying element across the campus and provides shelter from sun and rain. The remediation can also include renovations and additions to existing buildings.

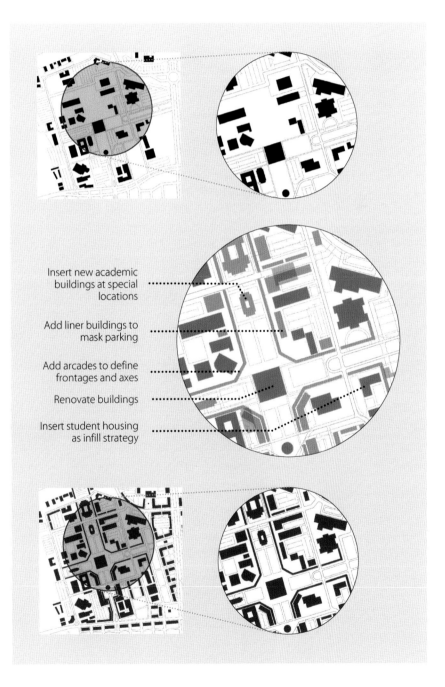

Deficiency: Freestanding building layout

Remedial Techniques: Introduce new buildings, liners, and arcades

Insert new academic buildings at special locations

Add liner buildings to mask parking

Add arcades to define frontages and axes

Renovate buildings

Insert student housing as infill strategy

Outcome: Traditional urban campus

Connect thoroughfares: The block structure of the university campus is oversized, unwalkable, and wastes developable space. These large blocks can easily be overlaid with a finer-grain pedestrian network to achieve better connectivity and pedestrian quality.

Dividing the megablocks into smaller ones also provides additional spaces for new buildings. The intervention rebalances the fabric. Multiple new choices for all forms of transportation are created in both north-south and east-west directions.

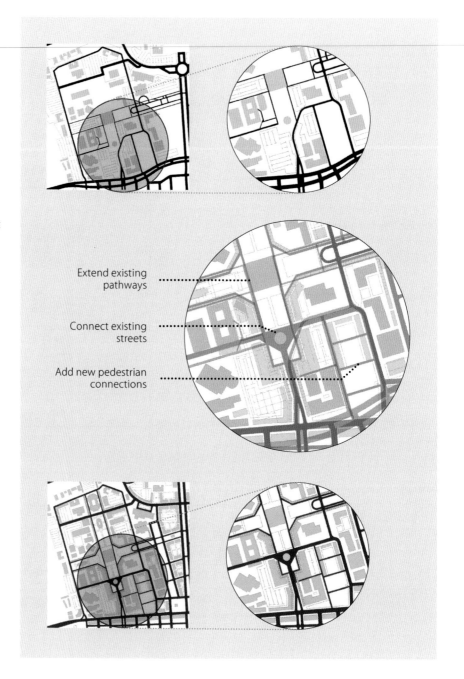

Deficiency: Lack of walkable block structure

Remedial Techniques: Connect thoroughfares; create blocks

Extend existing pathways

Connect existing streets

Add new pedestrian connections

Outcome: Connected network and walkable block structure

Rationalize parking: Suburban academic campuses have excessive parking. These large, under-utilized patches can be efficiently reorganized along the edges of the campus or concentrated in a few strategically located parking garages. New parking structures are embedded in perimeter blocks while existing lots are restriped and lined with masking structures. The main axes of movement and organization on campus will be designed as primary routes of excellent pedestrian quality, while the ones accommodating service and parking will be secondary. Analyzing existing building fronts to designate primary and secondary roads will help determine locations for parking.

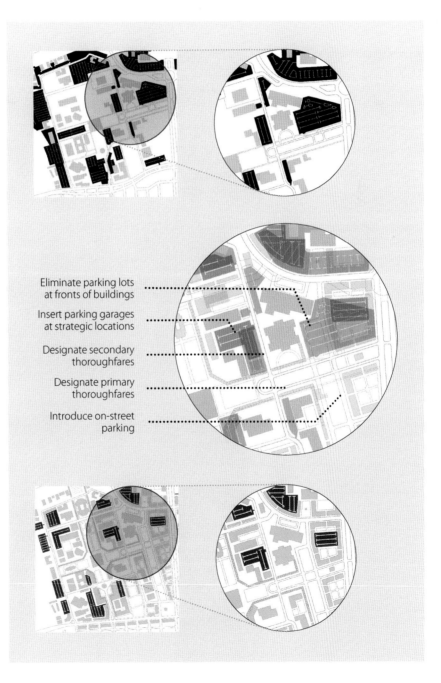

Deficiency: Dispersed and exposed parking

Remedial Techniques: Rationalize parking; add garages

Eliminate parking lots at fronts of buildings

Insert parking garages at strategic locations

Designate secondary thoroughfares

Designate primary thoroughfares

Introduce on-street parking

Outcome: Parking strategy to support campus growth and pedestrian-friendly environment

Define axial relationships: The deficiency of unstructured civic space stems from the combination of random building placement, the lack of a walkable block structure, and dispersed and exposed parking. The academic buildings are indiscriminately dispersed, with parking along their fronts. As shown here, axial relationships are recovered and defined, and the main axes are designated as primary frontages. This creates a hierarchy for the entire campus including buildings, street network, and parking strategy. New academic buildings strengthen the civic axes, serving as terminated vistas and landmarks.

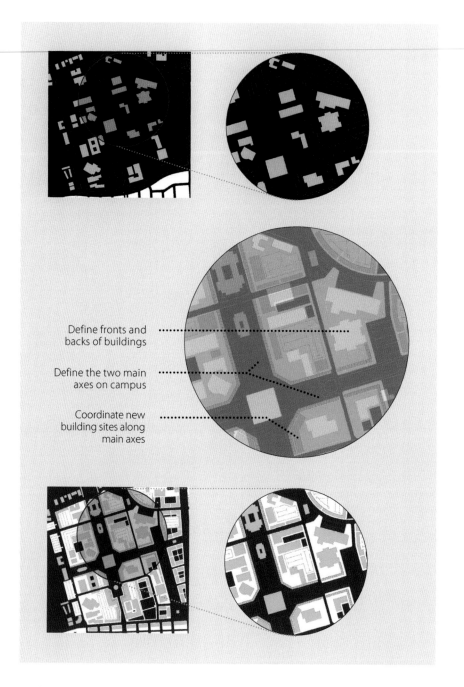

Deficiency: Unstructured civic space

Remedial Techniques: Define axial relationships

Define fronts and backs of buildings

Define the two main axes on campus

Coordinate new building sites along main axes

Outcome: Hierarchy of civic spaces

Integrate local food production: There is a lot of wasted space on academic campuses. As urban agriculture becomes widespread along the full spectrum of rural-to-urban environments, academic campuses can become laboratories for local food production at different scales. Many of the newly created public spaces – along the cross axes, on rooftops, and in the large medians, for example – can be used for student community gardens. The University of Virginia in Charlottesville and Texas A&M University in College Station are among the institutions that have already begun experimenting with community gardens on their campuses.

Deficiency: Lack of local food production

Remedial Techniques: Convert existing open spaces into organic gardens

Create new, dedicated spaces for urban agriculture throughout campus

Utilize existing open space for community gardens

Add rooftop gardens

Outcome: Create educational opportunities with food production

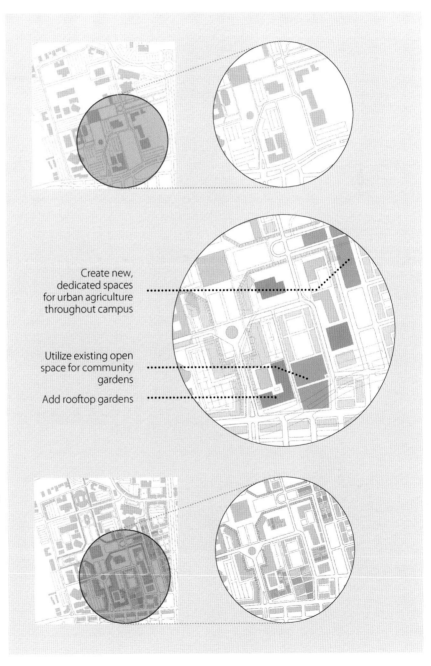

APPLICATION: REPAIRING STRATEGIES FOR MEDICAL CAMPUSES IN DIFFERENT SUBURBAN CONTEXTS

4-181. Medical campus in overdeveloped suburban context

4-182. New main street organizes the urban fabric of mixed-use, perimeter blocks

Medical campuses, as built in the last half century, have become very similar to academic campuses in their disconnectedness from communities and urban life. Hospitals and medical facilities once anchored whole urban districts and neighborhoods, but they have become overscaled mega campuses with vast fields of parking to accommodate the cars that are required to reach them. These parking lots are ideal resources for the transformation of a medical campus into an urban core.

The main difference between academic and medical campuses is that after repair the former remain focused on academic activities, while medical campuses can be embedded in a mixed-use fabric, becoming urban cores for their regions. The two main strategies for transforming medical campuses are urban infill and the diversification of uses. The medical office buildings and hospital facilities, which together represent a substantial employment

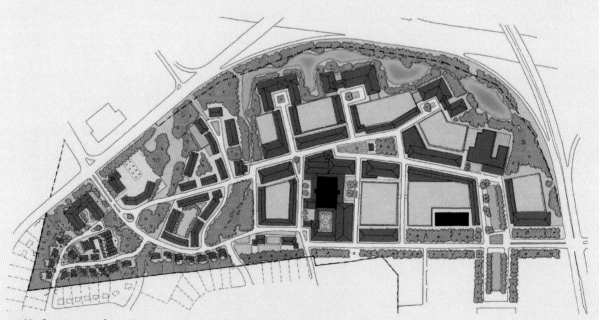

4-183. Campus transformed into a regional urban core with mixed-use buildings

■ Existing buildings   ■ Proposed buildings   ▢ Proposed parking garages

hub, can be incorporated into a dynamic and diverse fabric. This strategy combines the dedication to healing and wellness with the benefits of a healthy, walkable community. Adding residential, retail, hotel, and civic uses to a medical campus creates opportunities for hundreds or thousands of workers to also live, shop, and play there.

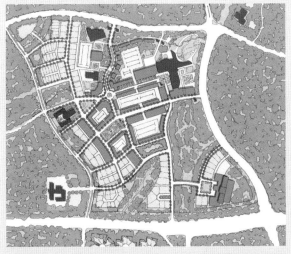

4-184. First phase of the campus incorporating existing buildings

■ Existing buildings   ■ Proposed buildings

The transformation of a medical campus into an urban core can be applied in different contexts: when the campus is located in an extensively developed suburban area, and when it is on a relatively undeveloped site that has potential for growth. In the first case, repair includes creating as many connections as possible and intensifying the campus to become the urban core of the surrounding region. A main street is introduced to link and organize the multiple medical destinations and accommodate a variety of shops, lofts, offices, and hotels (figures 4-182 and 4-183).

In the second case, repair addresses the immediate expansion plans of a medical center in an area where growth is expected to happen, while also developing a long-range vision for a new, mixed-use town center (figures 4-184 and 4-185). Demographic projections, possible transit connectivity, and the natural context of the region determine the potential intensity of development around the campus. Healthcare organizations willing to take visionary steps can broaden the scope of hospital expansions to include the creation of complete town centers with a balance of institutional, residential, commercial, and civic functions.

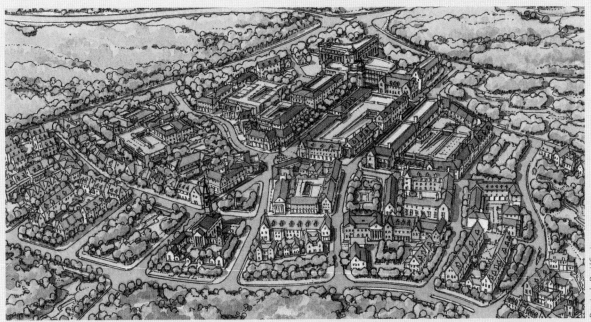

Drawing by David Carrico

4-185. Aerial view of completed first phase amidst land zoned for urban core uses

SPRAWL-TYPE OPEN SPACE

This series of examples explores the possibilities of re-conceptualizing and restructuring under-utilized open space in suburbia. Similar to the other land types in sprawl development, open space, both public and private, has frequently been handled with a generous but wasteful approach.

Underperforming golf courses are among the best sources of land for infill and urban intensification. After environmental mitigation, golf courses can also be used for organic farming and local food production.

Other leftover suburban space can be reshaped as parks, squares, playgrounds, and rain gardens for water retention. Other techniques to consider are the creation of bio-swales and the transformation of lawn strips, parkway edges, and wide suburban medians into edible landscapes, or at least planting less-damaging ground cover.

The sports field is another element that in suburbia is usually segregated and reachable only by car. It can be successfully embedded in urban fabric and used as a neighborhood anchor or destination, especially if paired with buildings of civic importance, as well as shops, restaurants, and cafés.

UNDERPERFORMING GOLF COURSE

Rising land prices, environmental concerns, and economic insolvency cause scores of golf courses to close every year. According to the National Golf Foundation, golf course closings in the U.S. outnumbered openings from 2006 to 2008, with one hundred and six golf courses folding in 2008 alone.[15] The vast swaths of land they leave behind can be attractive targets for mixed-use infill or community open space.

The case study analyzed in the following pages shows how a defunct golf course can be transformed into a neighborhood center that will include a mix of residential and commercial uses and a strong civic component. A school, a library, a swimming pool, and various public spaces such as parks and greens punctuate the development's fabric. The golf course shown is typical of many others in that it is bounded by suburban residential subdivisions, giving it great poten-

tial to become a walkable, mixed-use center for the surrounding area. Though in its heyday it might have looked as good as shown in figure 4-191, after several idle years its maintenance will become a burden, the land will go fallow, and the large, unsupervised space may become susceptible to crime.

Golf courses frequently have elevated levels of arsenic or other pollutants in the soil due to pesticide use. This can lead to groundwater contamination, but infill with clean soil can mitigate this damage and reduce the risk of further contamination. If the soil composition and water table allow, the fill can be obtained locally by digging new lakes or canals that will not only capture the stormwater runoff, but also offer amenities for the entire community and compensate adjacent residents for the loss of their golf course views.

DEFICIENCIES

The deficiencies of the defunct golf course are illustrated in figures 4-186, 4-187, and 4-188. Underutilized suburban spaces are often surrounded by single building types with single uses, usually residential, making good use of the space difficult. Large open grounds like these interrupt the urban fabric, making connectivity and block structure challenging. Golf courses are also typically private, with no public access along their edges.

4-186. Underutilized golf course

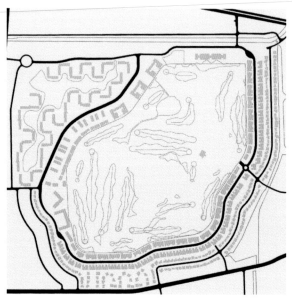

4-187. Lack of block structure

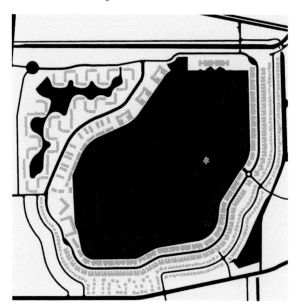

4-188. Unstructured open space

TRANSFORMATION INTO A NEIGHBORHOOD CENTER

This defunct suburban golf course occupies approximately one quarter of a square mile, which is an ideal size for a new neighborhood to serve as an anchor for the surrounding area (figure 4-189).

■ Existing buildings

4-189. Existing golf course

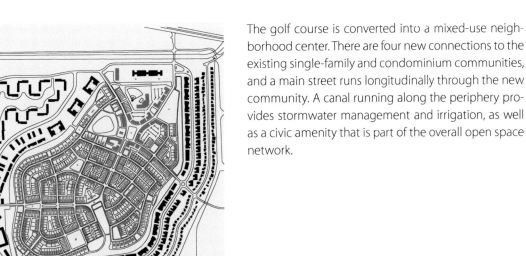

The golf course is converted into a mixed-use neighborhood center. There are four new connections to the existing single-family and condominium communities, and a main street runs longitudinally through the new community. A canal running along the periphery provides stormwater management and irrigation, as well as a civic amenity that is part of the overall open space network.

▬ Proposed buildings
■ Existing buildings

4-190. Golf course repurposed into a neighborhood center

4-191. Non-functioning golf course surrounded by suburban residential development

4-192. The new neighborhood center offers a variety of public spaces, community amenities, and housing choices

The new village, which resembles an island with the canal around it, has a compact and dense structure to accommodate all the functions that are missing from the surrounding single-use suburban development (figure 4-192). The blocks are much smaller than the adjacent ones, and they hold smaller lots, which create additional choices for younger residents or seniors who want to scale down. Various public spaces are framed by apartments, townhouses, and live-work units.

4-193. The view of the canal around the neighborhood center is shared by new and existing residents

Urbanize the golf course: The condition along the edges of a suburban golf course includes a limited variety of building types precluding the active use of the space by the larger community. This condition is exacerbated by the practice of putting backs of buildings along the golf course in contrast to the traditional golf courses, which had parkways along the edges. The remediation of this condition, in combination with the dysfunctional golf course, requires urbanization of the site by establishing a compact block structure filled with a variety of building types and spaces to accommodate public amenities.

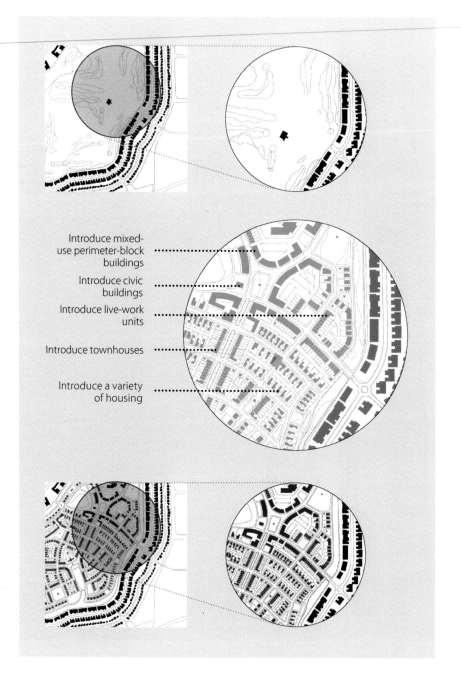

Deficiency: Underutilized golf course

Remedial Techniques: Urbanize golf course

Introduce mixed-use perimeter-block buildings

Introduce civic buildings

Introduce live-work units

Introduce townhouses

Introduce a variety of housing

Outcome: Variety of building types and mix of uses to support a village center

Connect existing thoroughfares and add new ones:
The vast expanse of the golf course disconnects the two sides of the surrounding community. Introducing a network of connected streets and urban-size blocks on the site creates the possibility of cross movement for pedestrians and cars. This movement will support the mixed uses that are clustered along the new main street and around the square in the upper portion of the site. A retail loop is formed between the two entrances from the north to provide access to the mixed use by passing traffic and will activate the square. A variety of streets and a secondary network of pedestrian passages, pathways, alleys, and lanes further enrich the connectivity of the neighborhood center.

Deficiency: Lack of walkable block structure

Remedial Techniques:
Connect existing thoroughfares and add new ones

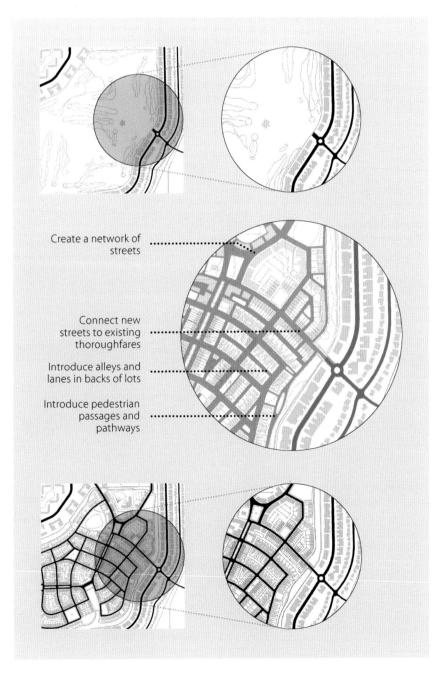

Create a network of streets

Connect new streets to existing thoroughfares

Introduce alleys and lanes in backs of lots

Introduce pedestrian passages and pathways

Outcome: Walkable network and block structure

Define open and civic spaces: The underutilized open space of the golf course is transformed into a pattern of useful public and private spaces. The empty site is overlaid with a layer of public spaces that are designed simultaneously with the urban fabric. A park around an existing body of water is the largest open space, followed by a school and its playgrounds. A main square is complemented by a series of smaller civic spaces such as attached greens, plazas, and playgrounds. A short (two-and-a-half-minute) pedestrian shed determines their location. The canal, incorporating a continuous jogging and bicycling path around the village center, is also an important component of the civic space network.

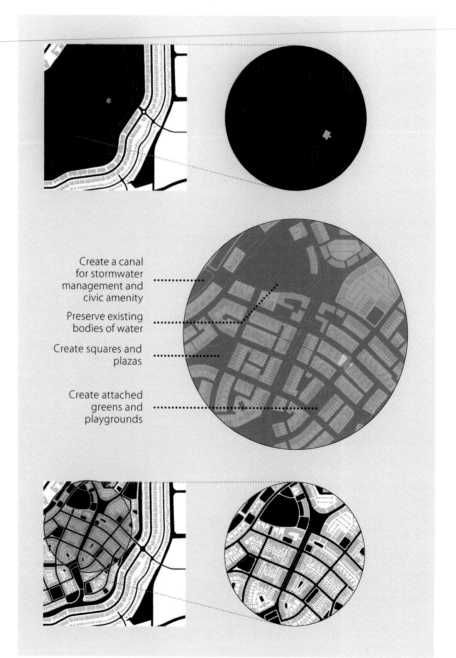

Deficiency: Unstructured open space

Remedial Techniques:
Define open and civic spaces

Create a canal for stormwater management and civic amenity

Preserve existing bodies of water

Create squares and plazas

Create attached greens and playgrounds

Outcome: Hierarchy and spatial definition of public realm

APPLICATION: TRANSFORMING SUBURBAN PLAYFIELDS INTO TOWN CENTERS

Playfields and sports facilities exemplify the wasteful use of space in sprawl developments. They are similar to schools, which used to anchor neighborhoods, but later were consolidated, grew in size, and migrated to the edges, where they could occupy vast parcels of land. The neighborhood ball field became an aggregation of multiple fields, a mega facility located outside of communities, accessible only by car, and therefore requiring massive parking lots.

One strategy to repair such large, regional facilities is to transform them into neighborhood or town centers, anchored by the open space. As shown in figure 4-195, existing playfields can be reorganized and clustered to better utilize the available land. The fields are embedded in the urban fabric, forming a town center and connecting to the existing suburban context. The town center includes a series of civic buildings, including a town hall, a theater, and an indoor recreational

4-194. Existing suburban playfields next to a highway

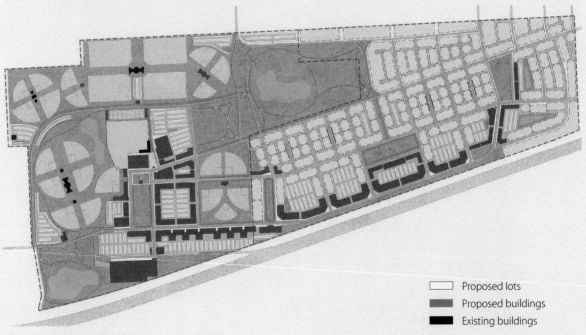

☐ Proposed lots
▨ Proposed buildings
■ Existing buildings

4-195. Playfields embedded in a new town center

facility for after-school care and community events. Conventional commercial businesses usually located on the periphery are brought into a main street, which includes a hotel and mixed-use buildings with shops, apartments, and offices. Denser office buildings along the fronting interstate shield the town center from the noise.

Families coming from farther away for competitions and regional events at the facilities can walk to shops, cafés, and restaurants at the new square and may be enticed to spend more time in the area.

While regional recreational facilities can be retrofitted into town centers, smaller surgical interventions can be considered in suburban communities. Many suburbanized towns across the country can use repair techniques for their existing ballparks and other fields.

Figures 4-198 and 4-199 demonstrate an intervention around an existing baseball field that is a civic amenity and an important gathering place for a suburban community. A strong urban frontage is introduced along three of the sides of the field, emphasizing the prominence of the location. A new city hall is placed at the corner of the ballpark, extending into mixed-use wings along the two streets. Live-work units and apartment buildings complete the streetscape.

A repair project of this type can dramatically affect the rest of a suburban community by showing the town's commitment to smart growth principles, and encouraging further densification and other redevelopment initiatives.

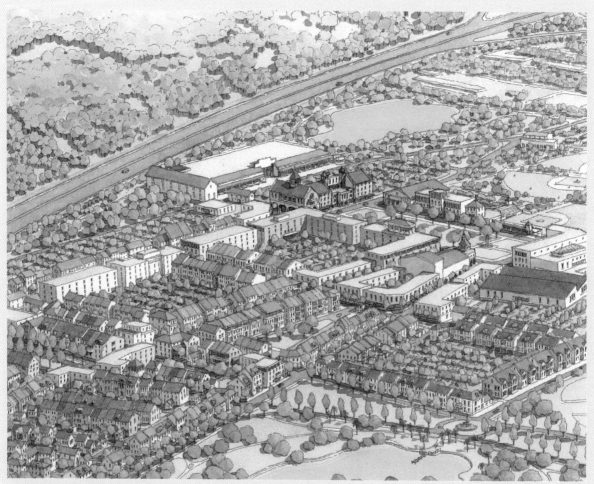

4-196. View of new town center with playfields integrated within its fabric; the playfields are a short walk from public spaces and community amenities

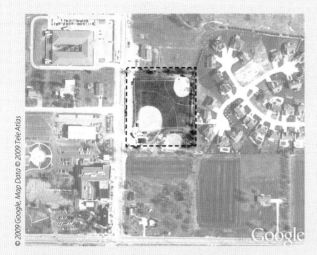

© 2009 Google, Map Data © 2009 Tele Atlas

4-197. Existing baseball fields in a suburban town

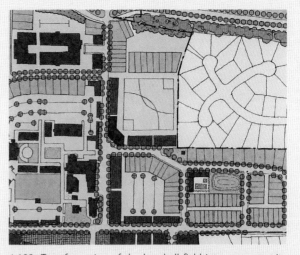

4-198. Transformation of the baseball field into a community center

Drawing by David Carrico

4-199. Baseball field with urbanized edges and a new, two-story city hall located at the corner

CHAPTER FIVE

REPAIR OF THOROUGHFARES AND PARKING

In American urban planning, thoroughfares are the predominant component of the public realm. This is in contrast to the European emphasis on networks of plazas and squares. Thoroughfares provide simultaneous circulation for pedestrians, bicyclists, and vehicles, but they also play an important social function – people meet, interact, shop, dine, and stroll along them. Attempts to separate the pedestrian and vehicle movement have proven in the past to undermine the purpose and complexity of streets as part of the public realm.

Thoroughfares have two main attributes: capacity and character. Capacity is the number of vehicles that can move safely through a segment of a thoroughfare in a given period, and is influenced by physical attributes such as number and width of lanes. Character is the suitability of a thoroughfare as a setting for pedestrian activities and as a location for various types of buildings. Character is influenced by physical attributes such as the ratio between the heights of facing buildings and the distance between them, as well as by building setbacks and the streetscape.

The capacity of a thoroughfare can be expressed in two-dimensional parameters, while its character is experienced three-dimensionally, combining spatial and streetscape features.

The complexity and social function of thoroughfares have been lost in the post-war suburban system, with capacity becoming more important than character. Pedestrian comfort, safety, and sociability are no longer considered during the design of thoroughfares. As a consequence, suburban thoroughfares have become simplistic, dendritic, unvaried, and over-engineered.

This chapter shows techniques for retrofitting typical suburban thoroughfares into complete, multimodal streets that safely and comfortably accommodate pedestrians, bicyclists, public transit, and vehicles, and create public spaces of specific character. In most cases the right-of-way and pavement widths have been kept the same, and the proposed changes are handled within these existing parameters.

Diagrams also demonstrate the transformation of sprawling intersections into more urban ones, including freeway interchanges and cloverleaves into urban roundabouts and complete intersections. The goal is to liberate substantial areas of real estate currently misallocated to the single function of handling fast-moving traffic. In a varied urban environment, intersections can calm traffic and become important landmarks. A variety of devices can be used to slow traffic flow without stopping it, benefitting pedestrians and bicyclists, as well as drivers and their passengers, as car accidents are reduced. One example is to reduce the turning radii at intersections. Overscaled radii are hostile to pedestrians because they increase the distances they have to cross at intersections and allow cars to take corners at excessive speeds. Other devices include traffic circles, roundabouts, and changing paving materials.

The drawings that follow are schematic, representing typical conditions, and simplified for clarity. Sprawl thoroughfares should be repaired according to the principles of context-sensitive design (see "Context Sensitive Solutions in Designing Major Urban Thoroughfares for Walkable Communities" by the Institute of Traffic Engineers and "SmartCode Version 9.2"). Just as buildings and all other elements of the built environment should be designed according to their rural-to-urban context and the needs of the local community, so should thoroughfares, intersections, and public frontages (everything between a property line and the pavement).

In most cases, a combination of techniques will be used to repair a thoroughfare and its buildings. The limited choice of suburban thoroughfares will be expanded to a full assortment of complete streets, from rural roads to urban avenues that provide comfortable, interesting, and safe environments.

Thoroughfares will ideally be repaired concurrently with the other elements of sprawl – buildings, open space, etc. – but they can also be used to start the process. For example, the repair of a strip shopping center can begin with improving the adjacent thoroughfares and creating a new fabric of streets within the parking lot. The next step can be to infill the fabric with buildings, and later replace the existing structures with new ones.

5-1. Types of sprawl thoroughfares   5-2. Level-of-service   5-3. Thoroughfare transformations

▬ Freeway
▓ Arterial
▬ Collector
— Local
⊶ Cul-de-sac

SPRAWL THOROUGHFARES

The five major types of thoroughfares found in sprawl are freeways, arterials, collectors, locals, and cul-de-sacs. Figure 5-1 shows these five types in an emblematic portion of suburbia. It is based on an approximate square-mile grid, though in real life the distances between thoroughfares are likely to be larger and the connectivity even worse.

The level-of-service diagram (figure 5-2) explains that the freeway has the most capacity and speed (mobility) and the fewest points of entry (land access). Capacity is reduced as points of entry increase, so that the cul-de-sac has the least capacity and the most points of entry. The standards assigned to these sprawl thoroughfares relate only to vehicular capacity, without consideration of character, walkability, or alternate forms of transportation.

Figure 5-3 shows the types of sprawl thoroughfares and some of the corresponding traditional thoroughfares. The former are limited in type, while the latter exhibit a wide variety and offer more choice depending on character and location within the rural-to-urban context. For example, the local, which is the typical wide street in suburban subdivisions,

can be "translated" into several traditional thoroughfares, such as a road, drive, street, and yield street, and a cul-de-sac translates into a road or a close.

As discussed in chapter three, "Repair at the Regional Scale," repair of the thoroughfare network should be conceived at the scale of the region, which may encompass one or many counties, several municipalities, or even a whole state. The decisions about where to locate public transportation will be based on a multitude of factors, the most important of which will be the locations of employment and commercial concentrations that have potential to become neighborhood centers, town centers, and regional urban cores for their suburban surroundings.

Because the thoroughfare network will become the armature for future transit and walkable fabric, it is essential that a toolkit of repair techniques is made available to planners, engineers, officials, and communities. These techniques are offered as the basis for discussion, local calibration, and implementation. The following "existing" and "proposed" drawings show the basic principles and the step-by-step process of how to transform a sprawl thoroughfare into a component of the public realm that is pedestrian- and bicycle-friendly and ready to accommodate transit.

5-4. Sprawl intersection

5-5. Neighborhood center intersection

FREEWAY

The freeway is a long-distance thoroughfare traversing open countryside. As it serves fast-moving traffic, it should have a limited number of intersections, driveways, and adjacent buildings; otherwise it invites strip development, which interferes with traffic flow and human comfort.[1] Sprawl repair of a freeway is necessary when the strip development has already occurred or when a highway enters a city and dismantles the urban fabric. There are two proposed designs for the repair of a freeway. In both, transit is included as the primary intervention. The first case transforms the freeway into a parkway with a large median that accommodates rail. The second is the more urban design, with the freeway becoming a boulevard.

Deficiency: Sprawl thoroughfare

Excessive number of lanes

Excessive lane widths

No landscape

No opportunity for transit

Outcome One: Parkway with transit

Remedial Techniques:

Reduce number of lanes

Reduce lane widths

Introduce a median

Introduce transit: light rail or bus rapid transit

Outcome Two: Boulevard with transit

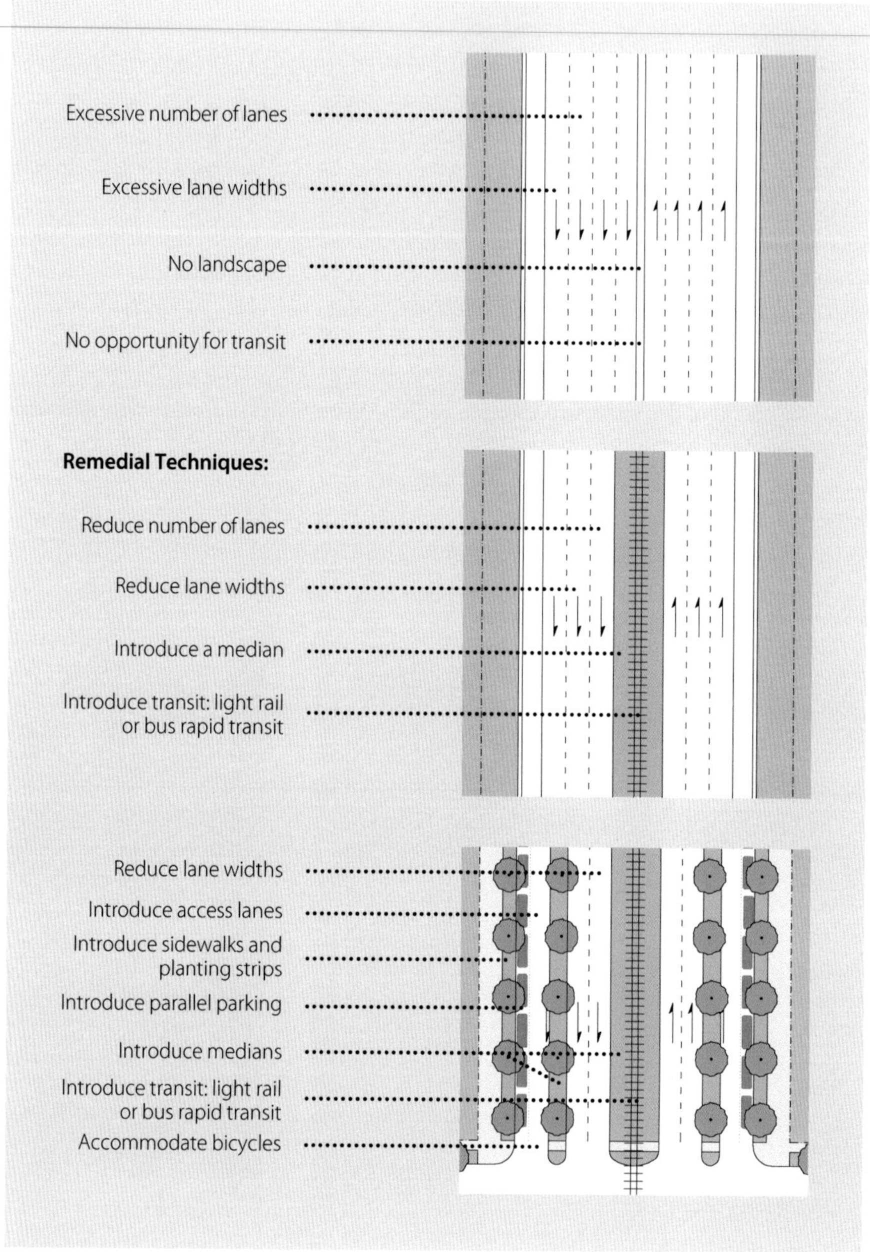

Reduce lane widths

Introduce access lanes

Introduce sidewalks and planting strips

Introduce parallel parking

Introduce medians

Introduce transit: light rail or bus rapid transit

Accommodate bicycles

Interchange: Freeway interchanges are the most challenging sprawl elements to transform. Freeways restrict access, usually through grade-separated interchanges where one thoroughfare goes above the other. One radical solution is to replace a cloverleaf intersection with an on-grade urban roundabout without reducing the number of lanes. The value of the developable recovered land factors into feasibility. (A variant of this repair is to have the freeway pass through a tunnel under the roundabout.) Another proposal takes the transformation further by making it into a boulevard intersection with the attributes of a walkable environment such as tight urban corners, pedestrian crossings, medians, and parallel parking.

Deficiency: Sprawl interchange

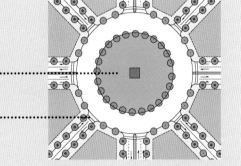

Car-oriented interchange ....

Outcome One: Parkway roundabout

Remedial Techniques:

Introduce a central green space ....

Introduce crosswalks ....

Outcome Two: Boulevard intersection

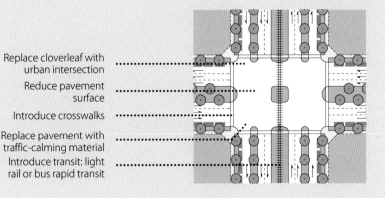

Replace cloverleaf with urban intersection ....

Reduce pavement surface ....

Introduce crosswalks ....

Replace pavement with traffic-calming material ....

Introduce transit: light rail or bus rapid transit ....

ARTERIAL

Arterials are heavily congested because they channel traffic coming from the collectors, locals, and cul-de-sacs. Some are laid out in one-mile grids, but connectivity is often interrupted. Arterials are more prone to strip development than freeways, as they have more points of access. Transforming arterials into urbanized thoroughfares is feasible only in the context of regional public transit. The two options show a six-lane arterial repaired as a boulevard and an avenue. The boulevard will have one-way access lanes and parallel parking, while the avenue will include a wide median for future light rail or BRT. Both streetscapes require sidewalks, pedestrian crossings, bicycle lanes, planting, and on-street parking.

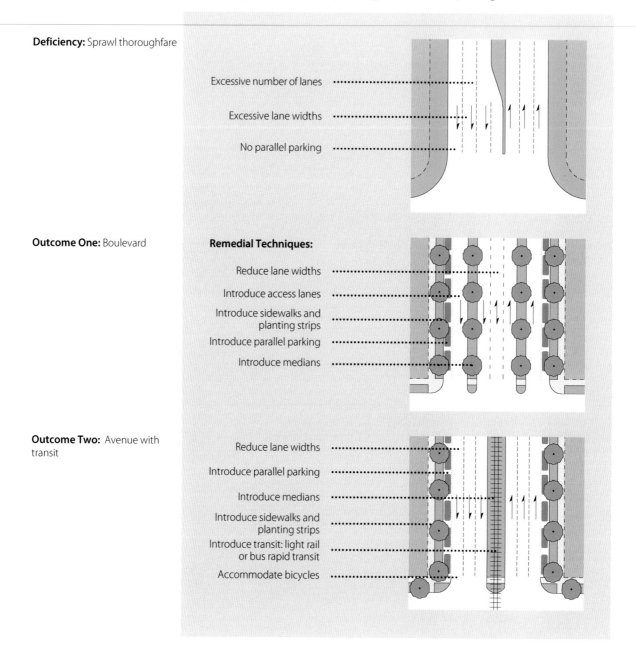

Deficiency: Sprawl thoroughfare

Excessive number of lanes

Excessive lane widths

No parallel parking

Outcome One: Boulevard

Remedial Techniques:

Reduce lane widths

Introduce access lanes

Introduce sidewalks and planting strips

Introduce parallel parking

Introduce medians

Outcome Two: Avenue with transit

Reduce lane widths

Introduce parallel parking

Introduce medians

Introduce sidewalks and planting strips

Introduce transit: light rail or bus rapid transit

Accommodate bicycles

Intersection: It is essential to provide urbanized alternatives to the conventional arterial intersections, as these are the locations of regional commercial nodes and employment hubs that will become the future urban centers. The ideal scenario is to urbanize all four corners of these intersections at the same time, but if not feasible the transforma-

tion can happen in phases, as the first step will be the streetscape transformation, with the buildings coming later. The two options for urban intersections correspond to the boulevard and avenue alternatives. In both cases the lane widths are reduced and parallel parking is introduced, as well as medians and access lanes.

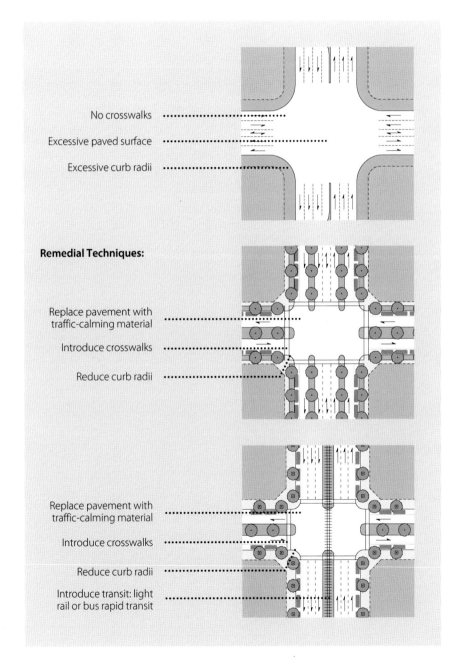

Deficiency: Sprawl intersection

No crosswalks

Excessive paved surface

Excessive curb radii

Outcome One: Boulevard intersection

Remedial Techniques:

Replace pavement with traffic-calming material

Introduce crosswalks

Reduce curb radii

Outcome Two: Avenue intersection

Replace pavement with traffic-calming material

Introduce crosswalks

Reduce curb radii

Introduce transit: light rail or bus rapid transit

COLLECTOR

Collectors are the thoroughfares that accumulate traffic from suburban enclaves and deliver it to the arterials. Like arterials, they often have heavy congestion, lack of connectivity, and haphazard strip development. Repairing a collector requires a comprehensive strategy, including reorganizing the fabric to create frontage along the collector and well-defined public space at important intersections. The first proposal shows a typical collector repaired into an avenue with a large median, and the second a main street.

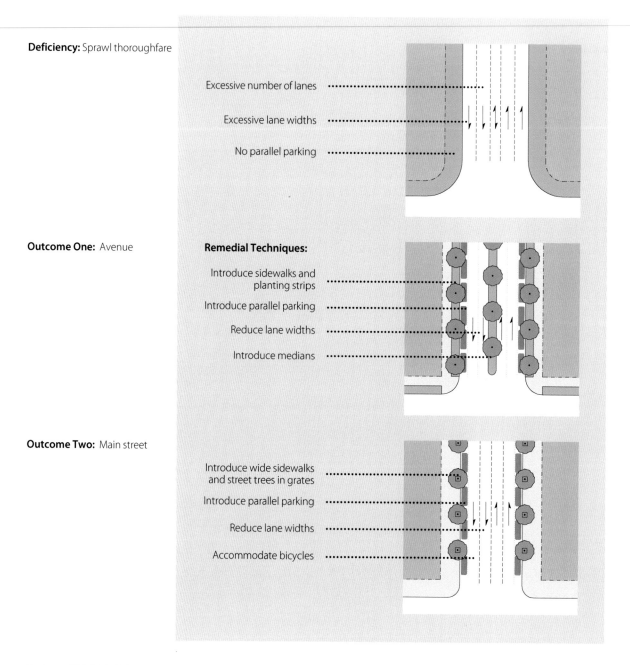

Deficiency: Sprawl thoroughfare

Excessive number of lanes

Excessive lane widths

No parallel parking

Outcome One: Avenue

Remedial Techniques:

Introduce sidewalks and planting strips

Introduce parallel parking

Reduce lane widths

Introduce medians

Outcome Two: Main street

Introduce wide sidewalks and street trees in grates

Introduce parallel parking

Reduce lane widths

Accommodate bicycles

Intersection: Intersections along collectors are often developed with commercial establishments such as gas stations, convenience stores, and strip shopping centers. Repair of these intersections should be coordinated with the repair of these sprawl elements and the surrounding area. These two proposals correspond to the avenue and main street retrofits. In both cases the lane widths and curb radii are reduced, and parallel parking, medians, and sidewalks with plantings are introduced.

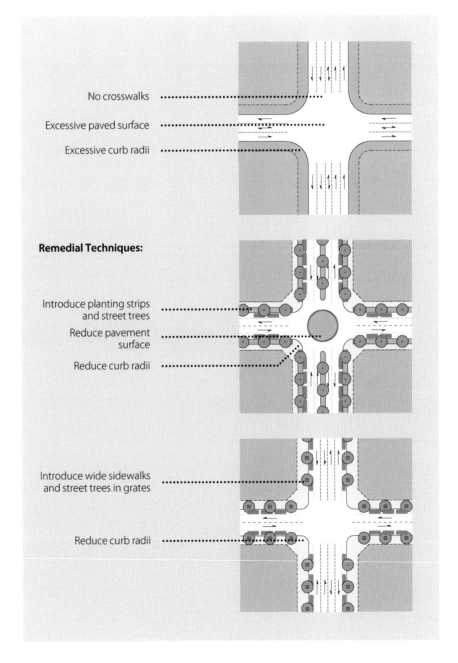

Deficiency: Sprawl intersection

No crosswalks ....

Excessive paved surface ....

Excessive curb radii ....

Outcome One: Avenue intersection

Remedial Techniques:

Introduce planting strips and street trees ....

Reduce pavement surface ....

Reduce curb radii ....

Outcome Two: Main street intersection

Introduce wide sidewalks and street trees in grates ....

Reduce curb radii ....

LOCAL

Local thoroughfares in suburban sprawl usually serve residential or commercial enclaves and feed collectors. They are often dead-ends or loops, and in rare cases connect with another collector. Local thoroughfares usually have two oversized lanes, and rarely include sidewalks or parallel parking. The goal of this repair is to create a pedestrian-friendly street with sidewalks, parallel parking, and bicycle routes. These two options cover a rural road and an urban street. In the first, large planting strips with informally arranged trees can serve as swales for stormwater management, while the second has wider sidewalks and trees planted in rows.

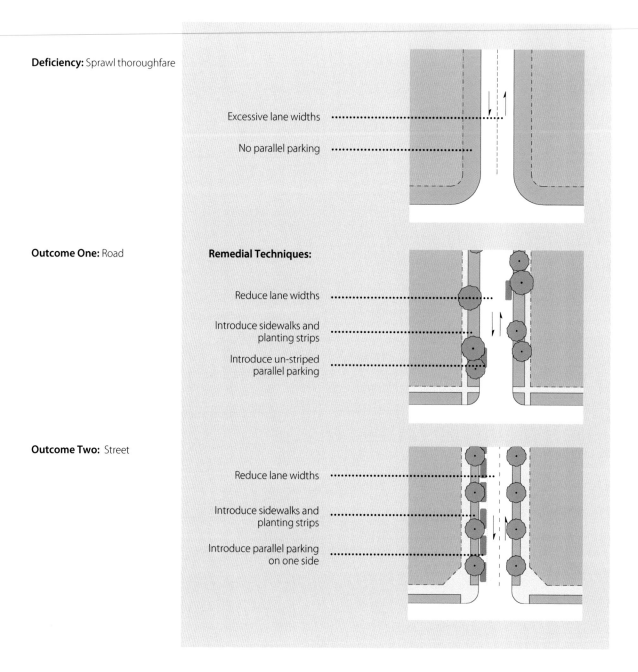

Deficiency: Sprawl thoroughfare

Excessive lane widths

No parallel parking

Outcome One: Road

Remedial Techniques:

Reduce lane widths

Introduce sidewalks and planting strips

Introduce un-striped parallel parking

Outcome Two: Street

Reduce lane widths

Introduce sidewalks and planting strips

Introduce parallel parking on one side

Intersection: The intersection of a local and a collector often contains a gated entrance to a residential or commercial enclave. Removing that gate should be included when repairing such an intersection because it will create connectivity between suburban pods and reduce traffic congestion. These two options for the transformation of local intersections correspond to the road and street repairs. In both alternatives the lane widths and curb radii are reduced, and parallel parking, sidewalks, and continuous planters are introduced.

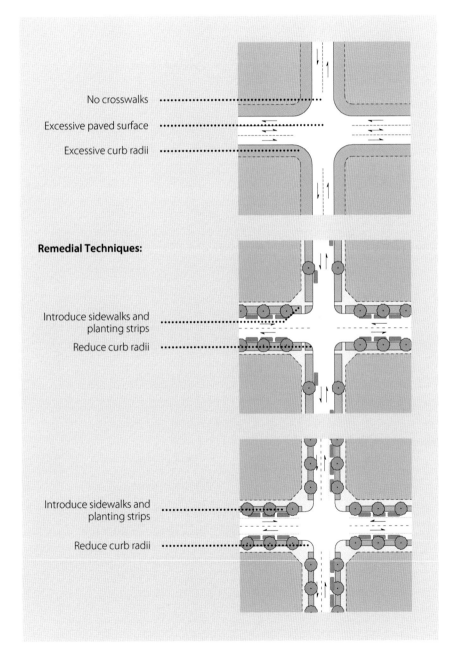

Deficiency: Sprawl intersection

No crosswalks
Excessive paved surface
Excessive curb radii

Outcome One: Road intersection

Remedial Techniques:

Introduce sidewalks and planting strips
Reduce curb radii

Outcome Two: Street intersection

Introduce sidewalks and planting strips
Reduce curb radii

CUL-DE-SAC

The cul-de-sac is the symbol of sprawl. Conceived as a device to deal with topography and environmental features such as wetlands, it later came to dominate the suburban pattern, interrupting thoroughfare networks and loading locals and collectors with traffic. These diagrams show a conservative and a radical approach. The conservative option keeps the cul-de-sac but adds a green space in the middle, forming a close (public space at a dead-end street). Pedestrian and bike connections are added where possible. The second proposal eliminates the cul-de-sac by introducing a road through it. This intervention requires the purchase of at least one property.

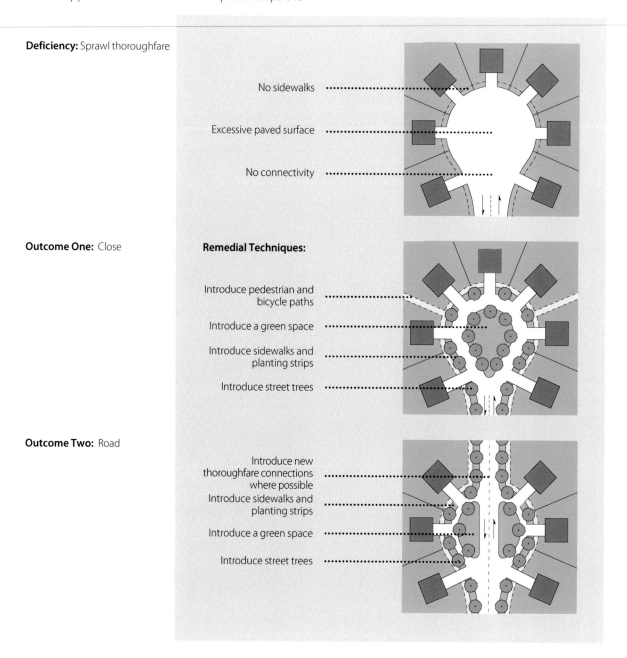

Deficiency: Sprawl thoroughfare

No sidewalks

Excessive paved surface

No connectivity

Outcome One: Close

Remedial Techniques:

Introduce pedestrian and bicycle paths

Introduce a green space

Introduce sidewalks and planting strips

Introduce street trees

Outcome Two: Road

Introduce new thoroughfare connections where possible

Introduce sidewalks and planting strips

Introduce a green space

Introduce street trees

PARKING STRATEGY

Parking plays a critical role in the functionality and quality of urbanism. In sprawl, driving is a necessity and cars are preeminent even when stationary. Parking lots overwhelm the fronts of buildings, discouraging walking and inhibiting the mix of uses and compactness required for good urbanism.

Cars must be accommodated, however, and a proper parking strategy is essential to sprawl repair. It helps the urbanization of oversized parking lots, thereby improving the pedestrian experience and supporting mixed uses and transit. The strategy also can be used to incentivize redevelopment, and to deal with the changing parking conditions that come with sprawl repair.

In sprawl, parking distorts, and even determines, the urban form. Because land in the suburbs has been inexpensive, surface parking lots have been easier and cheaper to build. Readily available parking is one of the main advantages that suburban development has over traditional urbanism. The overscaling of parking lots has been exacerbated by municipal parking requirements, which, more than any other code restraint, determine the size and shape of buildings. As a result, buildings in sprawl are usually freestanding, with large distances between them, which discourages walking.

A parking strategy should be a part of any sprawl repair project. Sprawl repair typically modifies the location, capacity, and form of parking facilities, and a parking strategy will help organize and optimize these changes. The urbanization of parking lots is among the primary techniques of sprawl repair. A strategy that ensures the adequate provision and utilization of parking encourages the redevelopment of those empty lots.

Sprawl repair often involves radical change of a site. This includes the concentration of surface parking into vertical structures on smaller plots, and the addition of on-street parking, resulting in an increase in the raw number of parking spots. Density, and therefore population, is also increased, but the mixed uses in proximity allow multiple options for transportation. The mixed uses also need the parking at different times (day/night, weekday/weekend), allowing it to be shared. This means the necessary parking per capita is reduced, and municipal parking requirements should be reduced accordingly.

Reuse of these parking lots creates large amounts of developable real estate. To enhance the value of this real estate and incentivize its redevelopment, municipalities (or even states) should consider subsidizing the construction of parking structures in sprawl repair projects. This will ensure the creation of a civic parking reserve, spur redevelopment, and achieve transit-supportive densities.

The parking strategy presented here consists of several interconnected policy recommendations and design techniques. Similar to strategies that have previously been used to repair suburbanized downtowns, it begins with the creation of a parking reserve to ease anxiety during sprawl repair. (Because of parking's economic implications, some property owners will consider new parking controls to be downzoning.) This strategy targets predominantly commercial areas, but can be modified for single-use residential and office enclaves. Whether a private or public-private venture, each sprawl repair project should include a management entity appointed to develop and implement a long-range parking policy. Following are suggestions for a parking strategy:[2]

1. Form a parking reserve. This is created from all sources of existing parking under municipal or private management. The parking reserve will be managed to enable the most efficient and flexible use of the supply. Parking from the reserve should be leased or sold on a first-come, first-served basis to encourage fast redevelopment. The parking reserve should include:

- All on-street parking along commercial frontages;
- All new on-street parking created by the repair of thoroughfares and traffic-calming practices (access lanes, medians, parallel and diagonal parking, etc.);
- All municipal parking garages and parking lots
- All parking associated with leases of commercial properties;
- Use of all private commercial parking garages and lots during their off hours (this may be controversial).

2. Transfer ownership of high-speed, suburban arterials and collector roads from DOT to the local municipality for complete-street design.

3. Allow on-street parking to count toward parking requirements, and introduce shared parking ratios for mixed uses. The more intense the mix of uses, the less parking should be required.

4. Reserve the most conveniently located parking places for short-term uses such as shopping, doctors' appointments, and business meetings. The lower spaces of parking garages should be reserved for customers, and the rest should be longer-term parking for employees and residents. On-street parking in front of stores should have short meter settings.

5. Analyze the feasibility of converting failed big boxes into parking garages to free the original front parking lots for redevelopment.

6. Provide showers and lockers in parking facilities and transit stops that connect with bike routes.

7. Before building vertical parking structures, reorganize the existing on-street and off-street parking. (Restripe spaces; install smart parking meters, street trees, access lanes, boulevard medians; employ techniques to calm traffic; and make sidewalk improvements such as widening them and installing benches and planters.) Some of the improvements can be paid for using a "point-of-sale" tax, meaning that the street frontage repairs will be paid for, or the repairs themselves will be deferred, until a property is sold.

8. Screen open parking lots with liner buildings or temporary buildings. Use pervious, pedestrian-friendly materials such as grass pavers in lots that have seasonal demand for parking and can be transformed into civic spaces at other times of the year.

9. Designate locations for future parking garages on the regulating plans. The construction of parking garages should be considered civic infrastructure, seeking similar public funding that is dedicated to utilities and thoroughfares.

10. Provide retail- or service-oriented frontages (community markets, fitness centers) at the ground level of parking garages that are on primary streets.

11. Design garages, when practical, for later conversion into habitable space (offices, lofts, or civic use), meaning horizontal floor plates and floor-to-ceiling heights feasible for later habitation. Accommodate vehicles powered by non-petroleum (electric and bio-diesel) sources with dedicated parking, power plugs, and bio-fueling stations.

12. Design parking signage to clearly show where the parking is. Pedestrian passages connecting streets to parking should be well lit and, ideally, lined by habitable space.

APPLICATION: MAIN STREET REPAIR

5-6. Suburban main street

This is a case study of the transformation of a suburban main street into an urban main street. Figure 5-6 shows commercial buildings fronting a narrow sidewalk and head-in parking lot.

5-7. First phase of repair includes parallel parking and streetscape improvements

Figure 5-7 illustrates the first phase, which includes widening the sidewalks, converting one moving lane to parallel parking, and adding tree grates.

5-8. Final phase includes building redevelopment and signage

Figure 5-8 shows the last phase, which incorporates the construction of new two-story buildings along the street, adding residential uses above the shops, and improving the signage. The other side of the street is redeveloped to create compatible frontages.

APPLICATION: COLLECTOR REPAIR

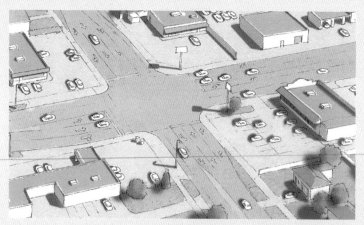

5-9. Existing collector with car-dominated character

Figures 5-9, 5-10, and 5-11 show the phased transformation of a suburban collector. The collector (running east to west) has four lanes and intersects another suburban thoroughfare. The intersection is hostile to pedestrians and bicyclists, with overscaled turning radii and limited landscaping. Outdated and underutilized parking lots dominate the streetscape.

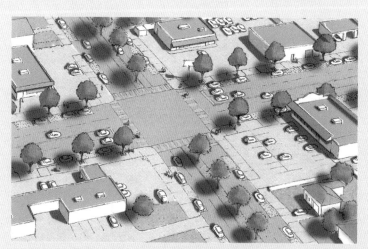

5-10. First phase of repair includes streetscape improvements

The first phase of the repair includes only streetscape changes – reducing lane widths, adding parallel parking, installing sidewalks, planting strips, and visible pedestrian crossings. This sets the stage for the building replacement and infill.

5-11. Final phase includes repair of the intersection and building redevelopment

The last phase includes the redevelopment of the suburban commercial structures to form a continuous, properly scaled frontage along the new main street and the repaired intersection.

APPLICATION: ARTERIAL REPAIR

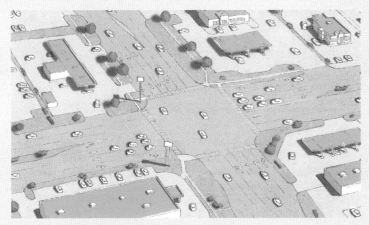

5-12. Existing arterial with car-dominated character

Figures 5-12, 5-13, and 5-14 illustrate the transformation of a six-lane suburban arterial into a transit corridor. The existing conditions have excessive pavement in the lanes and parking lots, and are unfriendly to pedestrians and bicyclists. The wide right-of-way has the potential for adding public transit.

5-13. First phase of repair includes streetscape improvements such as a wide median for future transit

The first phase includes the addition of parallel parking, wider sidewalks, landscaping, and a generous median, which will later accommodate a light rail line. The collector intersecting the arterial receives access lanes and medians on both sides, transforming it into an urban boulevard.

5-14. Final phase includes the addition of light rail and building redevelopment

The final phase incorporates the light rail line along the avenue, as well as the redevelopment of the buildings along its edges. The avenue becomes a pedestrian-friendly, sustainable avenue.

CHAPTER SIX

REPAIR AT THE BLOCK SCALE

This chapter explores techniques for transforming blocks and smaller urban increments, preparing them to become part of a future urban fabric. Large suburban megablocks can be broken down into a finer grain of smaller blocks by introducing new streets through their parking lots, thereby establishing a coherent pattern for future incremental development.

As the retrofitted increment grows, the surface parking, which is already organized into streets and blocks, can be filled in with structured parking and new construction. The transformation at the block scale can happen gradually, piece by piece, without requiring an unrealistic level of agreement and coordination between multiple property owners, and without entailing impractical amounts of public and private investment all at once.

The first case study is the megablock, which may be located in suburban sprawl or part of an urban fabric damaged by suburbanization. The tools for repairing such conditions are similar in both suburban and urban settings – a walkable block structure is created or reinstated, and the parking lots are filled with new, mixed-use construction at a higher urban intensity.

The slab and tower block is another essential case study of sprawl repair at this scale. In the U.S., slabs and towers were employed as the main tools of the urban renewal movement in the 1960s, when whole neighborhoods were razed and replaced by public housing. The concept of the megastructure in the park was also popular in Western and Eastern Europe during the first decades after World War II, when the demand for housing was high and modernist planning dismantled the traditional urban patterns. The result was that vast areas in the U.S. and Europe, within cities and on their peripheries, became desolate landscapes of tall buildings amidst undefined open space and asphalt. The tools for repair of such blocks incorporate re-platting, building new streets and connections, forming smaller blocks, and introducing building types to accommodate a mix of uses and make the streetscape more pedestrian friendly.

A critical remediation at the block scale is the transformation of McMansion-lined suburban blocks into more balanced environments. Most options involve the insertion of new building types such as townhouses, mews units, live-work units, and apartments into the suburban framework, achieving higher density and more pedestrian-friendly streetscapes. These techniques have previously been used in the successional redevelopment of the American city. For example, townhouses inserted behind mansions can be observed in Boston, Massachusetts. The mansions are converted into multifamily housing, with such interventions often tripling the existing density.

The next intervention is in the typical suburban residential block, where the deeper lots allow the introduction of back alleys and lanes and the addition of outbuildings to be used as granny flats or affordable rental housing. Further densification can be achieved by adding back buildings (structures between the main houses and the outbuildings).

The block scale also includes the most typical condition in sprawl development: residential blocks consisting entirely of cul-de-sacs. The most egregious deficiency in these subdivisions is a lack of connectivity. Opening the cul-de-sacs into streets may not be a feasible solution while the subdivision has high property values, but this tool should be considered for more radical repair when the appropriate conditions exist. With millions of properties foreclosed upon in 2007–2009, opportunities for retrofit at a larger scale materialized.

SUBURBAN MEGABLOCK

These diagrams illustrate the transformation of a suburban commercial block into walkable urban fabric.

The site has several large, freestanding structures surrounded by excessive parking lots, which waste land and discourage walking. The repair begins with the renovation of one of the buildings, dividing it in two to allow new streets and blocks. The others are kept intact. New streets are added, with discontinuous north-south streets to slow traffic. Two parking garages are built, with additional parking along the streets.

Three parcels are preserved for public spaces such as squares, plazas, and greens, while the other blocks are platted to accommodate a variety of building types. The perimeter blocks have garages in the middle, extending to live-work units and townhouses. If conditions allow, the surrounding suburban lots can be re-platted to allow higher density transitioning from the site.

Deficiency: Lack of urban fabric and mixed use

Oversized buildings

Exposed and excessive parking

No connectivity

Single-use buildings

Outcome: New urban fabric

Remedial Techniques:

Renovate and divide large building

Create urban blocks by introducing thoroughfares

Add liner buildings

Create plazas and greens

Introduce live-works and townhouses

Introduce perimeter block buildings with parking garages

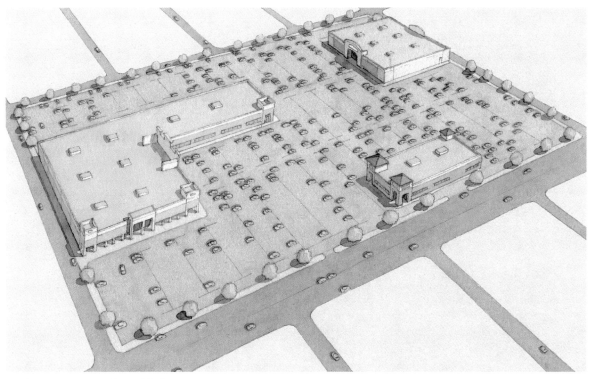

6-1. Existing commercial megablock

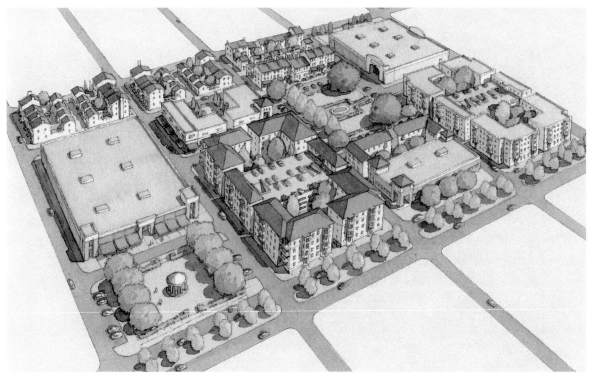

6-2. Repaired urban fabric with mix of uses and civic spaces

SLAB AND TOWER BLOCK

Slabs and towers have become symbolic of disastrous public housing experimentation.

The vast, unassigned spaces between buildings deteriorate fast, becoming unpleasant and dangerous to walk through. The goal is to transform the underutilized gaps between the structures into pedestrian-friendly, smaller-scale urban fabric. Privatizing some of the land, platting it into lots, and forming smaller blocks are the main remedial techniques used in this transformation. The process is applicable both when the buildings are preserved and when they are demolished.

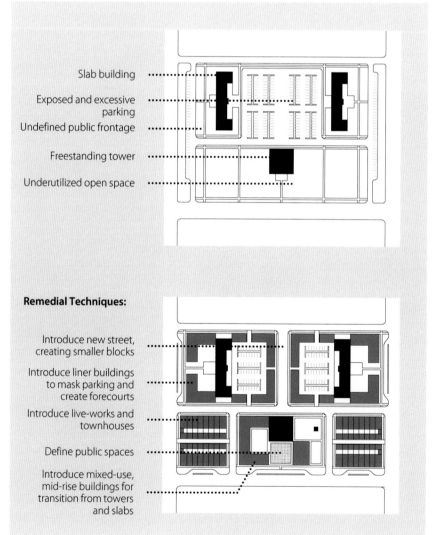

Deficiency: Oversized megablock

Slab building

Exposed and excessive parking

Undefined public frontage

Freestanding tower

Underutilized open space

Outcome: Walkable urban fabric

Remedial Techniques:

Introduce new street, creating smaller blocks

Introduce liner buildings to mask parking and create forecourts

Introduce live-works and townhouses

Define public spaces

Introduce mixed-use, mid-rise buildings for transition from towers and slabs

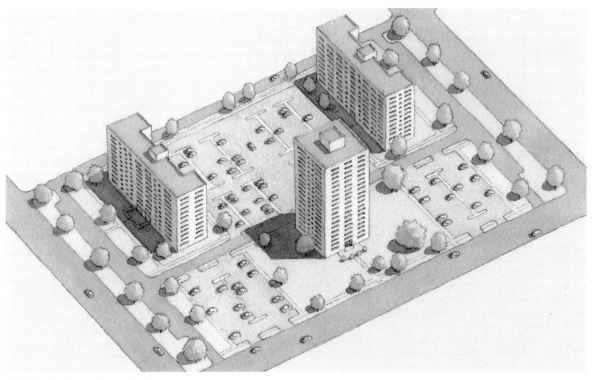

6-3. Existing slab and tower block

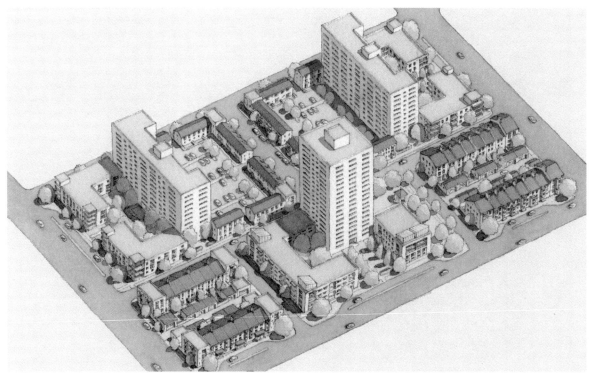

6-4. Repaired block with townhouses and mixed-use buildings

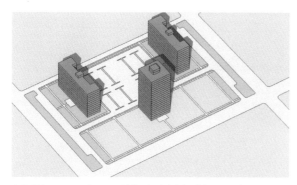

6-5. Existing conditions: A block of slab buildings and a tower

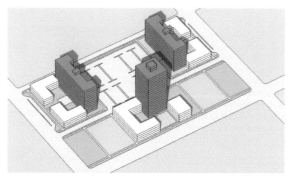

6-6. Phase One: Adding mixed-use buildings to create courtyards

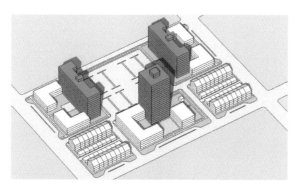

6-7. Phase Two: Adding townhouses and live-work units to create smaller increment of ownership

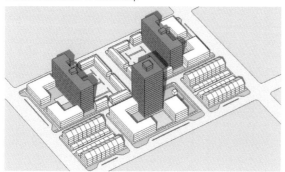

6-8. Phase Three: Completing the fabric with liner buildings to mask parking lots and create affordable spaces

A typical modernist megablock includes slab buildings and towers surrounded by excessive public space consisting mainly of surface parking lots. It is decidedly unfriendly to pedestrians (figure 6-5).

In the first phase (figure 6-6), mixed-use buildings are used to create courtyards in front of the slabs and the tower. The existing parking lots along the edges of the block are reorganized as on-street parking. Ground floors of the new buildings can be used for shops, offices, and cafés, as well as daycare facilities, meeting spaces, or other civic uses.

In phase two (figure 6-7), additional streets are introduced perpendicular to the length of the megablock, breaking it up into smaller increments. One street bisects the large parking lot and is framed by liner buildings. Townhouses and live-work units are inserted in the leftover space, fronting the surrounding streets. The newly created private ownership of smaller lots and buildings clarifies the relationship between private and public space.

In phase three (figure 6-8), a new street bisects the large parking lot between the slabs. The street is framed by liner buildings, which accommodate affordable lofts and live-work units. The final outcome of the sprawl repair of this oversized block is a finer grain of five smaller blocks, which reduce the scale and impact of the towers and slabs.

McMANSION BLOCK DENSIFICATION

The purpose of this case study is to analyze the possibilities for intensification of oversized McMansion lots in suburban conditions. At their minimum, McMansions' lots are 100 feet wide by 120 feet or more in depth, and can easily accept more density.

There are examples, specifically in urban environments, where this intensification has happened as a result of rising property values. In such cases, even underground parking for the additional units has been financially feasible. In suburban sprawl, especially during times of falling property values, urban intensification may be difficult to achieve on a block-by-block basis, and should therefore be applied in combination with community-scale techniques for sprawl repair, such as the introduction of mixed uses and thoroughfare transformation. However, the tools at the block scale are available to smaller developers and entrepreneurs who can purchase several McMansion lots, convert them into a dense cluster, and sell or rent the units. The regulatory mechanism to enable

such interventions can include a form-based code overlay if whole neighborhoods are retrofitted and made denser, or a PUD (Planned Unit Development) overlay in the case of smaller-scale up-zoning.

The examples shown illustrate densification by adding townhouses, mews units, and apartment villas to the backs of lots. These techniques can be combined with the conversion of the large houses into senior or student housing or apartments. By applying both methods, the average density can be substantially increased, in some cases even tripled. Even with the higher density, the character of the neighborhood is preserved because the detached, large houses remain.

The common technique used for this densification is the introduction of alleys, either parallel to the long sides of the blocks or intersecting them. The new units face the existing streets, visible between the existing McMansions. Parking is handled either underground or, in the case of the mews buildings, in a frontloaded garage as part of the unit, or in small pockets of surface parking in the example with the apartment villas.[1]

6-9. McMansions on large lots

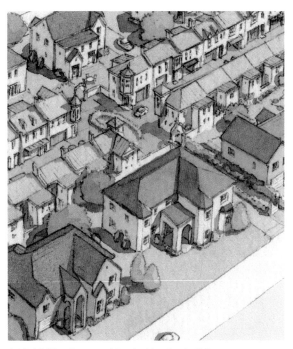

6-10. McMansions combined with other building types

INFILL WITH MEWS

The mews unit is a compact building type that is ideal to be used for infill of the McMansion block. Originating from the dense urban fabric of British towns, these buildings are small in size, two or three stories tall, and located along a back alley or lane (mews). McMansion garages are typically accessed from the front, so back alleys open the lots for another layer of housing. The mews lane can run perpendicular or parallel to the block. In the first case, fewer lots are affected but density is not increased as much as in the second outcome.

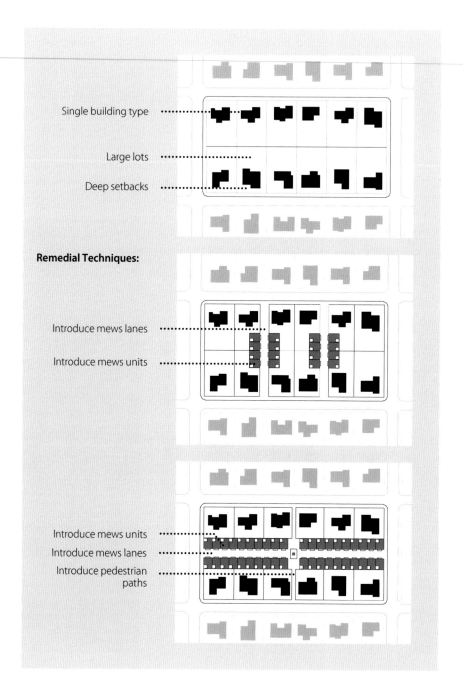

Deficiency: Oversized lots; 12 dwellings at 3 units per acre

Single building type

Large lots

Deep setbacks

Outcome One: Mews perpendicular to the block; 28 dwellings at 7 units per acre

Remedial Techniques:

Introduce mews lanes

Introduce mews units

Outcome Two: Mews parallel to the block; 52 dwellings at 13 units per acre

Introduce mews units

Introduce mews lanes

Introduce pedestrian paths

6-11. Existing block of McMansions

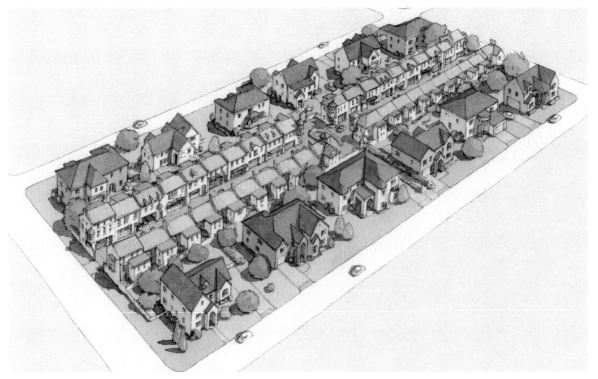

6-12. In outcome two, the McMansion block is made denser with mews

INFILL WITH TOWNHOUSES

Infilling the McMansion block with townhouses is a more radical intervention because they typically front on a vehicular or pedestrian thoroughfare rather than an alley. Townhouses can be built per- pendicular to the block, facing a narrow pedestrian street, or they can be built parallel to the block, with underground parking if the new density achieves sufficient returns.

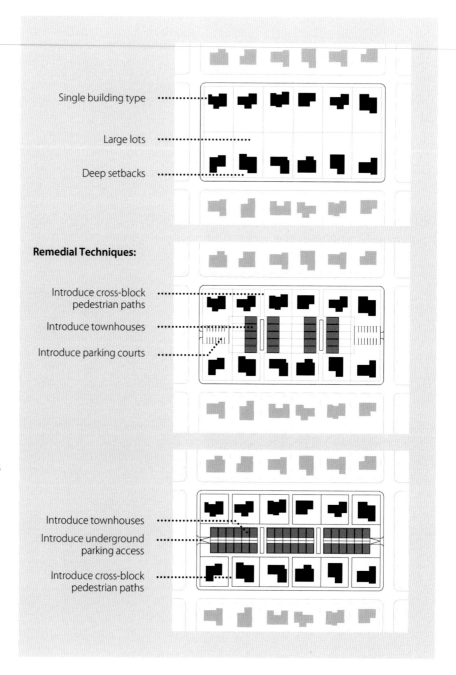

Deficiency: Oversized lots; 12 dwellings at 3 units per acre

Single building type

Large lots

Deep setbacks

Outcome One: Townhouses perpendicular to the block; 32 dwellings at 8 units per acre

Remedial Techniques:

Introduce cross-block pedestrian paths

Introduce townhouses

Introduce parking courts

Outcome Two: Townhouses parallel to the block; 48 dwellings at 12 units per acre

Introduce townhouses

Introduce underground parking access

Introduce cross-block pedestrian paths

6-13. Existing block of McMansions

6-14. In outcome one, the McMansion block is made denser with townhouses

INFILL WITH APARTMENT VILLAS

The apartment villa is a building type that can be inserted among existing McMansions with little disruption, as the two types are similar in size. Apartment villas are two or three stories tall, with four to six units in total. They can be inserted along alleys perpendicular to the McMansion block, or can be located at the two edges of the block, with parking clustered in a court in the middle. Conversion of all or some McMansions into multifamily housing is suggested, if possible.

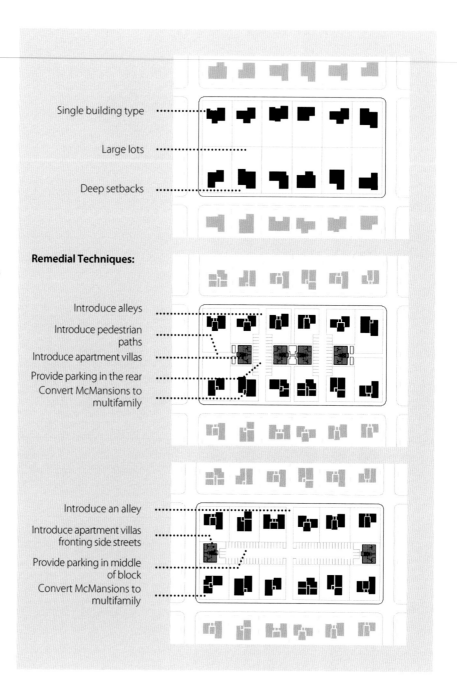

Deficiency: Oversized McMansions and lots; 12 dwellings at 3 units per acre

Single building type

Large lots

Deep setbacks

Outcome One: Infill with apartment villas and McMansions converted to multifamily; 84 dwellings at 21 units per acre

Remedial Techniques:

Introduce alleys

Introduce pedestrian paths

Introduce apartment villas

Provide parking in the rear
Convert McMansions to multifamily

Outcome Two: Apartment villas fronting side streets and McMansions converted to multifamily; 48 units per block at 12 units per acre

Introduce an alley

Introduce apartment villas fronting side streets

Provide parking in middle of block
Convert McMansions to multifamily

6-15. Existing block of McMansions

6-16. In outcome one, the McMansion block is made denser with apartment villas

RESIDENTIAL BLOCK DENSIFICATION

Most suburban residential blocks are deep (between 100 and 150 feet), and have the potential for increased density. This phased repair begins with the addition of alleys and lanes in the back to increase connectivity and allow outbuildings (for rentals, granny flats, or studios). The next phase can include the addition of backbuildings, further increasing the density. The corner lots can be converted to live-work units or corner stores.

Deficiency: Single building type and use. Suburban houses; oversized lots; 14 dwellings at 3.5 units per acre

Single building type

Deep setbacks

Phase One: Alleys and outbuildings along cross-block alley; 28 dwellings at 7 units per acre

Remedial Techniques:

Introduce alley

Introduce outbuildings

Phase Two: Outbuildings along alley and corner stores; 38 dwellings at 9.5 units per acre

Infill with backbuildings

Transform corner units into corner stores or live-work units

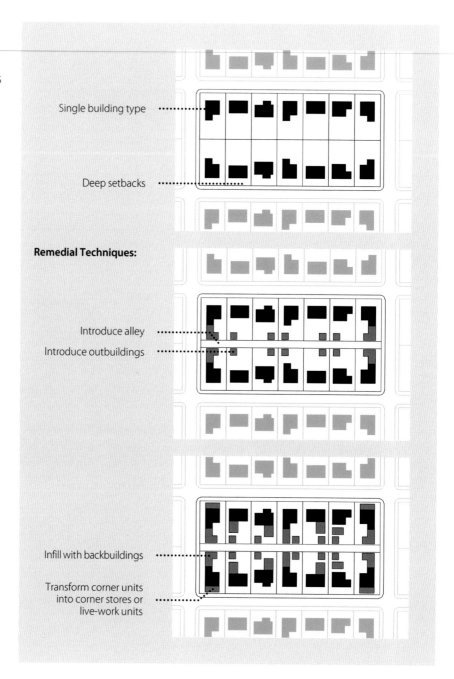

6-17. Existing condition: Typical suburban residential block

6-18. Phase One: New alleys and outbuildings

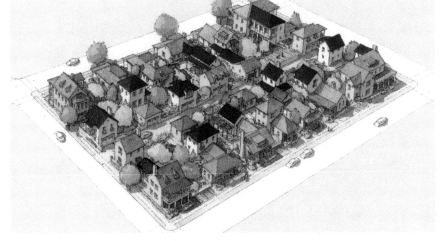

6-19. Phase Two: Backbuildings

RESIDENTIAL BLOCK DE-DENSIFICATION

Density at the block and lot scale can be reduced in places where deserted and blighted properties have become prevalent. Lots can be re-platted into larger parcels to be used for community gardens, stormwater-retention greens, or family compounds. Maintenance of such places will be best managed on a block-by-block basis.

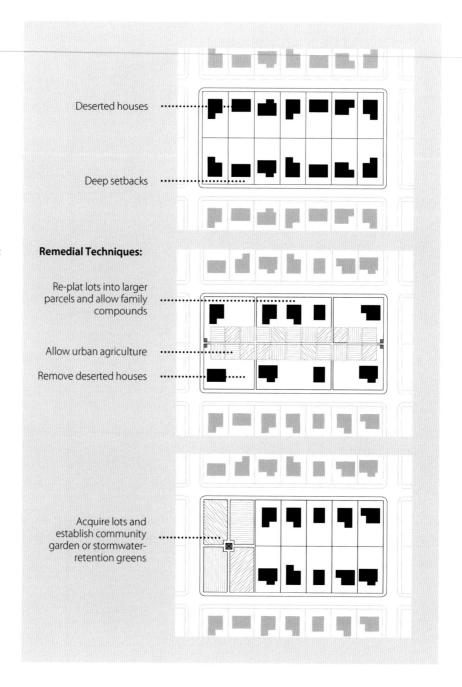

Deficiency: Deserted, blighted properties; 14 dwellings at 3.5 units per acre

Deserted houses

Deep setbacks

Outcome One: Agricultural lots; 6 dwellings at 1.5 unit per acre

Remedial Techniques:

Re-plat lots into larger parcels and allow family compounds

Allow urban agriculture

Remove deserted houses

Outcome Two: Civic green for stormwater management or community garden

Acquire lots and establish community garden or stormwater-retention greens

6-20. Existing condition: Typical suburban residential block

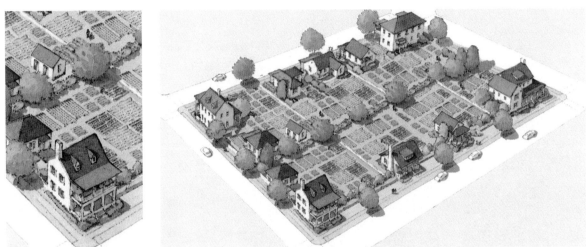

6-21. Outcome One: Agricultural lots and family compounds

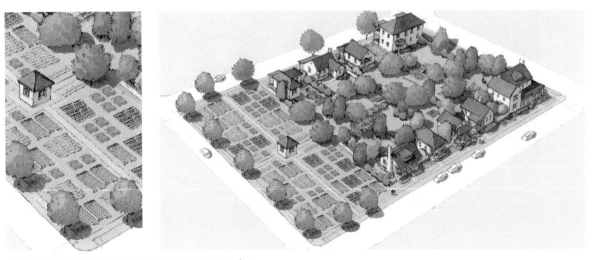

6-22. Outcome Two: Civic green as a community garden

RESIDENTIAL BLOCK WITH CUL-DE-SACS

The most emblematic and challenging element of sprawl is the suburban subdivision with disconnected cul-de-sacs. Repair begins with an analysis of the reasons for the disconnection. If there are no topographical impediments, the feasibility of opening the cul-de-sacs and connecting the streets is determined. Some properties may need to be purchased by the future developer, or even be subject to eminent domain, depending on the importance of their locations.

VEHICULAR CONNECTIVITY

If the open space in the back of lots is underutilized, the cul-de-sacs can be connected parallel to the blocks, creating additional frontage to subdivide into lots.

Deficiency: Suburban fabric with cul-de-sacs

Cul-de-sac

Residual open space

Disconnected street network

Remedial Techniques: Connect cul-de-sacs parallel to blocks

Purchase houses at tip of cul-de-sac

Connect street through cul-de-sac

Create a green to calm traffic

Create lots and houses fronting the new street

Outcome: Connected fabric

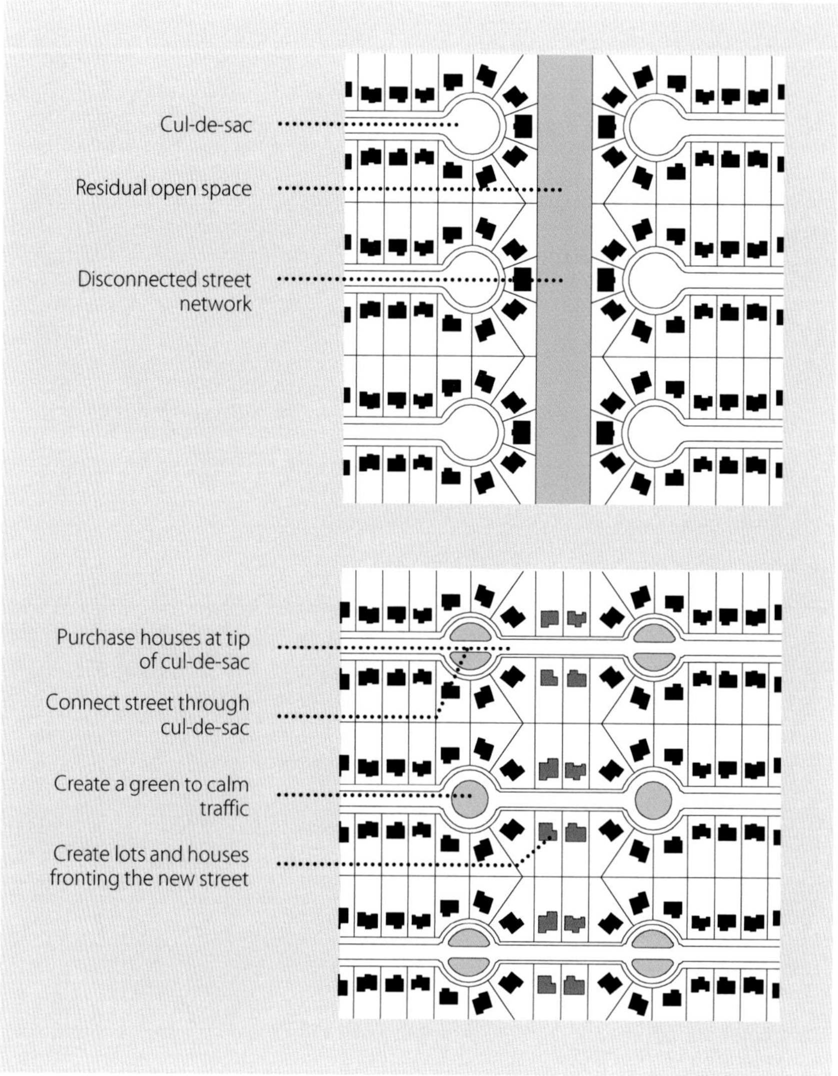

PEDESTRIAN AND BICYCLE CONNECTIVITY

Where there is an environmental easement in the back of the lots, the strategy for connectivity introduces pedestrian and bicycle pathways rather than vehicular thoroughfares. They are also delineated parallel to the blocks, as a narrow easement (eight to ten feet) that can be acquired from two adjacent properties. A more comprehensive pedestrian and bicycle network can be established within the greenway in the back, if the environmental assessment allows it.

Deficiency: Suburban fabric with cul-de-sacs

Cul-de-sac

Residual open space

Disconnected street network

Remedial Techniques: Connect cul-de-sacs with pedestrian and bicycle networks

Add pedestrian and bicycle paths for connectivity

Create, wherever possible, pedestrian and bicycle trails in residual space

Outcome: Pedestrian and bike paths

Create a green to reduce pavement surface

ONE-WAY VEHICULAR CONNECTIVITY

When it is not possible to acquire properties for connectivity, an alternative is to connect the cul-de-sacs perpendicular to the blocks. In this case, easements can be purchased from two adjacent property owners facing one of the cul-de-sacs and the same can be repeated for the adjacent cul-de-sac. The new street can be one-way if a larger easement cannot be secured.

Deficiency: Suburban fabric with cul-de-sacs

Cul-de-sac ·········

Disconnected street network ·········

Remedial Techniques: Connect cul-de-sacs perpendicular to blocks

Purchase right-of-way for new connections ·········

Connect street through cul-de-sac ·········

Create a green to calm traffic ·········

Outcome: Connected fabric

APPLICATION: COMMERCIAL BLOCK REPAIR PHASING

This sequence demonstrates the gradual urbanization of a typical megablock containing a defunct mall and several outparcels. The mall is repurposed into a high-tech hosting space, while its parking lot is transformed into a mixed-use urban square.

The first phase creates the square and a main street connecting to an adjacent property. The second phase adds to the liner buildings surrounding the square, creating urban blocks.

6-23. Existing conditions: The mall, its parking lots, and outparcels

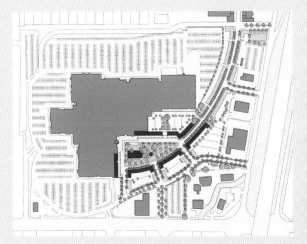

6-24. Phase One: Add a public square and a main street; the first buildings can be used as "billboards" for visibility from the highway

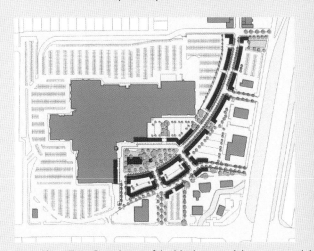

6-25. Phase Two: Completion of the blocks around the square and the main street

CHAPTER SEVEN

REPAIR AT THE BUILDING SCALE

The goal for this set of remediation techniques is to retrofit the primary building prototypes that define suburbia. These iconic, detached structures and their parcels have the potential, after modest interventions, to contribute to a more diverse, cohesive urban fabric.

The existing suburban buildings are repurposed and/or joined by new structures, often taking advantage of suburbia's typically excessive setbacks and parking lots. Some buildings, such as the drive-through restaurant, corner gas station, and the strip center, are more vulnerable than others. Because of their short life spans and large lots, demolition could be the first option or the eventual outcome of a phased repair.

Starting at the level of the single structure gives individual business owners and smaller investors the chance to participate in the transformation of sprawl. Structurally viable buildings are preserved, modified, expanded, and reused within a more sustainable urban context. Neighbors can replicate these small interventions and gradually redevelop more properties to form mixed-use and diverse environments. Requiring fewer resources, such projects can be the seeds of change necessary to start initiatives on the larger scale.

To be effective, the repair at the building scale must be combined with a regulatory framework at the scale of the community and the region that allows mix of uses and higher densities. Parking requirements must also be reduced and shared parking allowed between compatible uses.

7-1. Existing suburban houses

7-2. Repair by infill with outbuildings and backbuildings

McMANSION

The McMansion is the building type most often associated with residential sprawl. Once the symbol of success and achievement, the McMansion has become a liability for suburbanites who are strapped with upside-down mortgages and long commutes. As a result, thousands of McMansions have been subjected to foreclosure, aban-donment, and even demolition. Sprawl repair can be accomplished at the block scale (see chapter six, "Repair at the Block Scale"), or at the scale of a lot. One way to reuse McMansion structures is to transform them into senior or student housing or apartments. Parking moves to the rear, and the garage can be used as living space.

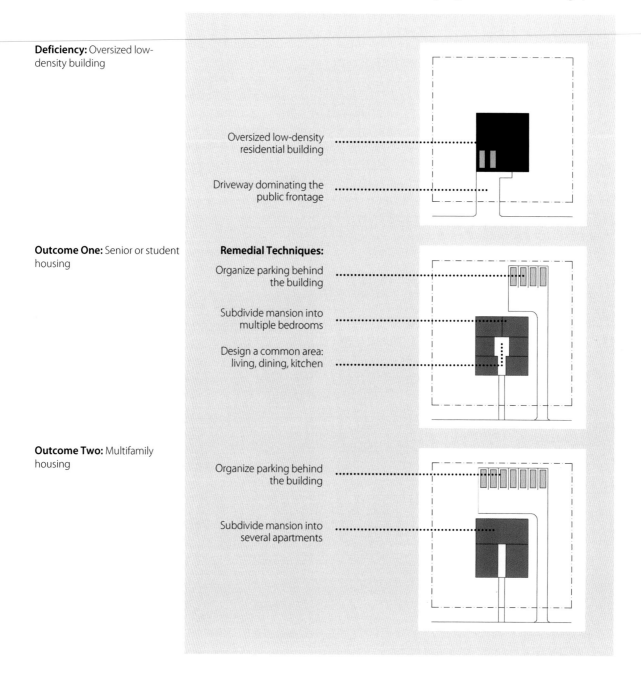

Deficiency: Oversized low-density building

Oversized low-density residential building

Driveway dominating the public frontage

Outcome One: Senior or student housing

Remedial Techniques:

Organize parking behind the building

Subdivide mansion into multiple bedrooms

Design a common area: living, dining, kitchen

Outcome Two: Multifamily housing

Organize parking behind the building

Subdivide mansion into several apartments

7-3. Existing McMansion:
First and second floor: five bedrooms,
five bathrooms, and three-car garage

(Labels in plan: GUEST BEDROOM, OPEN FAMILY ROOM, BREAKFAST ROOM, KITCHEN, 3-CAR GARAGE, OPEN FOYER, DINING ROOM, LIVING ROOM; RETREAT, OPEN TO BELOW, BEDROOM 2, BEDROOM 4, LAUNDRY ROOM, OWNER'S SUITE, OPEN TO BELOW, BEDROOM 3)

7-4. Outcome One: McMansion
converted into senior or student
housing. First and second floor: ten
bedrooms, nine bathrooms, and a
suite for a caretaker

7-5. Outcome Two: McMansion converted into multifamily housing.
First floor: one 1-bedroom and one
2-bedroom apartment
Second floor: two 2-bedroom apartments

■ Existing walls   ■ New walls

SUBURBAN RANCH HOUSE

Suburban ranch houses are not oversized like McMansions, but their lots often are. One solution is to subdivide the lot and build a second structure. The deep suburban setbacks, usually in the range of 20 to 30 feet, can be used to extend the first house, as shown in both diagrams. New zoning is needed to permit the redevelopment of the front yards, together with design guidelines to ensure a harmonious character along the street. Gardens for local food production should be allowed and encouraged.

Deficiency: Underutilized front setback and backyard

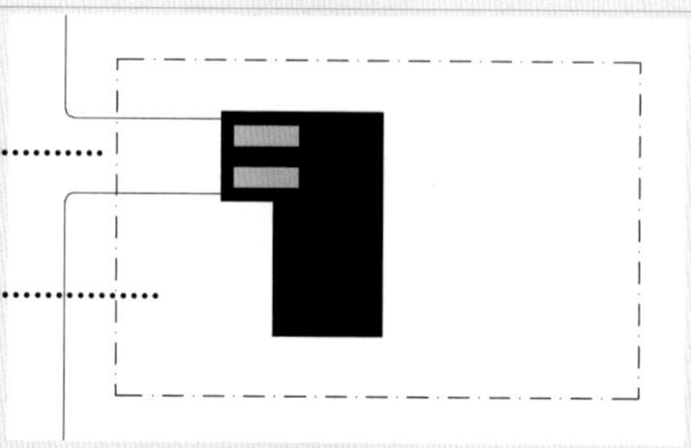

Driveway dominates the public frontage

Deep front setbacks

Outcome One: Two lots

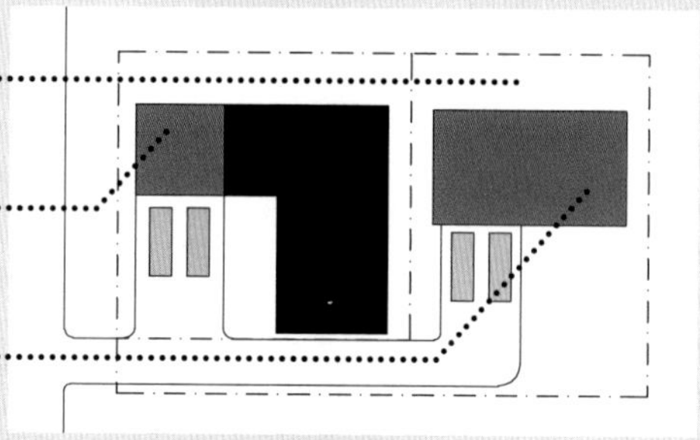

Remedial Techniques:

Subdivide the lot

Add to the house in the front setback, creating live-work, garage, family room, or bedroom

Add a second unit in the back

Outcome Two: Front auxiliary wing, garden in the back

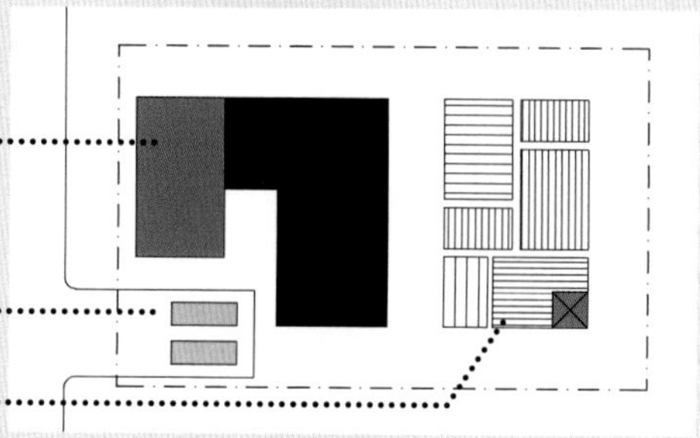

Add front auxiliary wing, replacing driveway

Add a driveway

Allow urban agriculture

Drawing by James Wassell

7-6. The existing condition is an excessive front setback dominated by a driveway and a parking garage

Drawing by James Wassell

7-7. The existing garage is converted into additional living space as a two-story structure built over the existing driveway

Drawing by James Wassell

7-8. A new wing is added, creating an entry courtyard and preventing the garage and driveway from dominating the street view

Drawing by James Wassell

7-9. A detached outbuilding is built in the front yard, creating a private interior courtyard and preventing the garage and driveway from dominating the street view

Drawing by James Wassell

7-10. The garage is removed altogether. In its place sits a one-story addition delineating the street. A garden is in the backyard

DRIVE-THROUGH

The deep setbacks, exposed parking, and under-utilized lots of the ever-present drive-through discourage walking and homogenize the streetscape. Figures 7-11 and 7-12 depict the phased transformation of a drive-through property into a contrib- uting element of a community. In outcome one, liner buildings are added along the street fronts. In outcome two, the restaurant is replaced with a parking garage. In some situations, this might be the first option.

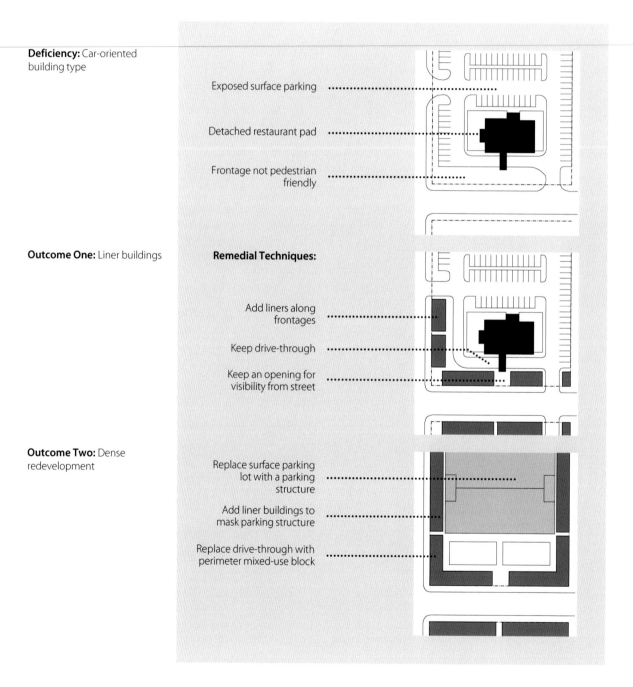

Deficiency: Car-oriented building type

Exposed surface parking

Detached restaurant pad

Frontage not pedestrian friendly

Outcome One: Liner buildings

Remedial Techniques:

Add liners along frontages

Keep drive-through

Keep an opening for visibility from street

Outcome Two: Dense redevelopment

Replace surface parking lot with a parking structure

Add liner buildings to mask parking structure

Replace drive-through with perimeter mixed-use block

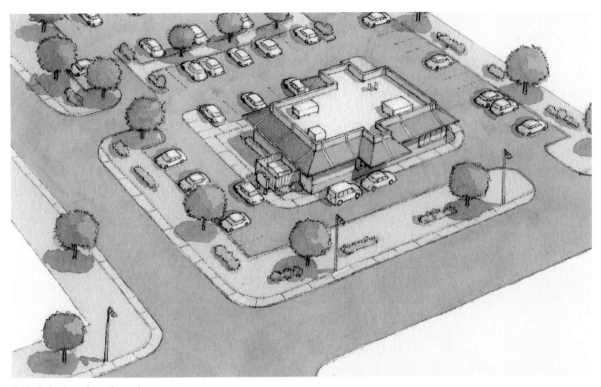

7-11. Suburban drive-through

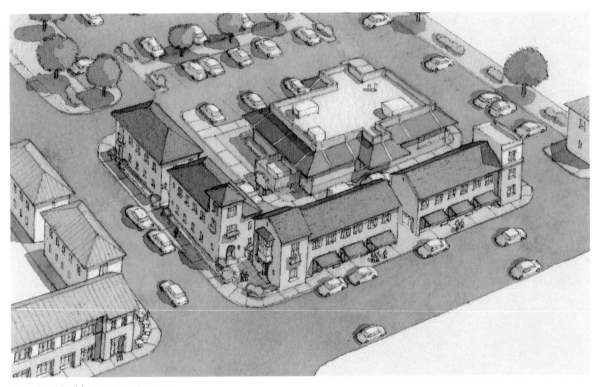

7-12. Liner buildings on a main street

GAS STATION

These drawings show two simple options for repairing a typical corner gas station. In the first, a two-story corner store is added to improve the intersection and screen the gas station (figure 7-14). The second option includes a larger store with two wings wrapping both corners and creating a plaza. In this case, the pumps are expanded in size while the original building is removed. Both options are viable when the location of the underground fuel storage does not interfere with the new construction. If the pumps are moved or eliminated, environmental remediation must be considered.

Deficiency: Car-oriented building type

Detached building in the rear

Pumps dominate the public frontage

Outcome One: Corner store

Remedial Techniques:

Connect shed structure to new building

Build a corner store at the intersection

Outcome Two: Corner store with front plaza

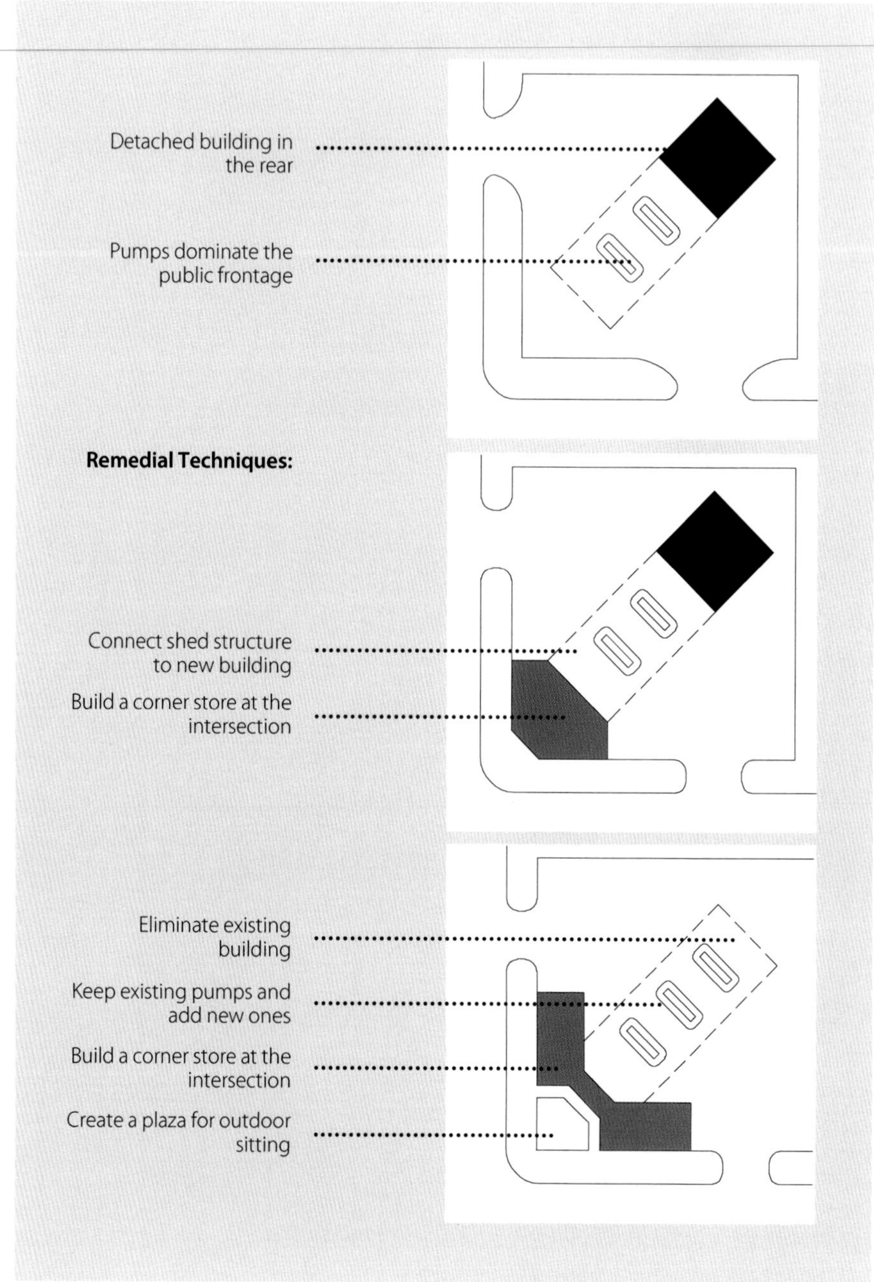

Eliminate existing building

Keep existing pumps and add new ones

Build a corner store at the intersection

Create a plaza for outdoor sitting

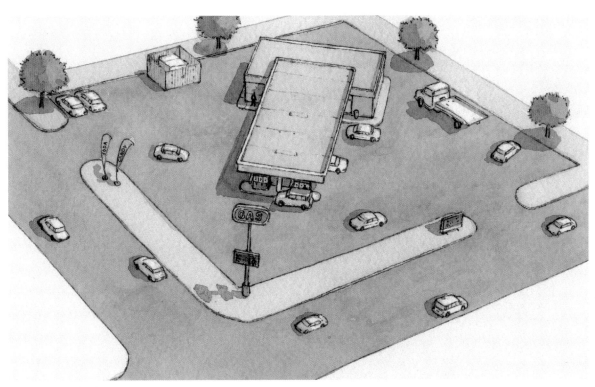

7-13. Existing suburban gas station

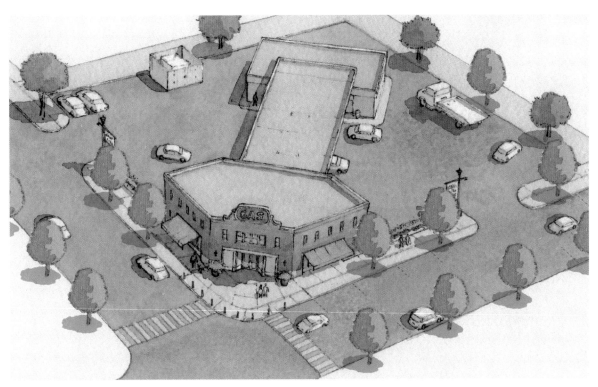

7-14. Corner store addition

PARKING GARAGE

Parking structures are elements of good urbanism only when they are well incorporated into the urban fabric. This is not the case with sprawl. One option for retrofit is to wrap the garage with mixed-use liner buildings (figure 7-16). These buildings will be single-loaded, 25 and 35 feet deep. Lofts or offices can be 45–50 feet deep. If the structure is not needed for parking, and its floors are horizontal, it can be converted into lofts or offices, with an atrium space in the middle. In all cases, it is essential to introduce streets and a block structure.

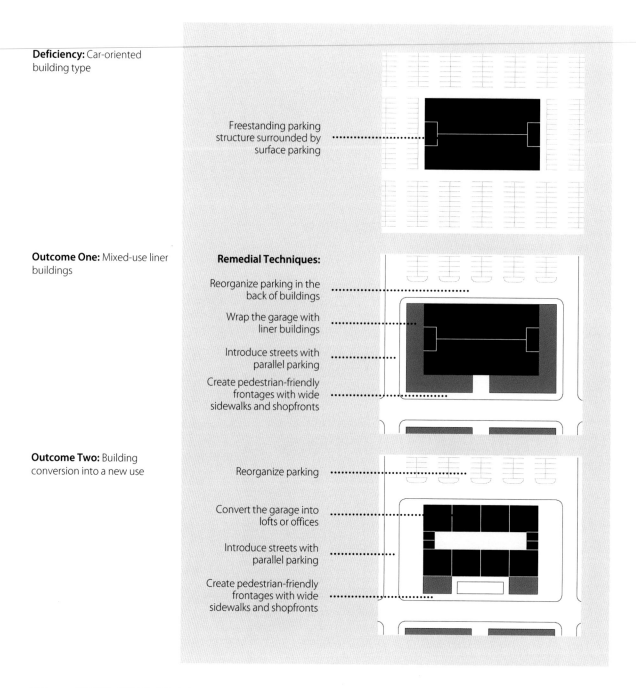

Deficiency: Car-oriented building type

Freestanding parking structure surrounded by surface parking

Outcome One: Mixed-use liner buildings

Remedial Techniques:

Reorganize parking in the back of buildings

Wrap the garage with liner buildings

Introduce streets with parallel parking

Create pedestrian-friendly frontages with wide sidewalks and shopfronts

Outcome Two: Building conversion into a new use

Reorganize parking

Convert the garage into lofts or offices

Introduce streets with parallel parking

Create pedestrian-friendly frontages with wide sidewalks and shopfronts

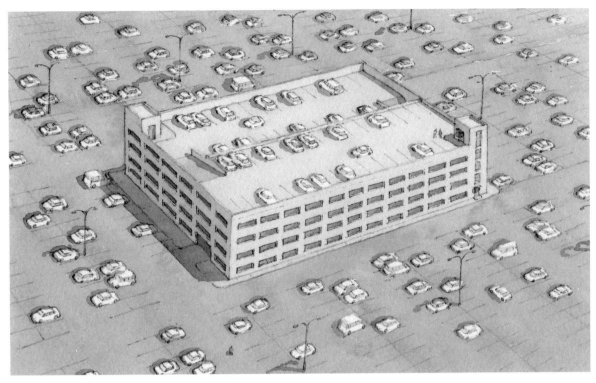

7-15. Existing parking garage

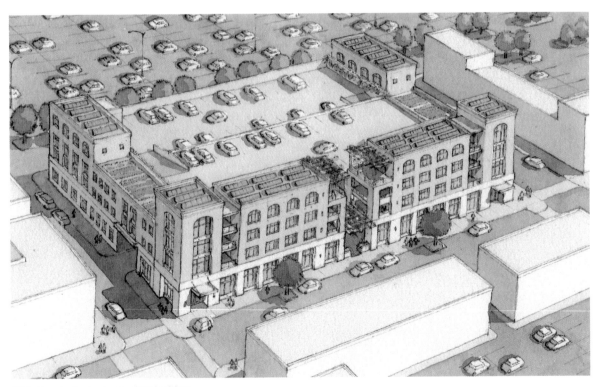

7-16. Repaired mixed-use urban building

STRIP CENTER

Following are two options for re-purposing a strip center. The first is to add two side wings that improve the street face by reaching the sidewalk and framing a courtyard. The center could be adapted for new uses, such as a recycling center (figure 7-18). The second option also improves the frontage by adding liner buildings, and divides the existing building to house multiple businesses.

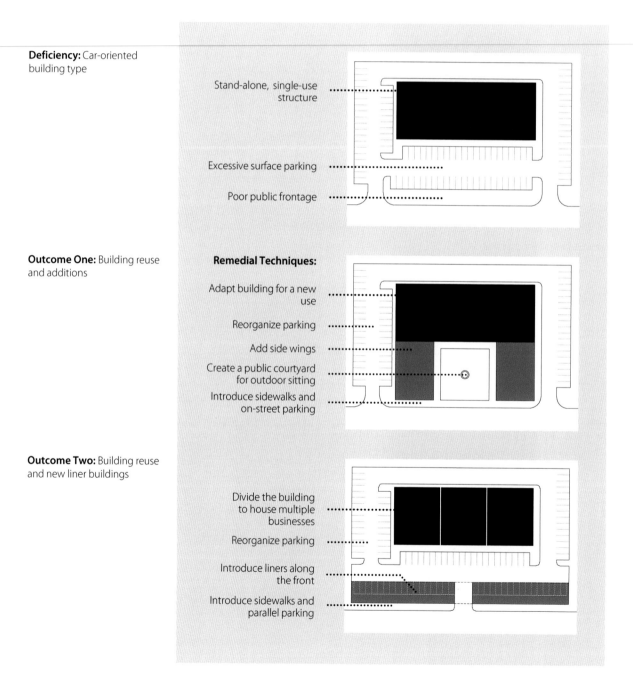

Deficiency: Car-oriented building type

Stand-alone, single-use structure

Excessive surface parking

Poor public frontage

Outcome One: Building reuse and additions

Remedial Techniques:

Adapt building for a new use

Reorganize parking

Add side wings

Create a public courtyard for outdoor sitting

Introduce sidewalks and on-street parking

Outcome Two: Building reuse and new liner buildings

Divide the building to house multiple businesses

Reorganize parking

Introduce liners along the front

Introduce sidewalks and parallel parking

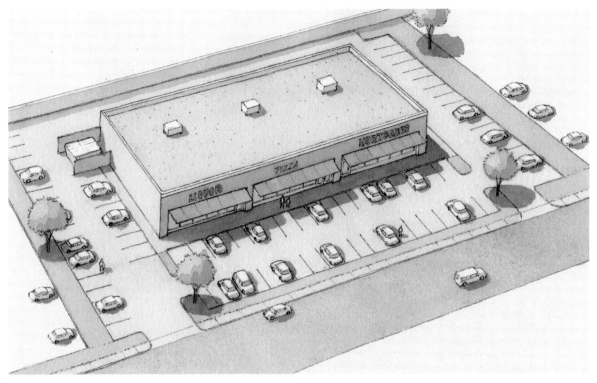

7-17. Existing strip center

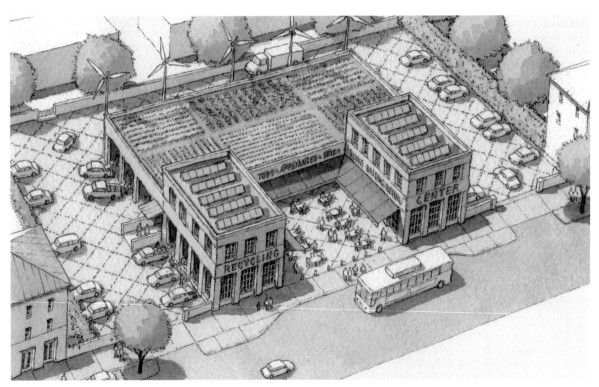

7-18. Conversion into a recycling center

BIG BOX

Big-box retailers often abandon buildings for new ones farther out. With so many going out of business, even more are available for redevelopment. These proposals offer different levels of intervention. The first keeps the building as is, with liner buildings in front. Its use may remain retail, or it can be converted for large occupants such as a satellite college campus, or even a parking garage. A more radical approach (figure 7-20) densely develops the entire site. Perimeter buildings and garages are added in front, and the building is renovated. The creation of new streets and a block structure is crucial to both options.

Deficiency: Car-oriented building type

Stand-alone, single-use structure

Excessive surface parking

Outcome One: Liner buildings

Remedial Techniques:

Convert building for a new use

Create block structure, with a main street terminating on building

Introduce high-density perimeter buildings

Outcome Two: Converted structure and complete urban blocks

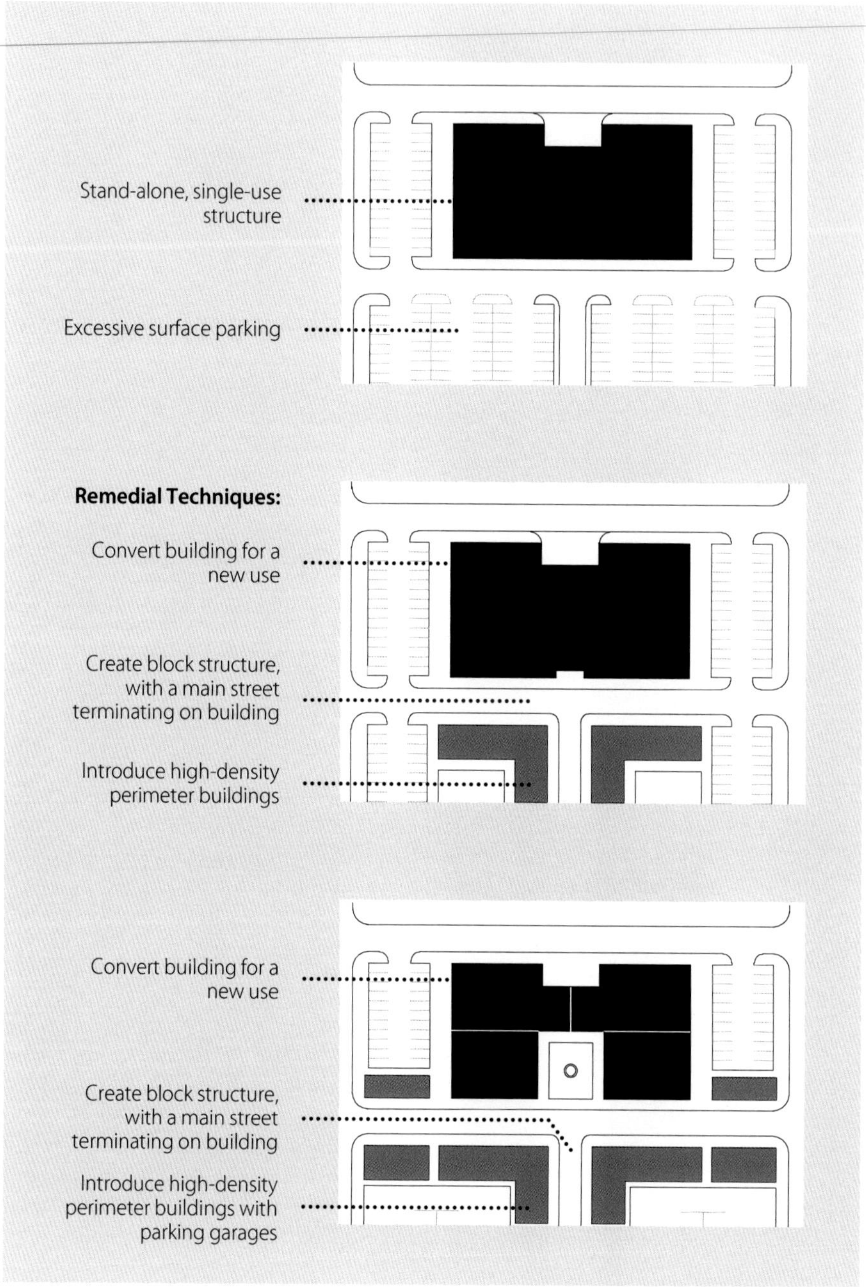

Convert building for a new use

Create block structure, with a main street terminating on building

Introduce high-density perimeter buildings with parking garages

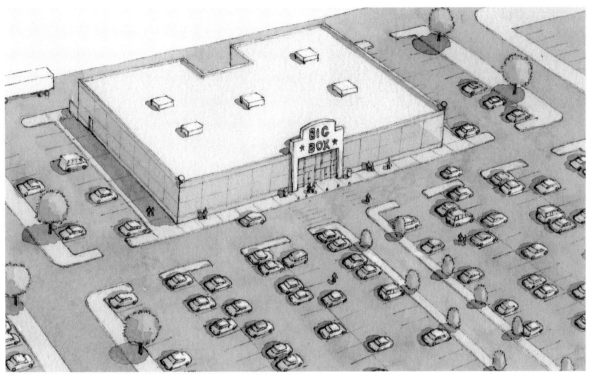

7-19. Existing big box

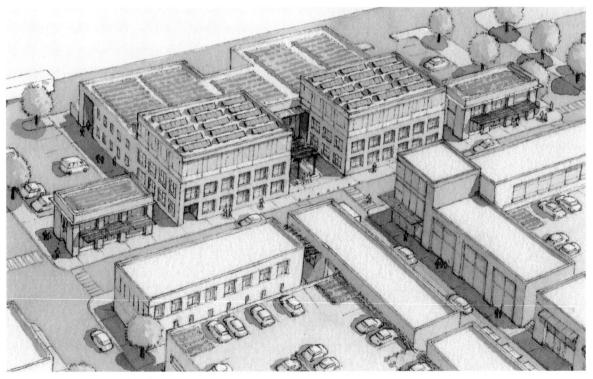

7-20. Renovated and reused big box terminating a new main street

RELIGIOUS BUILDING

Religious institutions can create additional revenue and improve their surrounding neighborhoods by urbanizing their underutilized parking lots with housing or mixed-use buildings. The first example proposes an infill with senior courtyard housing. Small, L-shaped buildings share walls and pedestrian passages (figure 7-22). The buildings can be used for independent or assisted living. The second option introduces mixed-use liner buildings that form a civic space terminating on the religious building.

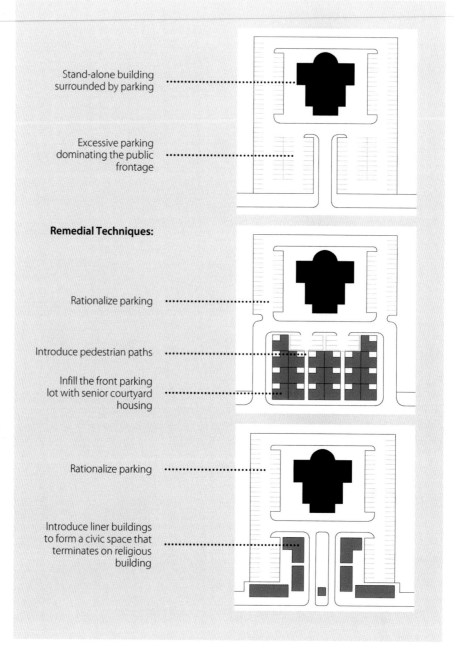

Deficiency: Civic structure with oversized, underutilized parking lot

Stand-alone building surrounded by parking

Excessive parking dominating the public frontage

Outcome One: Senior housing infill

Remedial Techniques:

Rationalize parking

Introduce pedestrian paths

Infill the front parking lot with senior courtyard housing

Outcome Two: Liner buildings and public space

Rationalize parking

Introduce liner buildings to form a civic space that terminates on religious building

7-21. Existing suburban religious building

7-22. Parking lot developed with courtyard senior housing

APPLICATION: REPAIR OF OUTDATED MULTIFAMILY HOUSING

Instead of demolishing out-of-date multifamily structures, they can be renovated and expanded to form better street frontages. The examples in figures 7-23 and 7-25 show British New Towns' terrace housing with deep, paved setbacks and nondescript, aging architecture. The proposal is to build attached or detached additions, in the form of extra rooms or studios, at the buildings' fronts, improving the proportions, size, and overall quality of the buildings while making their streets more pedestrian friendly (figures 7-24 and 7-26).

7-23. Outdated multifamily housing

7-24. Detached building additions

7-25. Outdated terrace housing

7-26. Attached, two-story building additions

APPLICATION: REPAIR OF A SUPERMARKET

Grocery stores and supermarkets are frequent contenders for sprawl repair. The example shows a redevelopment of a supermarket in the suburban fringes of a European town. The underutilized parking lots are urbanized with new apartment buildings and multistory parking garages "masked" with offices and affordable residences. The structure and the main entrance of the supermarket are preserved. The building can retain its retail use or if it is failing, it can be repurposed into a civic or office use. In either case, liner, mixed-use buildings are attached along its frontages to frame the new streets and public spaces.

7-27. Existing supermarket with excessive surface parking lots

7-28. Redevelopment of the supermarket and its parking lots into mixed-use fabric

POSTSCRIPT

Despite the severity of the building industry meltdown, the development of sprawl has not stopped. In the first months of 2009, the State of Florida processed an unprecedented number of proposals for new residential and commercial development. Megaprojects that were approved, pending, or proposed by the Department of Community Affairs included more than 470 million square feet of commercial space and more than 600,000 residential units on more than 430,000 acres across the state.[1] It is urgent that such efforts be redirected to the available places for redevelopment – defunct malls and empty parking lots – rather than build more unsustainable sprawl, replacing open space and productive farmland.

One of the goals for this manual is to demonstrate that there is good news. The tools presented here offer hope to those who recognize that sprawl must be and can be fixed. Suburban residents should not be worried – sprawl repair not only proposes ideas for regenerating their failing surroundings, but promises to enhance rather than obliterate their way of life. Most places will remain suburban in nature, but they will offer expanded choices for living, working, and socializing. Sprawl repair creates places for those who want to tend a garden in a quiet village and for those who are drawn to the liveliness of a town center.

The promise of a better life is more compelling than predictions of doom. The success of Dr. Dean Ornish, founder of the Preventive Medicine Research Institute, is a good example. Rather than scare heart patients with the "fear of death," he inspires them with a vision, the "joy of living."[2] Our approach to sprawl repair should be the same. Rather than threaten suburban residents with the demise of our way of life – or worse, blame them for it – we should entice them with the vision of thriving communities and the better life they provide.

ENDNOTES

CHAPTER ONE: FROM SPRAWL TO COMPLETE COMMUNITIES

1. Joel S. Hirschhorn. *Sprawl Kills: How Blandburbs Steal Your Time, Health, and Money* (New York: Sterling & Ross Publishers, 2005).

2. Jessica L. Furey. "Travel and Environmental Implications of School Siting," United States Environmental Protection Agency (2003) via EPA, <http://www.epa.gov/dced/pdf/school_travel.pdf> (19 February 2010).

3. Liz Chandler and Stella M. Hopkins. "Suburban Decay Stuns City Leaders," *The Charlotte Observer*, December 12, 2007.

4. Christopher B. Leinberger. "The Next Slum?" *The Atlantic*, March 2008. <http://www.theatlantic.com/doc/200803/subprime> (19 February 2010).

5. Reid Ewing et al. *Growing Cooler: The Evidence on Urban Development and Climate Change* (Washington, D.C.: Urban Land Institute, 2008).

6. "State Surgeon General Seal of Walkability," *Promoting Health One Step at a Time*. University of Miami School of Medicine, via CFS, November 18, 2009. <http://cfs.med.miami.edu/SG_Walkability_Criteria_Instructional_Slides.pdf> (19 February 2010).

7. Todd Litman. "Where We Want to Be: Home Location Preferences and Their Implications for Smart Growth," Victoria Transport Policy Institute (2010), via VTPI, <http://www.vtpi.org/sgcp.pdf> (19 February 2010).

8. Robert Fishman. *Bourgeois Utopias: The Rise and Fall of Suburbia* (New York: Basic Books, Inc., 1987).

9. Kenneth T. Jackson. *Crabgrass Frontier: The Suburbanization of the United States* (New York: Oxford University Press, Inc., 1985).

10. Bryan Walsh. "A New Blueprint for Levittown," *Time Magazine*, 17 January 2008, 36.

11. Brentin Mock. "Can They Save Youngstown?" *Next American City* (fall 2008), 6.

12. Karina Pallagst et al. *Cities Growing Smaller* (Kent State, Ohio: Kent State, 2008).

13. Volk Zimmerman. "Final presentation at the Lifelong Communities Charrette for the Atlanta Regional Commission," Atlanta, Georgia, February 17, 2009.

14. David Brooks. "A Nation of Villages," *New York Times*, 19 January 2006, Opinion section.

15. Arthur C. Nelson. "The Next 100 Million," *Making Great Communities Happen* (2003). American Planning Association, via MI, <http://www.mi.vt.edu/uploads/The%20Next%20100%20Million.pdf> (19 February 2010).

16. Elizabeth Kneebone. "Job Sprawl Revisited: The Changing Geography of Metropolitan Employment," The Brookings Institution (2009), <http://www.brookings.edu/reports/2009/0406_job_sprawl_kneebone.aspx> (19 February 2010).

17. Dean Murphy. "California Looks Ahead and Doesn't Like What It Sees," *New York Times*, 29 May 2005, sec. 4, Final late ed.

18. Treasure Coast Regional Planning Council. "Bringing Communities Together Since 1976," <http://www.tcrpc.org/index.html. (February 19, 2010)>.

CHAPTER TWO: THE SPRAWL REPAIR METHOD

1. Douglas Farr. *Sustainable Urbanism: Urban Design with Nature* (Hoboken, New Jersey: John Wiley & Sons, 2008), 111.

2. Andres Duany, Sandy Sorlien, and William Wright. "SmartCode Version 9 and Manual" (New York: New Urban News Publications, 2009).

3. Duany Plater-Zyberk & Company. "Sprawl Repair Smart Growth Module," Transect, <http://www.transect.org/docs/SPRAWL_REPAIR.pdf> (19 February 2010).

4. PlaceShakers and NewsMakers. "DPZ Promotes Mall Makeovers," Placeshakers, <http://placeshakers.wordpress.com/2009/04/18/dpz-promotes-mall-makeovers/> (19 April 2009).

CHAPTER THREE: REPAIR AT THE REGIONAL SCALE

1. "The Lexicon of The New Urbanism Version 3.2," Duany Plater-Zyberk & Company, 2002. <http://www.dpz.com/pdf/LEXICON.PDF> (19 February 2010).

2. Thomas Low. *Light Imprint Handbook: Integrating Sustainability and Community Design* (Washington, D.C.: Island Press, distributor, 2008).

CHAPTER FOUR: REPAIR AT THE COMMUNITY SCALE

1. Institute of Transportation Engineers. "Context Sensitive Solutions in Designing Major Urban Thoroughfares for Walkable Communities." ITE, 2010. <http://www.ite.org/css/> (19 February 2010).

2. U.S. Green Building Council. "LEED for Neighborhood Development," U.S. Green Building Council, November 9, 2009. <www.usgbc.org/leed/nd/> (19 February 2010).

3. Patrick M. Condon, Duncan Cavens, and Nicole Miller. *Urban Planning Tools for Climate Change Mitigation* (Cambridge, Massachusetts: Lincoln Institute of Land Policy, 2009).

4. For more on TIF districts see: <www.lincolninstitute.edu/pubs/1078_Tax-Increment-Financing> (19 February 2010).

5. Homes and Communities, U.S. Department of Housing and Urban Development. "Neighborhood Stabilization Program Grants," Housing and Urban Development, <http://hud.gov/offices/cpd/communitydevelopment/programs/neighborhoodspg/> (30 January 2010).

6. Wikipedia World Encyclopedia. "Special-purpose local-option sales tax," Wikipedia, <http://en.wikipedia.org/wiki/Special-purpose_local-option_sales_tax> (2 January 2010).

7. Belmar is one of the case studies in Ellen Dunham-Jones' and June Williamson's book, *Retrofitting Suburbia: Urban Design Solutions for Redesigning Suburbs* (Hoboken, New Jersey. John Wiley & Sons, Inc., 2009), 159.

8. Ellen Dunham-Jones and June Williamson review bonuses for public space as applied in Downtown Kendall, Florida, in their book, *Retrofitting Suburbia: Urban Design Solutions for Redesigning Suburbs* (Hoboken, New Jersey: John Wiley & Sons, Inc., 2009), 196.

9. Some of the steps in the protocols were discussed with the members of the Retrofit–Repair listserv (November 2009). John Anderson contributed in an e-mail message and phone conversation to the author, January 29, 2010.

10. The descriptions of retail types are adapted from "A Primer on Retail Types and Urban Centers," by Robert Gibbs in Robert Steuteville and Philip Langdon's book, *New Urbanism Best Practices Guide, Fourth Edition* (New York: New Urban News Publication, 2009), 79–80.

11. ICSC Serving the Global Retail Real Estate, "Frequently Asked Questions," ICSC, <http://www.icsc.org/srch/faq_category.php?cat_type=research&cat_id=3> (20 February 2010).

12. Mark Bulmash. "The Retail Development Crisis. What Now?" (presented by the Bulmash Real Estate Advisors, Congress for the New Urbanism VII, Denver, Colorado, 2009).

13. Robert Gibbs. "Retail Principles for New Urban Communities, Historic Downtowns, and Suburban Retrofitting" (presented at the Harvard University Graduate School of Design, Executive Education, July 10, 2009).

14. Werner Hegemann and Elbert Peets. *The American Vitruvius: An Architect's Handbook of Civic Art.* (New York: Princeton Architectural Press, 1988), 115.

15. Mlive.com. "Pending sales of Sunnybrook, Railside offer hope for future of local private golf clubs," Mlive, <http://www.mlive.com/golf/index.ssf/2009/10/pending_sales_of_sunnybrook_ra.html> (29 October 2009).

CHAPTER FIVE: REPAIR OF THOROUGHFARES AND PARKING

1. The descriptions of thoroughfares are adapted from "The Lexicon of The New Urbanism Version 3.2," Duany Plater-Zyberk & Company, 2002 <http://www.dpz.com/pdf/LEXICON.pdf> (10 February 2010)

2. The parking strategy was discussed and articulated with members of the Retrofit–Repair listserv, October 2009.

CHAPTER SIX: REPAIR AT THE BLOCK SCALE

1. Townhouse development as infill behind mansions was discussed by Sara Hines in an e-mail message to the author, June 15, 2009.

POSTSCRIPT

1. Florida Department of Community Affairs. "Florida Builders Poised to Pounce," Department of Community Affairs <http://www.dca.state.fl.us/News/Praises/Article3.cfm> (17 April 2009).

2. Alan Deutschman. "Change or Die," *Fast Company*, May 2005 <http://www.fastcompany.com/magazine/94/open_change-or-die.html?page=0,0> (1 May 2005).

RECOMMENDED READING

Christensen, Julia. *Big Box Reuse*. Cambridge, MA: The MIT Press, 2008.

Congress for the New Urbanism. "Malls into Mainstreets: An In-Depth Guide to Transforming Dead Malls into Communities." Chicago: Congress for the New Urbanism, 2006.

Dittmar, Hank, and Gloria Ohland, eds. *The New Transit Town: Best Practices in Transit-Oriented Development*. Washington, D.C.: Island Press, 2004.

Duany, Andres, Elizabeth Plater-Zyberk, and Robert Alminana. *The New Civic Art: Elements of Town Planning*. New York: Rizzoli, 2003.

Duany, Andres, Elizabeth Plater-Zyberk, and Jeff Speck. *Suburban Nation: The Rise of Sprawl and the Death of the American Dream*. New York: North Point Press, Farrar, Straus and Giroux, 2000.

Duany, Andres, Jeff Speck, and Mike Lydon. *The Smart Growth Manual*. N.p.: McGraw-Hill, 2010.

Dunham-Jones, Ellen, and June Williamson. *Retrofitting Suburbia*. Hoboken, NJ: John Wiley & Sons, 2008.

Ewing, Reid, et al. *Growing Cooler: The Evidence on Urban Development and Climate Change*. Washington, D.C.: Urban Land Institute, 2008.

Farr, Douglas. *Sustainable Urbanism: Urban Design with Nature*. Hoboken, NJ: John Wiley & Sons, 2008.

Fishman, Robert. *Bourgeois Utopias: The Rise and Fall of Suburbia*. New York: Basic Books, Inc., 1987.

Frumkin, Howard, Lawrence Frank, and Richard Jackson. *Urban Sprawl and Public Health: Designing, Planning, and Building for Healthy Communities*. Washington, D.C.: Island Press, 2004.

Garreau, Joel. *Edge City: Life on the Frontier*. New York: Anchor, 1992.

Gillham, Oliver. *The Limitless City: A Primer on the Urban Sprawl Debate*. Washington, D.C.: Island Press, 2002.

Hayden, Dolores. *Building Suburbia: Green Fields and Urban Growth, 1820-2000*. New York: Vintage Books, 2004.

Hayden, Dolores. *A Field Guide to Sprawl*. New York: W.W. Norton & Company, 2004.

Hegemann, Werner, and Elbert Peets. *The American Vitruvius: An Architect's Handbook of Civic Art*. New York: Princeton Architectural Press, 1988.

Hirschhorn, Joel S. *Sprawl Kills: How Blandburbs Steal Your Time, Health, and Money*. New York: Sterling and Ross, 2005.

Jackson, Kenneth T. *Crabgrass Frontier: The Suburbanization of the United States*. New York: Oxford University Press, 1985.

Krier, Leon. *The Architecture of Community*. Washington, D.C.: Island Press, 2009.

Kunstler, James H. *The Long Emergency: Surviving the Converging Catastrophes of the Twenty-First Century*. New York: Atlantic Monthly Press, 2005.

Lang, Robert E. *Edgeless Cities: Exploring the Elusive Metropolis*. Washington, D.C.: Brookings Institution Press, 2003.

Lang, Robert E. *Boomburbs: The Rise of America's Accidental Cities*. Washington, D.C.: Brookings Institution Press, 2007.

Leinberger, Christopher B. *The Option of Urbanism: Investing in a New American Dream*. Washington, D.C.: Island Press, 2007.

"The Lexicon of the New Urbanism. Version 3.2." Duany Plater-Zyberk & Company, 2002.

Low, Thomas. *Light Imprint Handbook: Integrating Sustainability and Community Design*. Washington, D.C.: Island Press, 2007 (distributor).

Lucy, William H., and David L. Phillips. *Tomorrow's Cities, Tomorrow's Suburbs*. Chicago: American Planning Association, 2006.

Lukez, Paul. *Suburban Transformations*. New York: Princeton Architectural Press, 2007.

MacLean, Alex S., and Bill McKibben. *Over: The American Landscape at the Tipping Point*. New York: Harry N. Abrams, Inc., 2008.

Pallagst, Karina, et al. *Cities Growing Smaller*. Kent, OH: Kent State University, 2008.

Pulleyblank, Sarah. "Civilizing Downtown Highways: Putting New Urbanism to Work on California's Highways." Chicago: Congress for the New Urbanism, 2002.

Smiley, David J. *Sprawl and Public Space: Redressing the Mall*. New York: Princeton Architectural Press, 2002.

Sobel, Lee S., and Steven Bodzin. *Greyfields into Goldfields: Dead Malls Become Living Neighborhoods*. Chicago: Congress for the New Urbanism, 2002.

Stanilov, Kiril, and Brenda Case Sheer, eds. *Suburban Form: An International Perspective*. New York: Routledge, 2003.

Steuteville, Robert, and Philip Langdon. *New Urbanism Best Practices Guide, Fourth Edition*. New York: New Urban News Publication, 2009.

Wasik, John F. *The Cul-de-Sac Syndrome: Turning Around the Unsustainable American Dream*. New York: Bloomberg Press, 2009.

INDEX

Note: Page numbers followed by "f" indicate figures.